Inside the Eye of Hurricane Katrina

By Warren J Riley

TABLE OF CONTENTS

Dedication

In loving memory of the 1300 plus lives tragically lost during Hurricane Katrina and the 700-plus fellow citizens who went missing, our hearts go out to all those who perished or remain unaccounted for.

To the unwavering heroes who selflessly stood on the front lines, the first responders, fire, police, and medical personnel, and the courageous citizens who risked everything to save their neighbors in their time of greatest need, we extend our deepest gratitude.

In particular, we honor the brave men and women of the Coast Guard, National Guard the NOPD, the fire department, and countless dedicated citizens who valiantly worked together to rescue and protect hundreds of lives in the immediate aftermath of Katrina.

This book is dedicated to the resilient spirit of the Gulf Coast and its people, those who endured unimaginable hardships and came together in a testament to the strength of community and the human spirit. Your actions and sacrifices will forever be remembered and celebrated within these pages.

Foreword

I've never read a book that made me cry. After all, I spent the first 10 of my 30 years in television working in the news. At my first fire, I saw a grandmother burned to death - still gripping the security bars she'd purchased to protect her. The first murder I reported on was a triple homicide - 3 people had been shot dead near a New Orleans movie theater. In Miami, I heard an 8-year-old screaming to a 911 operator that he'd just shot his 5-year-old sister. He killed her with the gun their father had purchased to protect his family.

I never shed a tear. Not because I wasn't moved by those experiences but because the news was like that. It was a job, and we were taught to treat it as such to protect our own mental health.

But everything changed when I read Warren Riley's book on Hurricane Katrina. He told the story of two NOPD officers who found themselves wading through neck-deep, foul-smelling water on the first floor of a New Orleans East hospital. They were there to clear the way for patients to be evacuated when they realized the things bumping into them in the pitch blackness were bodies that the storm's brutality had swept from the morgue. The swollen bodies of men, women, and children came at them from every direction almost like a scene from a zombie movie. The officers, knowing it wouldn't be alright for the evacuees to see such horror, worked until they put every single body into an empty room.

And when I thought it couldn't be more disturbing, the story went on to discuss the close relationship between the charge nurse and her patients. The patients loved the nurse, and she treated each of them as if they were members of her family. Then, she was told that only so many would be able to leave the hospital because there was only so much room available to get them out. Not only would she have to leave the oldest, most frail, helpless patients alone, but she'd have to leave them in a sweltering hot building with few supplies and not knowing when help would arrive.

One of the most touching moments was when the nurse had to tell an 80-plus-year-old woman that she would be left behind. The love and the kindness the elderly patient displayed forced me - just a reader - to regroup.

It's not like I haven't dealt with the destruction and trauma of hurricanes. I grew up in New Orleans and moved to Miami. I've always lived in the cone of uncertainty. In that time, I produced 5 hurricane series. The last one preceded Hurricane Andrew - a storm that both shattered and claimed the lives of so many people in South Florida. But I'd never witnessed anything like Riley's depiction of the New Orleans police officers and first responders in the aftermath of Hurricane Katrina.

Riley, who became the top cop overseeing one unimaginable disaster after another, was, in my opinion, probably the best person to make sense out of Katrina's chaos. And to the degree that this stranger-than-fiction storm would allow, he did.

I met Riley at a police and citizens' meeting when he was a sergeant. It seemed as if no time had passed before he was promoted to lieutenant. I remember when he was promoted to Commander of Cops (Community Oriented Policing Services)- a program that embedded police officers in New Orleans public housing developments. There, they not only kept order, but protected the people who just wanted a normal peaceful life. Riley and his officers worked diligently to make that possible.

He went on to headquarters with the brass. The "White Shirts." Then Katrina struck. I'd evacuated with my family days before and was safe and far away. Riley and his people were struggling to keep their heads above water.

Little did I know that Katrina - who killed over a thousand people, trapped others on their rooftops, wreaked havoc in the Superdome and caused a diaspora of New Orleans, was inflicting psychological torture on the men and women working to make the city safe.

After reading this book, I can never see New Orleans the same way. And I can never drive past that old hospital site in New Orleans East without remembering what went on behind closed doors, in the dark, in the floodwaters, that few people knew about until now.

- **Lisa Martin, TV Producer/Production Coordinator**

I am honored to introduce to you this book Inside the Eye of Hurricane Katrina as told by Warren Riley, Retired Superintendent of Police, New Orleans Police Department.

I've known Chief Riley for more than 40 years. We first met as young officers competing against one another in the touch football league and we became friends. As sergeants, we shared an office as Internal Affairs Investigators until our promotion to the rank of lieutenant. I then served as the Fifth District Commander under his command as FOB (Field Operations Bureau) Chief then on his staff in the FOB office. Never did I ever imagine, two weeks later, we would be hunkering down together in NOPD's headquarters in the eye of Hurricane Katrina, arguably one of the worst natural disasters in America's history.

Over the twenty-eight days following the storm, I spent every minute side by side with Chief Riley. As a front-row witness, I can testify as Commander of Field Operations he never wavered from his duties regardless of the insurmountable wrath and destruction we faced. He is truly one who could bring to life what it was like in the eye and days following Hurricane Katrina.

Inside The Eye of Hurricane Katrina is riveting, revealing and informative. As you read this book you can feel the stress, pain, and fear that all New Orleanians and first responders experienced that horrific day. The historical value from federal, state, and local levels regarding disaster preparation and response contained in its pages will help first responders for years to come.

We will never take the power of Mother Nature for granted again!

- **Lawrence T. Weathersby, Sr.**

  Senior Pastor (Living the Word International)

  Retired Deputy Superintendent (New Orleans Police Department)

Synopsis

Inside the Eye of Hurricane Katrina as told by Warren Riley, Retired

Superintendent of the New Orleans Police Department

Inside the Eye of Hurricane Katrina brings the reader to the Abyss of Hurricane Katrina. To a depth that has never been explored or expressed in writing or conversations. Retired Superintendent Warren Riley writes this story of NOPD, government officials, and its citizens just before Katrina's arrival and through the days to follow. Warren Riley rode the storm out in the eye; he was the second in command of NOPD and was appointed as the Superintendent of Police 29 days after Katrina destroyed the Big Easy. He directed operations for NOPD, the National Guard, and other agencies and first responders before, during, and in the aftermath of Katrina.

Riley brings you in 96 hours pre-landfall and takes you on a journey that does not end for another 21 days. He captures the cavalier manner that NOLA is known for and illustrates it in writing as you have never experienced. The joyful spirit as well as the indifferent or lackadaisical attitude that Nawlins people and leadership are known for around the world. The governor's office's combativeness and leery attitude toward the city and the federal government, including the white house. Riley captures the bravery of many officers and citizens who, when the shit hit the fan, rose, stood in the eye, and weathered this horrific event. He depicts those officers who fled the city, some out of concern for family and some because of cowardice.

Riley vividly captures your attention as NOLA goes from partying hours before landfall to concern, fear, chaos, death, destruction, politics, and the power or intimidation of the people in the shadows, the shadow government.

When Katrina made her horrendous advent on NOLA, the first responders and city leaders were on their own for the first five days. The days after Katrina left New Orleans naked, dysfunctional, and terrified. NOLA a city with no power, no lights, no potable water, little food for survivors, 90 plus degree heat, and sweltering humidity for the next 21days. However, through it all, New Orleans was bent but not broken.

Riley brings you into some of the rescues, the crime, the looters, police shootings, and the tragic toll on citizens and officers. He dives into the tragedy of racism and how it hides, but it never goes away, how racist seeks, and wait for an opportunity to pounce.

Politics, political foes, and some shady members of the shadow government jeopardized New Orleanians for selfishness, politics, and profit. Riley brings you into the 911 operations center as tornados make landfall and as levees break. He captures the heroic and mentally challenging events that occurred as 911 calls overwhelmed experienced police dispatchers. The heroic dispatchers listened as the water rose in citizens' homes from the most impoverished communities to wealthy communities when the levees broke. The calls came in one after another from Lakeview and the lower and upper ninth Wards and as New Orleans East flooded from the levees that were overtopped by Katrina's raging waters. Riley captures the dreadful citizens calls into 911 for help as they try to survive against terrible odds as waters rose from zero to 14 feet within 23 minutes. And when we came up from the abyss and the failure of leaders at every level of government, when we heard a radio or saw TV again after many days, we learned that some of our own media called our evacuees refugees.

The story is riveting; it is told from a unique vantage point, which is told from the perspective of the chief operations officer for the New Orleans Police Department. It is a first-hand account of America's greatest natural disaster and most significant failures! It will touch your emotions: anger, sadness, and fear as you read this true to life story, you will never choose to weather another hurricane again.

Chapter 1:
How Did We Get Here?

August 29, 2005

It has been 18 years since Hurricane Katrina made landfall on the coasts of Louisiana, Mississippi, and Alabama, and I often reflect on the many dreams, nightmares, and visions of the horrific hurricane that still creep into my mind from time to time.

Many nights, I would awaken to the screams of horrified women holding onto their crying babies, begging me, the police, and first responders to save them from their nearly submerged homes. I would see grown men reaching out to me, yelling to be pulled to safety from rooftops and tree limbs, but I couldn't reach them. The images in my dreams haunt me—men, women, and children blown from rooftops into the raging waters, the surge, the angry tides. The wrath of Hurricane Katrina showed no mercy to any person or thing in its path. The rage and fury cracked, breached, and crushed New Orleans' levees, overtopping the barriers that were supposed to protect its residents.

In my dreams, I still see the wind, just as I saw it that morning when it rolled into New Orleans. The wind was so strong, so powerful, so loud that you could not only hear its ferociousness, but also see its might. Katrina's winds were not invisible; they were eerie, ghostly, and thick. And then I heard the roar of the tornadoes that ravaged my beloved city—a frightening sound that made you wonder how many freight trains were rolling into the city and how much damage they were inflicting upon NOLA and its people.

I vividly recall the voice and image of Officer Chris Abbot as he said his goodbyes, trapped in his attic as the water rapidly rose from his knees to his waist and, within minutes, to his neck. He radioed for help as the water reached his neck, with no apparent way out. Every officer who heard his desperate plea for help over the police radio thought he was being claimed by the waters of Katrina.

I heard the frightening screams of a mother's cry "Oh my God, my babies are drowning!" as call after call came into the 911 center, pleading for help in the most desperate tones

I listened to the voice of a 21-year-old man whom I met on the interstate 24 hours after Katrina ravaged New Orleans. It was the sound only a devastated parent could make—the sound of a heartbroken father. We rescued him from Interstate-10 several hours after he was saved from his submerged house in the 9th Ward. In the pitch darkness around 2:00 am, with only first responders' flashlights illuminating the area, I walked and came across him crying, battered and beaten. I assured him that we would soon bring him to a safe, dry area, but he continued to cry. When I asked him what was wrong, he told me that he and his three-year-old daughter were trapped in his attic for hours. Exhausted and with the water inches away from the attic roof, he held his precious child in his arms, hoping for rescue, and eventually fell asleep.

When he woke up, his beautiful daughter was no longer in his arms. Frantically, he searched for her, diving into the water, swimming in the dark and filthy attic, desperately trying to find her, but she was never found. He was later rescued, never to see his beloved child again. Sometimes, when I see my own daughter, I think of this young man, and it fills me with sadness. I remember hearing his gut-wrenching cries, unable to suppress the grief and pain. He cried so intensely that it affected his breathing, causing him to hyperventilate. He was heartbroken, torn apart, shouting that he wanted to die. I embraced him as tears streamed down his face, mingling with mine in the pitch darkness of Katrina. To this day, I wonder how he is doing.

In my dreams, I witnessed half-naked indigent elderly people with vacant eyes wading through sewage-infested waters up to their chests, unsure of what to do or where to go. I longed to help them, but they always remained out of reach, silently vanishing beneath the turbulent rivers of sludge, their haunting empty gazes fixed upon me. Though my girlfriend never complained, I suspect that my outbursts of nightmarish distress occasionally startled her awake, particularly when I would abruptly rise to answer a phone that wasn't actually ringing.

There were moments when, in a half-asleep state, I would hold the phone to my ear, listening to my fellow police officers on the other end of the line shouting that the water was rising in their sheltered locations and they couldn't escape, and I couldn't reach them. I was haunted by the nightmares of two officers, both of whom I knew personally, who tragically took their own lives. I had seen one of them just an hour before he committed suicide. The memory of Officer Kevin Thomas, shot in the head by looters less than 48 hours after Katrina made landfall, plagued my dreams. I envisioned this kind-hearted, jovial man, always eager to help others, suffering such a violent fate over chips and drinks. Thankfully, he survived the ordeal.

The relentless havoc wreaked upon New Orleans by Katrina, even before she made landfall, is eternally ingrained in my mind. Not only did she destroy a beautiful city, its allure, and parts of its history and infrastructure, but Katrina also sowed chaos among the leadership. Mayor Nagin and Superintendent Compass, two of the city's top leaders, were at odds, nearly resorting to physical altercation just eight hours before the onset of NOLA's destruction. Other city officials had to intervene, defusing the heated confrontation and curbing the profanity-laden tirade against Chief Compass's leadership. Katrina eventually brought Superintendent Compass to tears, pushing him to the brink of anxiety and emotional breakdown, witnessed by the world on television, which raised doubts about his ability to lead during this crisis. The aftermath and subsequent attempts to revive the city resulted in the imprisonment of numerous individuals, including businessmen, police officers, and even the mayor.

My nightmare persists as I recall the anguish of realizing that help did not arrive promptly, despite our foreknowledge that Hurricane Katrina would be the most catastrophic disaster in American history. Local, state, and even the White House had been warned that this would be the "Mother of all Hurricanes" and that New Orleans would be decimated, yet we remained unprepared as a city, state, and nation. In my dreams, I find myself standing in the middle of Canal Street, just outside the French Quarter, in an abandoned and ruined city, with lifeless bodies strewn about and an overwhelming silence of immense death. Only a handful of first responders and citizens, including myself, are left as the sole survivors. We wait for our government, but we are utterly alone, while President Bush and Air Force One soar overhead, seemingly oblivious to the catastrophe that has befallen New Orleans, as my dream gradually fades away.

"The first choice of every citizen is to figure out a way to leave the city," Mayor Ray Nagin's booming voice filled the room.

Drip.

"We need to pray that the hurricane force winds will diminish," Governor Kathleen Blanco's voice echoed eerily.

Drip.

"We're told that Hurricane Katrina is now a Category 5 in strength," Nagin advised.

Drip.

"I-10 in the interior of the city is gridlocked," Governor Blanco announced.

Drip.

"This is a very serious storm that will likely topple our levee system," Nagin projected.

Drip.

"There may be intense flooding that is beyond our control," Blanco forecasted.

Drip.

"The Superdome will open at noon as a refuge of last resort," Nagin declared.

Drip.

Unconsciously, I wiped the water from my face, shoulder, and chest as I slowly stirred on the makeshift cot that I had been sleeping on in my office at the New Orleans Police Department Headquarters. Despite having slept for a few hours, my mind continued to race with the sobering details from

Mayor Nagin's press conference alongside Governor Blanco, which I had attended earlier.

Two more drops of water from the ceiling fell onto my head, serving as a reminder of the reality of my present surroundings. I winced slightly, feeling the persistent discomfort in the small of my back from sleeping on a makeshift cot that, technically, could be referred to as such, but in reality, felt more like a glorified bed of cement. With Hurricane Katrina looming, it was my responsibility as the Deputy Chief of Operations of the New Orleans Police Department to remain on high alert and ensure that the entire NOPD was prepared to respond effectively. While more comfortable accommodations were offered to me at the Hyatt Regency Hotel, where many city officials including Mayor Nagin, my boss Superintendent Edwin Compass of the New Orleans Police Department, and Terry Ebbert, the Director of Homeland Security were staying, it didn't feel right for our essential staff at the New Orleans Police Headquarters to be without any of the leadership team present during the storm. Furthermore, my role involved running operations from the Special Event Communication and Critical Incident Command Center, known as Base 9, located at NOPD Headquarters. It was both a matter of leadership and practicality for me to remain within reach of what I needed to fulfill my duties diligently, rather than seeking comfort in the hotel.

The sound of howling wind brought me back to the present. With tired eyes, I could see through the windows of my office that the wind had intensified significantly since last night's 75-mile-per-hour gusts. I stood up groggily and walked closer to the full-sized windows in my office to better assess the situation outside. Although I prided myself on being a resolute man not easily swayed by fear, I couldn't deny the twisting sensation of a million knots in my stomach as I looked out of the windows. Situated on the fifth floor of the building, I had a clear view of the ominous beginning of a nightmare. The wind itself seemed like a living organism, invisible appendages hurling and lifting debris into the air. I watched as license plates, wheels, garbage, and roofing materials were catapulted over our building as if they weighed mere ounces. Broken tree limbs and random objects cluttered the air, reminiscent of Mardi Gras confetti scattered carelessly. However, this was no festive parade; the occasion was anything but celebratory.

This was Hurricane Katrina making her ominous arrival upon the city of New Orleans. Alongside me at Headquarters were essential staff members, including police officers, administrators, 911 supervisors and operators, dispatchers, and critical members of my team. Having undergone countless compliance manuals and emergency preparedness meetings with the mayor and his staff, and having planned for every conceivable contingency, we bravely hunkered down at Headquarters, awaiting the inevitable but praying for the best. Like me, the majority of them utilized their offices to snatch a few hours of sleep.

The sound of water dripping into my office had escalated from occasional drops to a steady pour, a clear indication that the rain outside was intensifying. Glancing at the clock on the office wall near the door, I saw that it was just after six in the morning, confirming that sleep had eluded me, burdened as I was with the stress of an impending storm that could ravage our city. The reports were dismal, and the projected damage was even worse. As I gazed out of the window, witnessing the unfolding scene, I pushed thoughts of death and disaster out of my mind.

"What if I don't make it out of this storm?" I wondered aloud.

"What will happen to my precious daughter, Morgan?"

"What about my brother, older sisters, and their families?"

"What will happen to my fiancée? How will their lives be impacted?"

I felt overwhelming gratitude that they had followed my directive to evacuate the city earlier and were now safely in Houston, Texas. Initially, the projected path of Hurricane Katrina had the storm heading towards the Florida panhandle, with the left edge of the cone barely scraping Metro New Orleans. Such projections were not uncommon. Over the years, we had seen several hurricanes pose a threat to the New Orleans area, only to have the city escape the full force of the storm.

For days, we had clung to the hope that this would be another instance of narrowly dodging disaster. However, three days ago, in a dramatic shift, the forecast models projected Katrina's path through Southeast Louisiana and into the Mississippi Gulf Coast. Even the most optimistic among us couldn't help but feel concern. During one of the many briefing sessions with the mayor and the emergency response teams, some of the most respected meteorologists in the business uttered the words, "This is THE storm we have been dreading for years."

The wind outside intensified. Debris was no longer simply lifted into the air; things were now flying about with alarming speed. I witnessed small bicycles and tires sailing past my windows as if weightless. Not far from my location, on the Headquarters parking garage, stood a communication tower held secure by four cables. Amidst the chaos outside, I could see the wind mercilessly battering it. The tower swayed back and forth, defying the onslaught of the winds, but the cables strained to their limits. With the intensity of the wind, my fear was that we might lose the tower and, with it, our ability to communicate, amplifying the disastrous nature of the situation.

Another strong gust of wind pushed the tower to an impossible angle, and I silently prayed that it would hold its ground in this storm. In this moment, a sense of defiance and optimism overcame me, as if the communication tower symbolized the spirit of the city of New Orleans, and the cables represented the city's leadership team. Each gust of wind tested the tower's resilience, but the indomitable strength of the cables refused to yield. Just like those cables, we, too, would stretch and strain, but we would not allow the storm to break the spirit of the city we loved so dearly.

Suddenly, a noise resembling a half-dozen freight trains caused my mouth to go dry. The wind howled, flinging objects around, and a sick feeling settled in the pit of my stomach, suggesting that things were about to go from bad to worse. As I stood by the six-foot-tall windows in my office, I sensed a dramatic shift in pressure within the room. My ears popped, and a dull ache throbbed at my temples. When I attempted to refocus on the windows, I felt a sensation of the room spinning. Vertigo? I had never experienced it before, so what kind of equilibrium-shifting madness was this? The pressure changes in the room caused my head to swirl. The building trembled slightly, and I could hear the pounding of the winds on the roof above.

I had heard stories of tornadoes sounding like trains, and I knew that there were undoubtedly tornadoes tearing through our area. Despite concerns about the building's stability, I knew that leaving it was not an option in the face of winds reaching 130 to 140 miles per hour. My foremost concern was the safety of the staff members here, who, like myself, were seeking rest in their offices. Given the size of the windows, shattered glass would pose a severe threat, potentially causing life-threatening injuries if people were inside those offices. I heard growing confusion outside my office as people were roused from sleep by the ferocious winds assaulting NOPD Headquarters.

My immediate thought was that we were all going to die as the building imploded under the force of the gale outside. An image of the Twin Towers in New York on 9/11 flashed in my mind, reminding me of the horrific ordeal New Yorkers endured. I imagined the weeks it would take to recover our bodies from the rubble of this building, which threatened to become our final resting place. The thought of my family having to grieve my loss in such a manner infused me with the strength to set aside my emotions and approach the situation with a tactical mindset.

I forced myself to refocus on what was happening outside my window. Rain poured in torrents, whipped across the city by a fury that could only be described as vicious. At this point, it was evident that tornadoes were tearing through the city. Visibility was severely limited due to debris of all kinds hurtling through the air, damaging cars and buildings in their path. The sound of freight trains grew louder with each passing moment, indicating the dangerous proximity of tornadoes in our vicinity. Unconsciously, my hand rested on one of the windows for balance. Suddenly, I felt the window reverberate under my touch. The shift was so palpable that I had to step back, visually confirming what I had sensed physically.

The windows in my office were visibly pulsating, as if they were inhaling and exhaling. They seemed alive, moving in and out. "Shit! What the fuck!" I exclaimed. Realizing the gravity of the situation, I swiftly grabbed my wallet and cellphone, flung open the door to my office, and entered the shared hallway that led to my staff's offices. "Everybody, get into the hallway and take cover!" I commanded, opening office doors as I went from one office to another.

Many of the staff members were already in the hallway, but some were startled awake by my urgent announcement. "Captain," I said as I opened the door to my Chief of Staff, Captain Michael Pfeiffer. "Help me gather as many people into this hallway as possible. Tornadoes are in the area, and windows might blow out." Despite being roused from sleep, Captain Pfeiffer, a former Navy Officer, immediately sprang into action. We instructed the staff to move to the hallways and close their office doors. As we swiftly made our way from office to office, the sound of a freight train could still be heard, accompanied by occasional building shakes, booming thunder, and intense lightning. In less than two minutes, we had everyone in the hallway, positioned at the lowest points possible. Faced with imminent danger, staff members displayed concern, yet they remained courageous and calm. Murmured prayers filled the air as everyone sought divine protection from the force of the storm. We waited what felt like an eternity. Each passing minute seemed like an hour, and each hour felt like a lifetime. Thunder, lightning, and strong winds served as an insidious soundtrack, announcing the destruction and chaos befalling our beloved New Orleans.

I then directed Captain Lawrence Weathersby, another member of my staff, to check in with each commander at their designated locations throughout the city and provide a status update. "Chief, so far, none of the office windows have blown out," reported Captain Lawrence Weathersby, as he approached me, accompanied by Sergeant Cynthia Landry.

I nodded in confirmation of his observation. "I still believe transitioning everyone to the hallway was a wise move," Landry remarked. "If those windows were to give way under the wind's pressure..." "It would almost certainly be fatal," I interjected, finishing her statement. She nodded in agreement. "Have we received any status reports from the commanders?" I asked, referring to the commanders, 911 dispatchers, and supervisors at our Communications Special Event and Critical Incident Command Center, known as Base 9, for which I had oversight. "Nothing so far," replied Captain Weathersby. "We need to get a status check," I stated, as I made my way toward the elevators, with Landry, Pfeiffer, Weathersby, and Sergeant Andre Menzies following closely behind.

"This will help us better understand what's happening in the city." Although the Mayor had issued a mandatory evacuation order for the city, there were several thousand residents who were either unable to leave or chose not to. Despite the reports, many were unable to evacuate due to financial constraints and believed they would be better off in their homes rather than seeking refuge in designated shelters, such as the Superdome. As the elevator doors opened on the second floor, I immediately sensed an atmosphere of chaotic sorrow.

Dozens of dispatchers, wearing headsets, were stationed at their desks, answering and redirecting calls. The calm voices of the dispatchers filled the air. However, a stark contrast existed between what we heard and what we saw. Nearly every dispatcher, regardless of gender, was crying. Some were silently sobbing. While composed and professional when speaking on the phones, most couldn't contain their tears. Trying to comprehend the scene before us, Pfeiffer, Landry, and I were approached by one of the senior dispatcher supervisors, Andrea Deal. "Hi Andrea," I greeted her, unable to hide my confusion.

"What's happening down here? Why is everyone crying?" Andrea Deal was one of our most experienced and professional supervisors, a true leader who always remained composed in challenging situations. As I looked at her, tears welling in her eyes, struggling to maintain her composure, a wave of nausea washed over me. I had an unsettling feeling that this would not be good news. "Andrea," Sgt. Cynthia Landry moved closer to her, "What's the status? What's happening here?" Andrea stepped away briefly, then returned with a dispatcher's headset. "Chief, plug into one of the dispatch stations and listen," she directed.

I swiftly made my way to a dispatch station and plugged into the Fifth District channel, which covered the Lower and Upper 9th Ward sections of the city. What I heard will forever be etched in my memory. "Somebody please help us!" a frantic woman's voice crackled through my ears. "We're trapped in the attic, and the water is rising." The anguish in her voice struck me to the core. Fear permeated every word she spoke. The cries of young children could be heard in the background. "Grab your brother!" the mother shouted to one of the children. "Don't let him go under!" "Ma'am, we need you to get to the highest point in your home," a male dispatcher reassured the mother.

"We'll send help as soon as we can." "You have to send someone right now!" the mother replied in a hysterical tone. "My babies are drowning!" "We'll get to you as soon as we can," he responded. My heart sank as I scanned the room, searching for the dispatcher who was speaking with the desperate mother. He was a well-built man in his late thirties, holding his head with both hands, tears streaming down his face. With hurricane-force winds outside, it was impossible to dispatch any rescue vehicles. Wind speeds exceeding 60 miles per hour could easily overturn SUVs and other emergency vehicles. The dispatchers were in an impossible situation.

All they could offer was comfort and a listening ear. The screams, prayers, and sounds of people fighting for their lives, followed by an eerie silence, had become all too familiar. I switched to another call, hoping for a different outcome. "I'm scared," came the frightened voice of a little girl. "I can't find my mama. She went downstairs, and now she's gone." The little girl's sobs overwhelmed the call as the dispatcher did her best to console her. "Baby, tell me, where are you?" the dispatcher asked. "I'm upstairs in my room," the little girl replied between fear-filled sobs. "Is there water in your room?"

"Yes, and it's rising!" the terror in the little girl's voice echoed. DAMMIT! I screamed internally, feeling a lump forming in my throat. "Listen, sweetie, I want you to get on the highest thing in your room and stay there," the dispatcher instructed. "I'm not going to leave you." "I'm so scared. Can somebody please come and get me?" she pleaded. There was a moment of silence. I spotted the dispatcher at her station, sobbing into her hand to muffle the sound, pausing the call momentarily to regain her composure before continuing to project strength to the little girl. "Baby, we're going to get to you as soon as we can," she finally assured. Though I am not prone to emotional outbursts or displays, in that moment, it took every ounce of strength to maintain my composure.

This was a fucking nightmare, one of the saddest moments of my life. Our worst fears were being realized in ways that defied comprehension. As I switched from call to call, I heard the desperate cries of women, men, and children pleading for help. Their voices were filled with fear and terror as the storm's waters engulfed their homes. In the background, the sounds of men and women using tools and blunt objects to break through their attics, desperate to escape the rising water, blended with the confusion, panic, and fear that hung heavily in the air. "Shit! You guys have to get somebody here now!" a frightened man screamed into his phone.

"My mamas in a wheelchair with an oxygen tank. We can't move her!" "I'm in my attic, and the water is up to my neck," an alarmed female voice declared on another call. "Oh God! I can't swim. Please send help!" I, along with the dispatchers, knew that the projected wind speeds were not expected to drop below 60 miles per hour for at least another six hours, making it impossible to send assistance. My heart weighed heavily with instant grief. We were listening to the cries of dozens, if not hundreds, of people facing their final moments, pleading with God for help. The depth of grief I felt at that moment was comparable to the loss I experienced when my mother died when I was 18.

There was something profoundly haunting about hearing the panicked voice of a young child confronting the reality of death. The sound of men and women taking their last breaths, struggling for air, and splashing in water would forever be etched in my mind. One of the last calls I remember listening to in that moment was between a dispatcher and a young man who identified himself as David Baptiste. His brokenness resonated through the phone. "My baby is gone, bruh! She's gone!" he sobbed uncontrollably. "David, can you tell me what's happening?" the female dispatcher asked. Adjusting my headset slightly, I listened as he continued to speak. "I fucked up, man," he wept.

"We came to the attic because the whole house is flooded." "Who?" "Me and my baby girl," he answered through sobs. "The attic is flooded too, almost to the top. I've been trying to get us out of here, man. I've been using a hammer to try to break out of the attic." David burst into tears once more. It took him another 10 minutes to compose himself enough to continue speaking. He told the dispatcher that the attic was nearly submerged, the water reaching close to the roof.

Since the water was almost at the highest point, he was too tall to stand. Instead, he had found a sturdy wooden beam to lie upon, supporting his weight and providing enough space for his baby girl to rest safely on his chest. Exhausted from his attempts to break free, David lay on his back, with his hammer and phone resting to the left of him, while his daughter drifted off to sleep on his chest. Looking at the menacing dark water mere inches away, he said, "I fell asleep staring at that water, man." His voice quivered with emotion. "When I woke up..." David choked up, struggling to continue. "She was gone." "She fell into the water, David?" the dispatcher asked. "I don't know how it happened," he replied, sobbing once again. "She must've rolled off me into the water or something. I don't know." A lump formed in my throat. I couldn't fathom a greater pain than what this young man was describing.

"I've searched for her in the water so many times, man, and I can't find her!" he confessed. "Someone has to help me, man! Someone has to help me find my baby girl!" Overwhelmed by the heartbreaking plea, I abruptly stood up and removed the headset. I had reached my limit. The dispatchers continued to field calls, clinging to hope in the face of utter despair. This level of devastation surpassed our projections and fears. I questioned whether things would improve or if they could further deteriorate. How did we overlook this? Could we have been better prepared? Should we have evacuated the city sooner? How would we navigate the days ahead? What would the final death toll be? Would any of us make it out of this alive?

Call it a Freudian slip or the verbal expression of my inner turmoil, but as Pfeiffer and Landry approached me, words escaped from the depths of my soul: "How in the fuck did we end up here?"

Chapter 2:
Denial

Countdown to Katrina - T-144 Hours

Denial became the prevailing mindset as New Orleans headed toward a collision course with the devastating force of Hurricane Katrina. The city's residents, accustomed to hurricanes veering away from them in favor of other regions like Florida, found it easy to dismiss the looming destruction. The initial tropical depression system in the Southeast Bahamas on August 23, 2005, seemed inconsequential at the time, but little did we know that it marked the beginning of a countdown to cataclysmic devastation—the moment when Katrina would intersect with New Orleans.

On that humid August day, I swiftly parked my Ford Expedition next to Houston's Restaurant on St. Charles Avenue. This particular establishment held a special place in my heart, offering an upscale dining experience infused with the undeniable charm of New Orleans. Even from my insignificant vantage point in the parking lot, I admired the beauty of five grand oak trees lining the street, adding to the city's magical allure.

Oh, how I love this city!

I grabbed my phone and keys, exiting the truck. As the Chief of Operations for the New Orleans Police Department, leisurely weekday lunches were a rarity for me. Every meeting, even casual lunches, carried a purpose. Today's gathering with my longtime friend and a Criminal Court Judge, Arthur Hunter, was no exception. Mayor Ray Nagin appointed me to my current position just nine months ago, after firing my predecessor, Jerry Ursin Jr., for misrepresenting his qualifications on his resume. Nagin had made it clear that my priority and assignment were to tackle the daunting task of reducing the city's murder and violent crime rates. Achieving this goal would require deliberate effort and strategic planning.

Arthur and I had attended the police academy together, forging a fast friendship during those formative days. He had always expressed his desire to pursue a law degree and become a judge, and he had succeeded. His combination of tactical thinking, operational expertise, and a can-do attitude perfectly complemented my own personality, solidifying our friendship of over 25 years. I couldn't help but smile at the prospect of the good-natured banter that would surely ensue when Arthur and I were together. With those thoughts in mind, I made my way toward the bustling entrance of the restaurant, filled with patrons and busy waitstaff.

Stepping into the restaurant, I inwardly sighed as I surveyed the bustling lunch scene—a packed venue teeming with customers and waitstaff. I estimated that the wait time would easily exceed forty-five minutes with such a crowd, and I regretted choosing this place for our meeting. I couldn't afford to have my time consumed by a lengthy lunch. I had another meeting scheduled with my Chief of Staff, Captain Michael Pfeiffer, at 4:00 p.m., followed by dinner and drinks with my girlfriend Tiffany. A delay of this magnitude would disrupt my entire day. Just as I approached the hostess to provide my name, a voice called out to the left of me.

"Warren!" the voice exclaimed.

Following the sound of the voice, my eyes landed on Arthur waving me over to a nearby booth. Relief washed over me as I realized he had arrived before me and secured a table. It shouldn't have surprised me—Arthur Hunter always seemed to be a few steps ahead of everyone. "My man!" I exclaimed, shaking his hand and patting him on the shoulder once I reached the table. "You saved my day. I thought we'd be stuck waiting in this lunch crowd." "Come on, man," Arthur Hunter replied with a good-natured laugh. "You should've known I'd be here ahead of the crowd." As was our custom, we began with casual conversation about our personal lives before delving into business matters. Arthur Hunter and his wife Charlotte, married for over 20 years, still seemed like newlyweds.

Whenever he spoke about her, you could see the love, attraction, and admiration that radiated from him. They had a son who had just entered his senior year of high school. "When are you going to settle down with Tiffany?" he asked knowingly. It was no secret among our friends that while Tiffany and I were in a loving and healthy relationship, I didn't feel the need for marriage to define or solidify it. She enjoyed her work as a business owner in the private sector, while I dedicated my life to public service. Somehow, we found a balance that worked for both of us.

Additionally, my sixteen-year-old daughter from a previous relationship, Morgan, kept me busy. Morgan was my heart and soul, a typical teenager pushing her dad's buttons, but she was sweet and loved me immensely. "Ah, come on, man," I replied, laughing. "Don't start with the marriage talk. We're fine as we are." Laughter filled the air as we playfully bantered back and forth before diving into a serious discussion on practical measures to reduce violent crimes and murders in the city. I expressed my concern to the judge about the District Attorney releasing violent criminals and sometimes dropping charges, citing Article 701 of the Louisiana Code of Criminal Procedure.

Numerous murderers had been released under this rule, which, in my opinion, the District Attorney had misinterpreted. These releases had led to more violence, as some offenders went on to commit further crimes or became victims themselves in retaliatory acts. I had discussed this issue with the District Attorney during a previous dinner, and he had promised to address it, but nothing had changed. The body count continued to rise, and the release of murder suspects only contributed to the city's violence. Arthur assured me that he would arrange a meeting between the District Attorney, myself, and him to address the matter. After finishing lunch and bidding farewell, little did I know that it would be one of the last conversations I would have with Arthur for a long time.

I returned to NOPD Headquarters at 3:00 p.m., giving me ample time to review files and briefing documents related to policy revisions I was considering for the department. As I pulled into my parking space with my assistant, I noticed dozens of arrestees being escorted from a bus outside central lockup and into the facility for processing. Among them were petty thieves, small-time drug dealers, and individuals caught in a roundup, familiar with the routine of being arrested. While making my way through the main floor toward the elevator that would take me to my office on the fifth floor, I caught sight of a young man, no older than seventeen or eighteen, with a vacant but fearful expression. Two of our officers were speaking to him, undoubtedly preparing to process him through the system.

It was clear that despite his current predicament, he was a good kid who had likely made a foolish choice. I overheard one of the officers admonishing him, urging him to reconsider his path and warning him against a life he didn't want. I silently prayed and hoped that the young man would heed the officer's wise counsel. As a leader with several people reporting to me, it was rare for me to reach my office without being stopped for inquiries or asked to weigh in on specific matters. I always took the time to engage with officers and civilian employees, even if it was only for a brief moment. I remembered being a young officer, encountering chiefs who wouldn't acknowledge my presence and flaunted their superior status.

For that reason, I always maintained an open-door policy and made a point to acknowledge every person who worked under my command. When I stepped out of the elevator and reached my office unscathed, I chuckled at the rarity of the moment and resolved to review as much policy as possible within the hour. Just as I was finishing up one last note in the margin of a policy document, my Chief of Staff, Captain Michael Pfeiffer, knocked on my door. "Come in, Captain Mike," I replied, setting aside the document. "The door is open." Pfeiffer entered with only a few folders in his hands, much to my relief.

As my Chief of Staff, he took great care to ensure I was well-prepared for our staff meetings and had all the necessary information to address important matters concerning our department's functioning. With our weekly staff meeting scheduled for tomorrow, it was essential for us to go over any outstanding items and directives issued by Chief Compass to ensure their implementation.

Pfeiffer, an experienced and decorated graduate of the Merchant Marine Navy Academy and a law school graduate, was easygoing yet focused. He had a strong grasp of policies, which made him an invaluable asset to our team. Little did I know how much I would come to value his attention to detail in the weeks to come. We quickly went through the details for the next day's staff meeting, and all things considered, it promised to be a relatively relaxed gathering. "Oh yeah, Chief, one more thing," Captain Pfeiffer said after we covered the last detail.

"There's a tropical depression system developing in the Southeastern Bahamas. We should keep an eye on it since we're in hurricane season." Even to this day, I am astounded by the casual manner in which most of us dismissed the beginnings of what would become the defining event of our careers. Abject denial was deeply ingrained in our collective mindset when it came to hurricanes. "Is that right, Mike?" I responded, giving it little thought. "Keep an eye on it and let me know, alright?" "Certainly," he complied. After the meeting with Captain Pfeiffer, I attended to a few lingering matters before wrapping up my day at the office. I was eagerly looking forward to my evening with Tiffany.

Our conflicting schedules had kept us apart for over a week, so I was excited to spend some quality time together. As I made my way out of the office, I ran into my boss, Superintendent Edwin Compass, near the elevator. Chief Compass, a 28-year veteran who had risen through the ranks of the department, was a well-educated man with bachelor's and master's degrees from Loyola University. He was also a proud graduate of the FBI Academy. Chief Compass had a reputation as a formidable street cop in his earlier years and was highly respected in the community.

He possessed a comical charm that made him likable and an outgoing personality that put people at ease. We shared an easy working relationship, characterized by mutual respect. During our conversation in the elevator, we discussed various topics related to the department and brought up the tropical depression in the Caribbean Sea. Unsurprisingly, Chief Compass had a similar reaction to mine. "I don't think it's much to worry about right now," he said dismissively as we exited the elevator. "It's too early to get worked up about a depression that's so far away." I nodded in agreement.

As a New Orleanian who had witnessed similar scenarios countless times before, I was certain it didn't warrant more thought than a passing discussion. Little did I know that later that evening, I would enjoy a delightful evening with Tiffany, completely oblivious to the ticking time bomb counting down to the intersection of Hurricane Katrina and the city of New Orleans.

August 24, 2005 (T-120 hours)

As per our protocol, our staff meeting commenced promptly at 10:00 a.m. with all members of my immediate staff present. My immediate staff consisted of Captains Michael Pfeiffer and Lawrence Weathersby, Sergeants Cynthia Landry, Michael Levasseur, and Gervais Allison, Officer Derek Brumfield, Officer Andre Menzies, and my civilian staff Lisa Brown and Cheryl Finley.

The meeting proceeded as usual, covering much of the same topics Captain Pfeiffer and I had discussed the day before. I was fortunate to have an excellent and cohesive team that worked efficiently together, and leading them was a pleasure. As we concluded the meeting, Captain Pfeiffer provided us with an update on the tropical system in the Bahamas. "The tropical depression I mentioned yesterday has evolved into a more organized system and has gained strength," Pfeiffer candidly announced. "It has been upgraded to a tropical storm and has been named Katrina." "It's still quite far away, right?" Officer Brumfield inquired.

"Yes, it is," Captain Pfeiffer responded. "This simply means that the storm's winds now fall within a range of thirty-nine to seventy-three miles per hour." Even in that moment, there was no sense of alarm or panic. After all, it was just a tropical storm, and there was no immediate indication that it was heading towards us. However, being a person guided by protocols and procedures, I retrieved our department's Hurricane Preparedness Manual to have it readily available in the unlikely event that we would need to utilize it. While my staff engaged in casual conversation about Tropical Storm Katrina in the meeting space, I excused myself to inform Chief Compass.

As the Assistant Superintendent, it was my responsibility to ensure he remained up-to-date on matters such as this. At that moment, the tropical storm posed no significant concern, but should he be questioned about it, he needed the most recent information to provide an informed response. "Hey chief, do you have a moment?" I asked, lightly tapping on his already open door. "Sure," he replied from behind his desk. "Come on in." "I have an update on the storm system in the Bahamas that I mentioned to you last night," I said, taking a seat across from him.

"It has intensified and organized into a tropical storm now named Katrina." "Heading towards Florida, I presume?" Compass inquired. "Yes," I nodded in confirmation. According to Captain Pfeiffer, Tropical Storm Katrina was generally moving westward towards Florida, which was not an uncommon trajectory. "I've always found the naming conventions for these storms intriguing," Compass said, reaching for a book behind him. "The World Meteorological Organization has a strict protocol for a list of male and female names used on a six-year rotation. Did you know that?" "Honestly, I can say I did not," I chuckled in response. "What does 'Katrina' mean, anyway?" Chief Compass pondered aloud as he began looking up the definition on his computer without waiting for a reply.

"Right here, it says that Katrina means purification and cleansing." Chief Compass and I exchanged a meaningful glance. "Hell, Warren, we all know plenty of areas in New Orleans that could use some cleansing," he remarked, and we shared a laugh at the irony. Little did we know that the literal and metaphorical cleansing of New Orleans, symbolized by the name Katrina, was far closer than any of us could have imagined in that moment. Later in the day, from my office, I observed Captain Pfeiffer putting up our department's magnetic map outside his office to track Tropical Storm Katrina. As I approached for a closer look, I overheard Sergeant Cynthia Landry teasing him about it. Sgt. Landry was an easygoing person who took her job seriously, rarely indulging in jokes.

However, she occasionally surprised us with a well-timed one-liner that brought laughter. "Why are you putting up that map?" she asked him. "It's not a hurricane. It's not even in the Gulf of Mexico. You're a lawyer and a cop, not a damn weatherman." Captain Pfeiffer, a highly intelligent graduate of the Merchant Marine Academy, stood firm in his preparedness while the rest of us had grown complacent about hurricanes. "I hear you, Sergeant Landry," he replied with a smile.

"Just stay tuned, Sgt. Just stay tuned. These storms are unpredictable and can change direction at any moment. Within 24 to 36 hours, this storm could become a hurricane. I think we should all pay attention to it." "I hear you," Sergeant Landry responded half-heartedly. I must admit, even I didn't believe the storm warranted that much attention at this point. If Pfeiffer was committed to monitoring Tropical Storm Katrina, I would let him do so, and I appreciated his focus. Meanwhile, my top priority remained the task of reducing the city's murder rate and violent crimes. Although, acutely aware that we had time it was T-120 hours.

Thursday, August 25, 2005 (T-96 hours)

The next day started like any other as I enjoyed breakfast with the two important women in my life, my girlfriend Tiffany and my beautiful daughter Morgan, before we each went about our respective work and school activities. Work proceeded smoothly for most of the day, and I made satisfactory progress on some policy revisions. Around midday, as I returned to my office after a short break, my office phone rang. Seeing that it was Chief Compass calling from his office, I promptly answered.

"Hey Warren, Mayor Nagin has called an Emergency Preparedness meeting later this afternoon at City Hall," he informed me. "Both you and I need to be there." "Is it about the tropical storm?" I inquired. "Yes," Chief confirmed. "Apparently Tropical Storm Katrina seems to be gaining strength, and we need to be proactive in case it poses any implications for New Orleans." For the first time since I heard about the storm named Katrina, I felt a sense of concern. Although it still seemed unlikely that Louisiana would be significantly affected based on its current location and trajectory, Captain Pfeiffer's words from the previous day regarding the unpredictability of storms echoed in my mind.

Hours later, at 4:00 p.m., Chief Compass and I arrived at City Hall for the Emergency Preparedness meeting. The meeting took place in the Chief Administrative Officer Dr. Brenda Hatfield's conference room on the 9th floor. It was attended by all the city's department heads and essential personnel. Mayor Nagin chaired the meeting, greeting everyone with a calm and authoritative demeanor. Mayor Clarence Ray Nagin, Jr., was considered a maverick, distinguished from previous mayors as a new and different type of leader.

A graduate of Tuskegee College in Alabama, he became a successful businessman and served as the President of COX Cable of New Orleans. As the first businessman to hold the position of mayor instead of a career politician, Nagin exuded confidence and charisma, appealing to people from various social and economic backgrounds. As a proud native of New Orleans,

Nagin often mentioned that he was born in Charity Hospital, where many low-income individuals sought medical care. New Orleanians sought a change from typical politicians of the past, electing Ray Nagin by a landslide of 68 percent, expecting him to deliver favorable results. The meeting began precisely at 4:02 p.m., with the following key individuals in attendance: Mayor Nagin, Dr. Brenda Hatfield, Director of Homeland Security Terry Ebbert, Director of Finance Reggie Zeno, Acting City Attorney Sherry Landry, Health Department Director Dr. Kevin Stevens, Director of Emergency Medical Services Dr. Juliette Saussy, Fire Chief Charles Parent, Superintendent Compass, and myself.

"Good afternoon, everyone," Mayor Nagin began, commencing the meeting. "I appreciate you all gathering so quickly." "Without further ado, I'll get straight to the point," he continued. "We've been informed that Tropical Storm Katrina has intensified and been upgraded to a full-fledged hurricane bearing the same name." "Currently, Hurricane Katrina is classified as a Category 1 hurricane, meaning it has sustained winds of 74 to 95 miles per hour and storm surges of up to 4 to 5 feet high." "Do they expect it to make landfall anytime soon?" I heard a female voice inquire, though I couldn't discern who it was. "It is expected to make landfall in Florida around 7:00 p.m. Eastern Standard Time," Nagin responded. Upon hearing those words, two immediate thoughts crossed my mind.

Firstly, a Category 1 hurricane did not pose an immediate threat to the city of New Orleans. At that level, we might experience some minor street flooding in low-lying areas and perhaps some damage to unanchored motor homes. Our levee system was designed to withstand winds of up to 111 miles per hour. In the best-case scenario, it would entail a one to three-day cleanup, and we could resume normal operations. Secondly, I primarily considered the possibility that Katrina could cross the Florida peninsula and enter the Gulf of Mexico. The warm waters of the Gulf had the potential to significantly strengthen the hurricane, posing a serious threat to the states in Hurricane Alley: Louisiana, Mississippi, Texas, and Alabama. Throughout my career as a police officer, I had developed a curiosity about hurricanes, their causes, and the factors that contributed to their severity.

While scientists generally agree on the mechanics of hurricane formation and their increasing frequency and intensity worldwide, consensus ends there. One school of thought attributes to the rise in severe hurricanes to human activity and global warming, resulting in higher air and water temperatures that facilitate hurricane formation and intensification. Another school of thought suggests that the increase in severe hurricanes over the past few decades is a natural cycle driven by changes in salinity and temperature deep in the Atlantic Ocean, fluctuating every 40 to 60 years. Regardless of the cause, we were now on high alert and needed to closely monitor Hurricane Katrina.

If it reached the Gulf, the game would change exponentially. For the remainder of the meeting, we discussed cross-departmental responsibilities and the potential implications if Hurricane Katrina headed our way. The faces and expressions around the room shifted from earlier relaxation to growing concern. What had previously been an abstract thought was now a reality. We could be affected by this hurricane, and depending on its severity, the consequences could be catastrophic. Just before the meeting concluded, Mayor Nagin instructed all department heads to put their essential personnel on alert status.

"In accordance with the City of New Orleans' Emergency Preparedness Policy, all essential personnel must be placed on alert status at least 72 hours prior to a hurricane making landfall," Nagin declared. "This means all time-off requests are suspended until we get through this period." "Warren, make sure you notify all personnel of the alert status," Chief Compass directed me. "I'll send the message through the Command Center to ensure everyone is informed." I acknowledged his instruction, replying, "I'll take care of it."

Approximately two hours later, around 6:10 p.m. Central Standard Time, Hurricane Katrina made landfall in Florida. When I arrived home later that evening, both Tiffany and Morgan were waiting for me. It had been a long day, filled with information overload, but seeing them gave me a sense of relief amid everything. I waited until after dinner to inform them that Hurricane Katrina had made landfall in Florida and that there was a possibility it might reach New Orleans. Before I could utter a word, they both expressed their intention to leave the city. "I recommend that Morgan and I leave immediately," Tiffany asserted, with Morgan emphatically nodding in agreement. "You remember what happened last year with Hurricane Ivan. Getting out of the city was a nightmare."

In August 2004, Hurricane Ivan caused catastrophic damage as a Category 3 hurricane in Grenada and even greater devastation as a Category 4 hurricane in Jamaica. When it reached the Gulf of Mexico, it was the size of Texas and had the potential to be a major disaster. Most residents of New Orleans with the means to do so evacuated the city. The traffic congestion and counterflow were horrendous. What would typically be a six-hour drive to Houston took Tiffany and Morgan nearly 20 hours to complete. "I agree with Tiffany, Dad," Morgan added.

"My mom Gwendy, and my brother Quinn will be here shortly, and we're leaving tonight. Tiffany will leave in the morning, heading towards the Houston area." Later that evening, as Tiffany and Morgan packed the last of their belongings, I released a breath I hadn't realized I was holding. I then began contacting other family members and close friends, advising them to evacuate as soon as possible. If New Orleans were to be struck by Hurricane Katrina, at least the people I loved most would be safe in Houston, out of harm's way. With a multitude of thoughts swirling in my mind, I decided to step outside into the backyard and take in the night air.

Sitting by the pool, sipping on some Hennessy, and listening to R&B music, the sky was clear, and the temperature was perfect. I reflected on the events of the day and all that we had learned within a mere 24 hours. I wondered what lay ahead for the city of New Orleans in the coming days. Would life continue as usual? Would this be another hurricane that spared our city?

As I sat there, Aaron Neville's "Bridge Over Troubled Water" began to play. Little did I know the significance of that moment—a bridge over troubled water. Just as I was about to return inside, Chief Compass's remark about the name Katrina resurfaced in my thoughts. "Hell Warren, we know a lot of areas in New Orleans that could use some cleansing." Initially, we had laughed at his statement, but on this night, it sent a shiver down to the core of my soul.

Chapter 3:
Category 1

Countdown to Katrina T-72 Hours

I woke up the next morning to the sound of one of my favorite news-casters on WWL Channel 4, reporting on various news stories. Still half asleep, I glanced at the clock on the nightstand next to me. It read 6:30 a.m. Just an hour and a half earlier, I had said goodbye to Tiffany, while Morgan had left the night before. Both had set out for Houston.

Though I didn't think it was possible for me to fall back asleep, I sur-prisingly drifted off almost immediately after getting back into bed. As I was dozing off, trying to catch a few more minutes of sleep, the newscaster started reporting on Hurricane Katrina and its impact on South Florida. I sat up and listened attentively. The news was disheartening. Katrina had struck Broward-Miami-Dade County the previous night as a Category 1 hurricane with winds exceeding 80 mph. The report mentioned 7 fatalities, 33 torna-does believed to have been spawned, a collapsed highway in Miami-Dade, and over 14 inches of rainfall. Additionally, more than 1 million people were without power.

The worst news yet was that it had entered the Gulf of Mexico as a Cat-egory 1 hurricane. The warm waters would only serve to strengthen it, in-creasing its destructive power for whichever unfortunate city lay in its path. "This can't be happening," I muttered to myself. Before succumbing to full-scale worry, I reminded myself that it was still early in the game and Katrina's path was merely a projection. Nothing was set in stone. How many hurri-canes in the past had appeared to be heading directly for New Orleans, only to shift course? Katrina would be no different, I reassured myself. Yet, there was an underlying sense of foreboding that I couldn't shake, no matter how hard I tried.

Later that morning, a little after 8 o'clock, our weekly CompStat meeting was scheduled to begin in the conference room adjacent to my office at NOPD Headquarters. CompStat was a meeting where we discussed the lat-est crime trends based on computer statistics with the district commanders, aiming to identify patterns in crime and devise strategies to combat them. A significant portion of the meeting revolved around following up on crime-fighting strategies from the previous week and formulating new approaches based on current developments. Eventually, the conversation turned to Katrina. How could it not? It was on the minds of every officer and commander present.

What struck me as interesting was that, at that very moment, we were experiencing 90-degree weather with mostly sunny skies. There were no indicators whatsoever that New Orleans was in any immediate danger from this monstrous storm named Katrina that had wreaked havoc in South Florida. Most of us had shifted from denial to a state of unconscious avoidance. While we no longer denied the possibility of danger, we engaged in psychological avoidance to shield ourselves from the potential reality. It was easy to avoid contemplating the danger of Katrina.

The Gulf Coast was constantly under the threat of hurricanes, but how many of them had truly caused significant damage to New Orleans in recent years? Moreover, if past patterns were any indication, the hurricane would likely veer away from the city as others had done before. However, complete avoidance would be reckless, and Katrina was the type of storm that one couldn't afford to take lightly. We discussed the devastation in South Florida and the current position of Katrina in the Gulf of Mexico, where it was steadily gaining strength from the warm waters.

"Commanders, I want to inform you that all members of the department are now officially on standby and emergency alert status," I announced, standing at the center of the conference room, facing the commanders. "All vacations are canceled until further notice."

As I observed their expressions, I could see a mix of concern and mild irritation at the implications of their updated statuses. Many of them had families and loved ones in the city, and navigating the uncertainty of the situation was undoubtedly challenging.

"This morning, we received reports that Hurricane Katrina caused moderate damage in South Florida, resulting in at least 7 fatalities and 33 tornado sightings," I continued. "With Katrina moving into the Gulf of Mexico as a Category 1 hurricane, there is a high likelihood of it gaining strength and posing a significant threat to those of us in 'Hurricane Alley'." It felt as if I was forcing them to confront what none of us wanted to consider: Hurricane Katrina was becoming a genuine danger to the city of New Orleans.

"Make sure to check the generators in your stations," I advised. "And don't forget to thoroughly review your hurricane preparedness manuals. Familiarize yourselves with the content." "Lastly," I added, "inform the members of your commands to prepare for the evacuation of their families as soon as possible. With Katrina in the Gulf of Mexico, we need everyone fully engaged, and that can only happen when we know our families are safe." Additionally, we will issue a message stating that if officers are married to another officer, only one officer has to stay. The partner will be allowed to take leave to care for their families.

The rest of the meeting focused on discussing various communication scenarios and emphasizing the importance of commanders being present for any future meetings that may be called. We dismissed them shortly afterward.

Around 10:00 a.m., we received information that Hurricane Katrina was projected to reach Category 2 hurricane strength and had the potential to intensify further. Despite some still holding on to the belief that Katrina would veer away from New Orleans, there was a palpable buzz around NOPD headquarters about the impending hurricane. Would Katrina finally be the "big one" for the city of New Orleans? How prepared was our city to handle a major weather event like Katrina? For years, New Orleans had been known as the City of Nine Lives when it came to major hurricanes. It seemed that almost every other year, there was a threat of a hurricane approaching, only for it to change course at the last minute. We had grown accustomed to the threat of severe hurricanes with minimal impact on our city.

Deep down, we hoped that Katrina would follow the same pattern. However, I decided to spend the rest of my afternoon reviewing my hurricane preparedness manual. While hopeful that I wouldn't need to put what I was reading into action, my strategic mindset wouldn't allow me to ignore the situation. I delved into topics such as acquiring and prepositioning assets that could potentially be needed during a weather crisis, as well as the tactics and objectives to address the possible challenges that lay ahead. Lost in my thoughts and preparations, I was interrupted by Superintendent Compass, who brought urgent news.

"Warren, the mayor has called for a mandatory staff meeting at City Hall, and he needs us to be there as soon as possible," Compass informed me.

I glanced up from the manual I had been reading to find Chief Compass standing in my office doorway. Though his voice remained calm, I could see a troubled expression on his face regarding our summons to City Hall. His typically composed light-hearted demeanor was replaced with an unfamiliar sense of vacancy and distance.

Perhaps he, like the rest of us, was grappling with the potential impact of Hurricane Katrina on New Orleans.

"Sure," I replied, closing the manual and swiftly packing up my desk. "I'll be ready in a minute and head over there right away."

"Okay, I'll see you there," Compass responded before leaving.

Upon arriving at City Hall for the staff meeting, the conference room was once again filled with various essential personnel, just as it had been during the emergency preparedness meeting the previous day. Alongside assistants and executives, notable figures like Dr. Brenda Hatfield, Director of Homeland Security, Terry Ebbert, Director of Finance, Reggie Zeno, Acting City Attorney, Sherry Landry, Health Department Director, Dr. Kevin Stevens, Director of Emergency Medical Services, Dr. Juliette Saussy, and Fire Chief Charles Parent were all present. Mayor Nagin stood at the epicenter of activity, seeking updates and issuing instructions seemingly simultaneously. The room buzzed with energy and movement.

Within the gathering, I noticed a young African-American man representing the United States National Guard with Captain bars on, despite his youth. He exuded professionalism and confidence, carrying himself commendably. While others engaged in social or business banter prior to the meeting's commencement, he sat quietly, diligently taking notes.

Deciding to establish a connection, I approached him. "Hello there," I greeted him, extending my hand. "I'm Warren Riley, Chief of Operations for the New Orleans Police Department."

"Hello, sir," he responded, standing to shake my hand as I took a seat next to him. "I'm Lieutenant Gregory Post with the National Guard. Nice to meet you."

Being strategic in my interactions, I engaged Lieutenant Post in a brief conversation about Hurricane Katrina, its potential dangers, and the involvement of the National Guard. Mayor Nagin then called the meeting to order, and discussions revolved around crucial matters at hand. With the weather system in the Gulf developing, the likelihood of Hurricane Katrina impacting New Orleans was increasing. While we maintained hope that it would spare our city, it would be unwise to ignore the potential threat. One of the initial topics of discussion centered around the timing and necessity of the first-ever mandatory evacuation in the city's history.

"We have already received calls from concerned business owners who fear the financial repercussions of a mandatory evacuation," Director of Finance Reggie Zeno shared.

In response, Mayor Nagin expressed exasperation, rolling his eyes. "I understand their concerns," he replied. "But I can't prioritize their bottom lines over the safety and security of the citizens of New Orleans."

A city attorney added, "Some have even threatened to sue the city if we issue a mandatory evacuation. However, there are provisions within the law that allow for such a call by the city when the safety of our citizens is at risk.

Silently, I marveled at the notion that some business owners were willing to sue the city over lost revenue due to a potential mandatory evacuation. The allure of money could blind people to what truly mattered.

"Here's the bottom line," Mayor Nagin asserted resolutely. "If conditions worsen in the Gulf and we determine that the safety of our citizens is at risk, we will call for a mandatory evacuation of the city. I don't give a damn how the business owners feel about it." Ray Nagin was not one to be swayed by other politicians or businessmen. Someone in the meeting sarcastically commented, "You know that's the old money of New Orleans always wanting to control everything." One of the staff members interjected, urging everyone to refocus.

The discussion then shifted to the potential implementation of contra-flow and its role in facilitating the evacuation of as many citizens as possible. Contraflow lane reversal, doubling the number of lanes available for evacuation traffic, involved using crossover sections to redirect outgoing traffic, thereby increasing capacity. The critical concern here was determining the optimal timing for initiating contraflow to prevent traffic bottlenecks.

Further discussions centered around the balance of our Emergency Fund and the available financial resources for emergency preparations. Lieutenant Gregory Post contributed to the conversation as the focus shifted toward the involvement of the National Guard and the logistics of their deployment in an emergency scenario. Despite being succinct and concise in his presentation, he exuded professionalism and demonstrated thorough knowledge. He confidently fielded every question thrown his way, and there were quite a few. In that moment, I felt a sense of pride, akin to a proud uncle witnessing the younger generation coming into their own.

Once again, the conversation veered toward the political aspects of decision-making, particularly regarding the economic implications and anticipated resistance. I felt a surge of pride knowing that not a single person in the room prioritized business or politics over safety. As our discussion continued, Mayor Nagin stepped out to take a call with Governor Kathleen Blanco. With the mayor occupied, many of us seized the opportunity to check emails or engage in light work.

Turning to Lieutenant Post, I suggested, "Given the developments thus far, I believe we should consider acquiring and prepositioning high-water vehicles, boats, and meals-ready-to-eat."

"Specifically, how many boats and trucks would you need?" he asked, jotting down a few notes on a pad. "And I'm assuming you would want Deuce and a Half trucks since they have an apparatus that allows them to drive in water as high as five and a half feet."

"That's correct," I confirmed, recalling the information from my hurricane preparedness manual. "We would need at least 40 flat boats and 40 Deuce and a Half trucks."

"Okay, I can place that request immediately," Lieutenant Post stated.

"Great," I replied. "I believe it's also necessary for us to request water supplies and a backup as well."

"Not a problem. I'll submit those requests right away to stay ahead of everything," he responded before promptly leaving the room.

I was grateful that I had taken the time to familiarize myself with the city's potential needs during a hurricane through the manual. Armed with that knowledge, I felt empowered and fortunate to be sitting next to Lieutenant Post, seizing the unexpected opportunity. At least in this moment, I believed I could contribute something tangible amidst what often felt like helplessness.

Approximately fifteen minutes later, Mayor Nagin returned to the conference room from his phone call with Governor Blanco. He informed us that Governor Blanco would be declaring a state of emergency for Louisiana later that afternoon around 4:00 p.m. CST. Before he could delve into further details, his executive assistant handed him his phone and whispered something in his ear. Mayor Nagin briefly stepped outside the conference room and returned, still engaged in an evidently important call.

"I'm in a staff meeting with essential personnel of the city of New Orleans," Mayor Nagin finally said to the person on the other end of the phone. "I'm going to put you on speaker."

The person on the phone turned out to be Max Mayfield, the Director of the National Hurricane Center. Once on speakerphone, he greeted all of us with news that we dreaded hearing.

"At this moment, Hurricane Katrina is officially a Category 2 hurricane and is strengthening."

It was as if all the air had been sucked out of the room. The expressions on people's faces ran the gamut. Some displayed shocked disbelief, while others wore silent expressions of panic. A few faces turned red with fear, and one woman in the room audibly began to weep. I simply asked myself, "Did he just say it was a Category 2 hurricane and that it was strengthening?" Although Mayor Nagin displayed concern, he maintained a confident and composed demeanor, navigating the room with grace. In the face of this distressing news, his composure was truly admirable. Many of us felt the weight of the information hitting us hard.

"The environmental conditions in the Gulf of Mexico are optimal for the development and strengthening of this hurricane, so it does not bode well for wherever it will ultimately make landfall. This has the potential to become a catastrophic category 4 or 5," Max concluded.

"Thank you, Max. I'll be in touch," Mayor Nagin said before ending the call.

Apart from the representatives present from the National Weather Service and local meteorologists discussing Katrina's projected path and trajectory, the room fell silent. For a long moment, no one spoke. It was as if everyone needed time to come to terms with the information we had just received. The longer Katrina lingered in the Gulf, the stronger it would become. If its path continued towards New Orleans, we would undoubtedly be facing a Category 4 or 5 hurricane.

For the first time, I contemplated what would become of Tiffany and Morgan if I died here in New Orleans. If Katrina hit as a Category 4 or 5, there was a significant possibility that I, along with many of the men and women staying behind to serve our city, would lose our lives. The thought hit me like a ton of bricks. I envisioned Morgan growing up without me, facing the challenges of school and college without my guidance. The prospect of missing out on these precious moments darkened my heart. I couldn't bear the idea of not being there for my daughter or any of my loved ones. In the room, a sense of concern for our families permeated the atmosphere, although the men were less vocal about articulating their worries compared to the women. Nonetheless, their expressions conveyed the shared anxiety.

Lieutenant Post returned to his seat next to me, informing me that he had already made progress on my requests. "The forty flat boats and 40 Deuce and a Half trucks have been ordered, and I'll inform you once the request is approved," he stated, glancing back and forth between me and his notepad. "We need to determine where you want the assets prepositioned."

I had contemplated this beforehand while reading through the hurricane preparedness manual. I had no idea then that I would end up sitting next to the person who could make it happen for me. "We need five boats and five trucks positioned at each of the eight district stations in the city," I responded. "This will allow us to respond immediately in every area, provided the hurricane winds subside."

"Sounds good," Lieutenant Post replied. "Let me go ahead and submit that. Given recent developments, we want to stay ahead as much as possible in case we need them."

Lieutenant Post left the room once again, and I appreciated his prompt and proactive approach.

I glanced across the room and noticed Colonel Terry Ebbert and Chief Compass engaging in light banter. Occasionally, Terry would join Mayor Nagin in conversation, but he always returned to his seat next to Chief Compass. What struck me was the contrast in their expressions and demeanors. Colonel Terry Ebbert, the Director of Homeland Security and a Vietnam war veteran, exuded a calm and poised demeanor that reassured many of us. This was a man who had faced life-threatening situations and remained composed. His posture seemed to convey the sentiment, "I've been through tough shit before! We've got this!"

On the other hand, Chief Compass appeared quietly distressed. To be clear, he wasn't visibly shaken or panicked, but there was a certain emptiness in his gaze that suggested a level of avoidance possibly rooted in fear—the same fear that seemed to be present in all of us.

Furthermore, I found it interesting that Chief Compass hadn't approached me yet to discuss strategy or the items outlined in the hurricane preparedness manual. As the second-in-command in the NOPD, it was my responsibility to ensure that things were in motion and that we were prepared. I expected him to be engaged and interested in the details.

In that moment, I resolved that he and I would have to debrief after the meeting to discuss our strategy. Awkwardness could not take precedence over the needs of our citizens or the effectiveness of our police department.

The remainder of the afternoon was filled with updates and planning sessions with the staff, ensuring that we were well-positioned to respond to any further unfavorable developments. As we worked diligently, someone in the conference room announced that Governor Blanco would be making an announcement on television. We knew that this would be the moment she declared a state of emergency.

Someone turned on the large television in the conference room and adjusted the volume so that we could hear what was being said. After a brief introduction, the newscaster tossed it to the reporter covering the live press conference with Governor Blanco. She began by stating that the National Hurricane Center had officially shifted the potential track of Katrina from the Florida Panhandle to the Mississippi/Alabama coast. In light of this update, she declared a state of emergency for Louisiana. The declaration activated the state's emergency response and recovery program, under the command of the director of the state office of Homeland Security and Emergency Preparedness, to provide emergency support services.

Governor Blanco spoke with assurance and confidence as she outlined the action plan for the state of Louisiana under the state of emergency. She reassured her constituents that we were resilient and prepared to face what could be one of the most challenging weather events to date if conditions continued to develop as they appeared. As Governor Blanco delved into the granular details, the newscaster chimed in to report that the governor of Mississippi, Haley Barbour, had also declared a state of emergency for Mississippi.

As the news coverage concluded, another wave of silence washed over the room. Even Mayor Nagin appeared subdued in this moment. It was sinking in: this was really happening. My mind immediately turned to the reports of the devastation caused by a Category 1 Hurricane Katrina in South Florida. Now that it had grown into a Category 2 and was gaining size and strength, what would happen to our beloved city? Were we truly prepared to face what could be "The Big One"? The countdown to the epic destruction wrought by Hurricane Katrina upon New Orleans was now less than 72 hours away.

Interlude

February 2005 - almost six months earlier.

Cafe' Rose Nicaud Coffee House was undoubtedly one of the most exclusive coffee shops in the French Quarter. Situated on the outskirts of the Quarter located at 632 Frenchmen Street, it served as a discreet meeting place for high-ranking city officials, businessmen tourists and locals. They used to gather in the mornings to start their days and to wine down from libations, jazz, and the nightly NOLA carnival atmosphere, and many temptations of the French Quarter.

When I received Mayor Nagin's call the previous night, inviting me to meet him at Cafe' Rose Nicaud, I knew the conversation would carry weight based on the venue alone. Ray Nagin was not one to engage in frivolous pleasantries with staff. While his charismatic personality and Southern gentleman charm allowed him to effortlessly work a room, his street smarts anchored his political persona with a no-nonsense ethic. He meant what he said, and he said what he meant.

After a day of reviewing policies and devising crime-fighting strategies, I settled in when I received a call from his executive assistant inquiring about my availability for an informal meeting at 9:00 p.m. the following evening. I confirmed my availability, and she informed me that Mayor Nagin would be calling me directly with further details. Shortly after, he called and casually invited me to join him at Cafe' Rose Nicaud for coffee.

"Riley, I want to talk to you about a few things," Nagin said in a relaxed manner. "This is just between us, alright?" he added quickly. I understood his message: Keep this meeting confidential. Even as I exited my parked car a half a block down on Frenchmen Street, I could still faintly hear the music and festivities of the French Quarter in the distance. The warm and humid air of New Orleans embraced me as I walked down to the front of the building.

Upon entering the coffee shop, I immediately spotted two of Nagin's bodyguards at a table near the entrance. They acknowledged me with a nod, and one discreetly pointed out Nagin's table across the room. As I approached Nagin's table, I noticed that apart from a couple who appeared to be finishing up their evening, the shop was empty. Although I knew that this was the Mayor of New Orleans and that there was no imminent danger, I still instinctively surveyed my surroundings and assessed the situation. Normally, I would have a staff with me to ensure a safe environment, but this was obviously a clandestine meeting which is why I decided to travel solo.

Nagin was seated at a table in the corner of the shop, and besides the bodyguards, we were essentially alone. It was officially 9:00 p.m., and the owner was turning the 'open' sign to 'closed,' preventing any further entry. It was clear that Nagin desired privacy for this meeting. He stood up to greet me as I reached the table. Ray Nagin exuded effortless swagger. It was evident that he spent time in the gym, given his physique, and his confidence permeated his entire being. Dressed in jeans and a polo shirt, he was still the most well-groomed individual in the room.

"Mayor Nagin," I greeted him as we both took our seats. "Chief, thanks for meeting me, man," he said, taking a sip of his drink. "No problem at all," I replied.

I ordered a coffee, and for the next 15 minutes, we engaged in casual conversation, covering topics that ranged from sports to religion. In a sudden shift, the mayor made a remark, "You know Eddie (Chief Edwin Compass) has some powerful preachers here on his side," referring to our previous discussion on religion. "Is that right?" I asked, although I was well aware of what he meant. New Orleans was a city with a complex political landscape, where a mix of influential figures held sway. Old-moneyed families, wealthy businessmen, and charismatic preachers who commanded the loyalty of their congregations all played a role in shaping policies and elections. It was an open secret that Edwin Compass had the support of prominent preachers in New Orleans, and had befriended a few of the super-rich and his gregarious personality, however, many thought it was more of a foolery than charisma that endeared him to them and their constituents. They embraced him as their guy. Nagin, frustrated, responded, "Ah, fuck Riley. You know exactly what I mean." I smiled knowingly, neither confirming nor denying my understanding. What I did know was that there was tension between Nagin and Compass, stemming from their differing views on focus and approach. "You know I don't indulge in all that political bullshit that Compass is into," Nagin remarked after a pause. "My goal is to reduce the crime rate in this city, not cozy up to politicians."

"I hear you, Sir" I replied. Nagin continued, "Eddie Compass wasn't my choice for Chief of Police. You were. My committee selected you," The selection for Superintendent of the New Orleans Police Department came down to three candidates, including Eddie and me. If I had a flaw in my career, it was my refusal to align myself with a political agenda in a city as politically driven as New Orleans. It wasn't my style, and honestly, it wasn't worth compromising my principles just to fit in. Eddie, on the other hand, was politically savvy, and in the end, it worked to his advantage.

Compass had worked for former Mayor Sidney Barthelemy's administration from 1986 through 1994 as a member of his security team. During that period of time Chief Compass met and entertained many highly influential people i.e., billionaires, millionaires, powerful preachers and politicians. He was gregarious, a bit high strung, but if you could deal with his highly upbeat, attention grabbing personality, you'd love him. He met with a lot of influential people while on Mayor Barthelemy's staff and many liked him and supported him.

"Hmmm," was all I could muster in response to Nagin's admission. What could I say? My boss's boss was essentially telling me that I should have been in his position. I knew better than to misinterpret his words, so I carefully chose my response. "You don't have to say anything," Nagin interjected. "I know where things stand."

"His political connections with the preachers and some powerful businessmen and families here made it easy to bring him into this position," Nagin continued. "What impressed me about you is your knowledge and composure. Not a single politician, preacher, or millionaire business person called me to advocate for your appointment as the new chief. But every other finalist had someone lobbying on their behalf. I respect that you stood on your own."

"At the end of the day, I went with Chief Compass to appease some of my supporters, Chief Policitis is a mother!", I listened intently as my eyebrows raised, my eyes squinted and my teeth quietly grind listening to Mayor

Nagin while trying not to react to this admission. Nagin continued: but Compass' focus is all wrong," Nagin stated. "Crime reduction should be the focal point," I responded, articulating what Nagin had been advocating for months. "Damn right!" he affirmed. "Reducing the violent crime rate in the city has been one of my platforms for years. He knew that when I interviewed him."

To the average person, the tension between Chief Compass and Mayor Nagin might not be apparent, but for those of us who were aware of it, it felt palpable at times. As the mayor spoke, I recalled a conversation I had with Chief Compass weeks earlier. He had mentioned that he and the mayor weren't getting along, describing a disagreement and alluding to some demands the mayor made that Compass refused to comply with. Based on my current conversation with the mayor, I knew this discussion was not going to be pleasant.

As the second-in-command in the NOPD, I sometimes felt caught in the crossfire of their dynamics, but I made a conscious effort to stay focused on the task at hand. I had only been in the position of Chief of Operations for a few months, succeeding my predecessor who was fired for lying on his resume. Mayor Nagin had appointed me with a clear mandate to reduce the violent crime rate in the city, and so far, we were making progress with an overall reduction across the board.

"Mayor Nagin, I believe that with my team's continued focus on crime reduction, we can achieve that objective," I offered.

"I have no doubt that you can do it, Chief," he responded. "That's why I brought you here. You deserve a bigger role. I need you to take a bigger seat at the table."

I wasn't quite sure what he meant by a "bigger seat at the table." "Are you saying I should take over as the Superintendent?" I asked, seeking clarification.

"It's not working out with Eddie," Nagin said, as if reading my thoughts. "He knows it. Are you ready to step up? I'm giving him six months to find another job. Are you ready?"

As a wave of mixed emotions washed over me, considering Eddie as a friend, I knew that as the second-in-command, it was my duty to be prepared to step up when the time came. "Yes, sir," I replied. Even though I knew we were essentially alone, I still glanced around the coffee house. We were indeed alone.

"How?" I inquired, seeking more details.

"Eddie is not suited for the type of department I need," Nagin answered. "He's a good guy, but not the right fit for my vision. He has accepted it. I just need to know that when I call you to take over, you will be ready."

I liked Eddie and considered him a friend to some extent. Running a police department had always been one of my goals, but this was not how I expected it to happen. Now, knowing that I was in fact the mayor and the committees first choice, and knowing that I was well prepared I assured the mayor that as the second-in-command, my job was to be prepared to step up at a moment's notice. "I'll be ready," I affirmed.

Chapter 4:
Category 3

Countdown to Katrina T-48 Hours

As Katrina near I dream of my child hood 1965, I was six years old and Hurricane Betsy. The sound of the rain and wind was deafening, only matched by the overwhelming fear inside me. I was convinced that my mom, my brother Rickie, my older sister Freda, her fiancé Roland, and I were going to die. Roland had nearly been blown off the roof as he tried to protect us from the powerful storm Hurricane Betsy by boarding up windows. Huddled together in the main room of our two-story shotgun house, I looked into my mother's eyes. Even as a child, I could see the fear in her gaze as she tried to project strength and courage while the hurricane relentlessly pounded our home.

My father, working for New Orleans Public Service, was considered essential personnel and was on duty in the city. So, it was just the four of us enduring the storm at home. Nestling closer to my mother, I could hear water pouring in from various parts of the house where leaks were not uncommon, but this time they felt like omens of impending destruction. Sensing my fear, my mother held me tighter, providing a momentary sense of comfort.

Then, a loud CRASH! echoed through the house as one of the back upstairs windows gave way to the force of the hurricane. We all cried out in surprise and alarm. In that instant, my young mind and heart braced themselves for the inevitable. And just then, the phone began to ring, piercing through the chaos.

RING! RING! RING!

Saturday – August 27, 2005

The incessant ringing of my telephone jolted me out of a dream, where the fear and memories of Hurricane Betsy haunted me. Still half-asleep, I fumbled around my room, searching for the source of the sound. Through the haze of sleep, I glanced at the clock, indicating it was 6:25 a.m. The realization that a call at this hour couldn't bring good news caused the thick fear from my dream to resurface. Reluctantly, I looked toward the faint morning light seeping through the dark curtains, gradually illuminating my room. Finally, I located my phone—it was still ringing persistently.

"Hello," I answered, my voice laced with trepidation.

"Warren, it's Terry," said Colonel Terry Ebbert, the Director of Homeland Security, on the other end. His voice lacked panic, but there was an unmistakable sense of urgency that caught my attention.

"Good morning, colonel," I replied. "What's going on?" It was clear he wasn't calling for casual conversation at this early hour, and I preferred to get to the point without delay.

"Warren, we received a briefing from NOAA (National Oceanic and Atmospheric Administration) today. Hurricane Katrina is heading straight for New Orleans, and the impact is expected to be catastrophic," Colonel Ebbert informed me. Shit, he wasted no time getting to the point.

"We need you and Chief Compass at City Hall immediately for an emergency strategy session with the mayor and city leaders," Colonel Ebbert continued. "I've been trying to reach Eddie, but I haven't been able to get through."

"Don't worry, Colonel. I'll find him," I assured him. "Eddie lives nearby, probably out jogging. I'll locate him, and we'll head over as soon as possible."

"Thanks," Ebbert acknowledged before ending the call. As I sat on the edge of my bed, adrenaline surged through my veins. I had hoped that Katrina wouldn't develop into a devastating storm with dire consequences for New Orleans, but it seemed that was exactly what was happening. Our city was in grave danger, and the next few days would be crucial for our survival and that of our community.

Before allowing my tactical instincts to take over completely, I had to address one immediate concern—Tiffany and Morgan. Though they were safely in Houston, recent developments suggested that I would have limited contact with them during the storm as my duties would consume me. I needed to hear their voices, drawing strength from their presence to face the unknown ahead. I dialed Tiffany's number first, and we exchanged heartfelt expressions of love. She voiced her concern for my well-being and emphasized her worry about my safety and mental state. The call to Morgan, however, filled me with a sense of dread. As parents, we instinctively love our children unconditionally, willing to sacrifice everything for them. But what do you do when you realize your own mortality may be imminent, leaving so much unshared? At sixteen, Morgan had a lifetime ahead of her, and nobody could understand and love her as deeply as I did. The thought of leaving her terrified me more than the dangers of Hurricane Katrina.

When Morgan's voice came through the phone, her concern and uncertainty were evident. Dammit! My heart ached instantly. As long as I had breath in my body, though, I was determined to be her protector, providing a sense of security even in uncertain times. "I've been hearing that New Orleans is going to be hit hard by Katrina," she said after our greetings. "It's going to be a rough ride for us, baby girl," I admitted. "But we will get through it, okay?" I would never lie to my daughter, but despite the challenges ahead, I fully intended to keep my promise to Morgan that everything would be okay. Our call ended with professions of love and my assurance to keep her updated as much as possible. The tenderness in her voice as she said, "Please be careful, Dad," touched me deeply.

Having connected with my family, I swiftly selected my attire for the day and headed to the shower. The water cascading over me reminded me of the significance of my bond with them and the jeopardy it faced due to the current circumstances. Melancholy and depression subtly tried to seep in, but I knew that if I wanted a chance at overcoming the impending challenges, I couldn't afford to spend my emotional energy on them.

There must be some sort of atmospheric or cosmic loophole that ensures New Orleans won't take a direct hit from Hurricane Katrina, I thought, reflecting the pervasive culture of denial deeply ingrained in the city. It was hard to fathom that after years of near misses and last-minute hurricane redirects, we would be faced with a direct hit from a super hurricane like Katrina.

Even as I dressed for the emergency meeting, a glimmer of hope clung to me, wishing for a last-minute change in the storm's course. I gathered the necessary items—snacks, laptop, and writing utensils—for the meeting, knowing I wouldn't have time to stop by my office beforehand. The urgency conveyed by Colonel Ebbert indicated the critical importance of the meeting, and we needed to be there immediately. Furthermore, I still had to locate Superintendent Compass, but I anticipated it wouldn't be a difficult task. Keys and supplies in hand, I left my home, stepping into a day that I knew would be life-changing.

Superintendent Edwin Compass was a man of routine and consistency, and our proximity allowed for chance encounters in our neighboring subdivisions. Each morning, you could find him jogging through the area, a ritual that he engaged in unless circumstances prevented it. I've heard many runners express how early morning runs serve as a time for free-flowing thoughts, allowing them to strategize and plan. Given our city's current predicament, I was confident Eddie would be jogging through the subdivision, his mind wandering in search of solutions beneficial to our city.

It took me no more than five minutes to spot Eddie, smoothly maintaining his rhythm and stride as he jogged along one of the service roads adjacent to his subdivision. Unaware of my presence, he suddenly stopped when I called out his name. "Eddie!" I shouted, prompting him to turn around, squinting to adjust his eyes to the morning sun peeking through the clouds. Pulling up beside him in my SUV, I rolled down the passenger window.

"I just got a call from Colonel Ebbert about Katrina," I informed him. "The mayor needs us at City Hall for an emergency meeting ASAP." Chief Compass showed no signs of surprise, but deep concern emanated from him. It was as if he had anticipated this moment. Compass stated dropped me at my house, we were only three blocks from his house. I dropped him off and waited, he was in and out within three minutes, he jumped into his SUV. With the lights and sirens, we headed to City Hall. As we started driving, it dawned on me that Deputy Chief Steven Nicholas should join us at the meeting.

Chief Nicholas oversaw the Technical Services Bureau for NOPD, responsible for IT, logistics, and equipment. Considering his role, I believed his participation in the meeting would be prudent. "I think Chief Nicholas should join us," I suggested to Superintendent Compass. "Okay," Eddie responded simply, somewhat detached. "I'll call him now and ask him to meet us there," I declared.

I immediately contacted Deputy Chief Steven Nicholas, explaining the situation and the urgent need for his presence at City Hall. Like the rest of us, he had been monitoring the storm and sleep had been elusive, so he welcomed the opportunity to be at the forefront of new information. He informed me that he wasn't far and would likely arrive before us.

Fifteen minutes later, we arrived at City Hall, carrying a heavy sense of the intensity of the impending meeting. Chief Compass had shared that around 4 a.m., while watching the Weather Channel, he learned that Katrina was gaining speed and could potentially become a Category 4 hurricane by 8 a.m. Upon entering City Hall, I spotted Deputy Chief Nicholas waiting by the elevator, seemingly anticipating our arrival as he immediately pressed the UP button. "Good morning, chief compass, Chief Riley," he greeted us as we approached him. "Good morning," Eddie and I echoed in response.

The three of us delved into the gravity of the circumstances that had brought us here so early in the morning. Chief Compass reiterated the news reports he had heard, confirming that Katrina was on track to become a Category 4 hurricane. The elevator arrived, and in silence, we rode up to the 8th floor, perhaps attempting to process the information we had just shared or grappling with the reality of our mortality.

Stepping out of the elevator, we made our way towards the mayor's conference room, where we were instructed to gather. Before reaching the conference room, Colonel Terry Ebbert spotted us as he exited an office nearby. As soon as he saw us, he approached with purpose. "Good morning, gentlemen," he greeted us. "Thank you for arriving as quickly as you could."

Each of us reciprocated his greeting, eager to understand the urgency behind the immediate meeting. "Around 4 this morning, we were advised that Hurricane Katrina is a CAT 3 and larger than the states of Louisiana and Mississippi combined," Colonel Ebbert informed us as he led the way to the mayor's conference room. "Moreover, many projections indicate that New Orleans is in its direct path." His words struck hard. New Orleans would indeed take a direct hit. I could feel my face expressing a mix of disbelief and shock, berating myself internally for even allowing a moment of hope. However, when I looked at Chief Compass and Nicholas, their expressions mirrored my own: utter astonishment.

Entering the Mayor's conference room, I fleetingly considered the weight of the decisions and conclusions we would reach in this meeting—an impact that would reverberate through the lives of thousands. Even at this early hour, the room buzzed with activity. City leaders representing various government factions and structures were present, attempting to multi-task and prepare their offices, departments, and staff for the impending demands.

Typing on laptops, cell phone conversations, and hushed discussions around the oversized conference table created an atmosphere reminiscent of a "High Alert Situation Room." The three of us took our seats just as Mayor Nagin entered the room. Although he donned slacks and a button-up polo shirt, his usual confident swagger seemed absent. He appeared disheveled, with scattered gray hairs piercing through his typically well-groomed five o'clock shadow. It was evident that he had endured a sleepless night. Skirting pleasantries and formalities, Mayor Nagin got straight to the point.

"Good morning, everybody," he stated. "Around 4 this morning, Dr. Brenda Hatfield, Colonel Terry Ebbert, and I spoke with Max Mayfield of the National Oceanic and Atmospheric Administration, and he advised that Hurricane Katrina is now a CAT 3 hurricane, possibly heading directly for New Orleans." "There's a high probability that within the next hour or so, Katrina will strengthen to a CAT 4 or even a CAT 5 hurricane," he continued. "As it stands, our levee system should handle a low to medium CAT 3 hurricane, but anything stronger is uncertain." The intensity in the room was palpable. We hung on his every word. Based on my research and preparations for this hurricane, I knew that a Category 4 hurricane carried winds of 131 to 155 miles per hour with storm surges of 13 to 18 feet.

These figures alone indicated that the storm would undoubtedly overwhelm our levees, breach them, and cause significant damage. "Currently, Katrina is larger than the combined size of Louisiana and Mississippi, and it's still growing," Mayor Nagin continued. "A direct hit would have a cata-strophic impact on our city." "With that in mind, we need to evacuate as many people as possible," he added.

"Hurricane Katrina is expected to make landfall on the morning of August 29th, possibly as a Category 5 hurricane." "I am exploring the legal implications of issuing the first mandatory evacuation in our city's history." "Governor Blanco and I will hold a joint press conference to inform the public about the severity of our situation and encourage anyone who can leave the city to do so." Mayor Nagin and Colonel Ebbert went on to explain that Phase 1 of Louisiana's emergency evacuation plan would commence around 9:00 a.m. Under Phase 1, citizens in coastal areas south of the Intracoastal waterways would begin evacuating 50 hours before landfall of a Category 3 hurricane or stronger.

Phase 2 would begin at 12:00 p.m. Furthermore, the mayor contemplated the possibility of issuing a mandatory evacuation order to ensure the safe departure of over 465,000 residents of New Orleans within 36 hours. It was an immense challenge that had to be met. To facilitate a smooth evacuation, cooperation from surrounding parishes in the New Orleans metro area and several counties in Mississippi would be necessary.

The state of Mississippi had already extended its cooperation by allowing citizens of New Orleans to evacuate first, preventing additional traffic congestion on the eastbound interstates. All department heads were instructed to have non-essential personnel evacuate the city immediately, while essential personnel were to prepare for the imminent arrival of Hurricane Katrina.

These essential personnel would seek shelter at the Hyatt Regency Hotel in downtown New Orleans and be ready to report by 9:00 p.m. on Sunday night, August 28th. The final instruction was for all department heads to convene in City Hall's media room at 1:00 p.m. for the mayor's joint press conference with Governor Blanco.

Like me, it seemed that every department head present instantly shifted into tactical mode. As soon as the meeting concluded, calls resumed, and individual departments began strategizing. "Chief Riley, I need you to notify all commanders that we will have an emergency hurricane advisory and preparedness meeting at 2:00 p.m.," Chief Compass directed.

He further explained that the meeting would take place in the large conference room at NOPD Headquarters and attendance was mandatory. Surprisingly, Chief Compass then approached me privately. "Warren, I want you to conduct the briefing," he said. "You've studied the hurricane preparedness manual more than any of us, so you're better equipped to address the instructions related to it."

I strongly opposed this idea. In times of uncertainty and apprehension, soldiers need to hear directly from their leader, not a representative or someone else in charge. I didn't hide my feelings and expressed my concern that the commanders needed to hear from their leader. I offered to compile a bullet list of talking points that he could easily navigate while ensuring that all crucial points were covered. He agreed, and we decided to proceed with the meeting in this manner.

However, Superintendent Compass's behavior continued to raise suspicions. I couldn't quite pinpoint what was off, but something was definitely amiss. I considered voicing my concern but then one of the mayor's assistants called for Superintendent Compass, and he left with them. As worried as I was about Compass's demeanor and unusual actions, I realized that now was not the time for a potentially negative discussion. We were on the verge of facing a historic hurricane of epic proportions with New Orleans in its direct path. This was a moment that required a united front, and any substantial concerns could be addressed later.

While preparing for the 1:00 p.m. joint press conference and our departmental meeting, I couldn't shake the feeling that this storm had caught us unprepared. With much of the city situated below sea level, any major breaches in the levee system caused by the storm could have catastrophic consequences. Adding to this precarious situation was the "bowl factor" of New Orleans. The city was nestled between levees along the Mississippi River and those surrounding Lake Pontchartrain. If water were to enter the city, it would be an immense challenge to remove it.

Fortunately, Phases 1 and 2 of the evacuation plans began successfully at 9:00 a.m. and noon, respectively. Citizens were leaving the city, which meant fewer people remaining to ride out the storm. I couldn't help but feel relieved that many were heeding the warnings and evacuating. However, it still wasn't enough. News reports showed some residents planning to stay, either because they had always done so or because they lacked the means to evacuate.

Mayor Nagin intended to announce that the Superdome would open as a last resort refuge for citizens with special needs. However, he was waiting to make the announcement, fearing it might discourage those who intended to leave the city. I hoped that the joint press conference with Governor Blanco would be enough to persuade our citizens to evacuate.

Precisely at 1:00 p.m., the media room at City Hall was filled with reporters and state and city officials as Mayor Nagin, Governor Kathleen Blanco, Chief Compass, and numerous officials from Southeastern Louisiana parishes held a special press conference to urge residents to evacuate. Mayor Nagin stood at the center of the podium, flanked by Governor Kathleen Blanco on his left and Councilman Oliver Thomas standing behind him. Clad in a button-up polo and a dark blazer, he exuded the natural swagger and confidence we were accustomed to seeing from him at such events. Governor Blanco displayed a professionally composed demeanor, completely aligned with the words of Mayor Nagin and the other officials. Her presence underscored the seriousness of the situation, with all levels of government fully engaged.

"This is not a test. This is the real deal," Mayor Nagin proclaimed. He continued, "Things could change, but as of right now, New Orleans is definitely the target for this hurricane." He explained that the city was following the state's evacuation plan and that he would not officially order evacuations until 30 hours before the expected landfall, allowing residents in low-lying areas to leave first. "By the first light in the morning, we may have the first-ever mandatory evacuation of New Orleans," he added. Urging immediate action, he addressed those without means of transportation or unable to evacuate, mentioning the possibility of using the Superdome as a shelter of last resort. He emphasized that those who chose to seek refuge there would need to bring their own food, drinks, and other essential items.

Aaron Broussard, President of Jefferson Parish, provided further details about the evacuations, emphasizing that residents in low-lying regions needed to leave immediately to allow others to follow suit. When Superintendent Compass took the center of the podium, I was relieved to see that he appeared to be in a positive mindset. He quickly mentioned that NOPD would likely impose a curfew and deploy officers throughout the city, especially around shopping centers, to prevent and discourage looting. He reassured everyone that NOPD would support the city throughout the storm.

"In the past, we have been fortunate to escape the worst of the hurricanes," Governor Blanco stated as she approached the podium. "But now, it seems we will have to face the full force of this storm." Cameras clicked, and reporters furiously transcribed statements, capturing the historic nature of the situation. "I am thankful that the parishes are cooperating in accordance with the Louisiana evacuation plan," Blanco continued. "Please listen to your parish leaders regarding when to leave your area. At this point, it could very well be a matter of life and death."

Throughout the press conference, Mayor Nagin and Governor Blanco presented a compelling case for evacuation. They advised citizens that Hurricane Katrina was directly targeting our city and would likely cause extensive destruction. Unlike previous hurricanes, where riding out the storm was presented as a cautious option, city and state officials made it clear that Hurricane Katrina was not a storm to be trifled with. The message was unequivocal: evacuate the city as soon as possible. Governor Blanco even made a striking statement, urging those who chose not to evacuate to write their names and social security numbers on their arms with a permanent marker so they could be identified, emphasizing the potentially fatal consequences of staying behind.

However, what concerned me was that there was still no official mandatory evacuation order. It was likely to be announced the following morning, but with less than 48 hours remaining, would it be attainable? I could only hope that the citizens were heeding this plea and evacuating the city immediately. The countdown to Katrina's devastating arrival in New Orleans was less than 48 hours away.

Chapter 5:
Gladiators in police uniforms

Mayor Nagin's joint press conference with Governor Blanco provided us with a clearer understanding of the gravity of the situation. Hurricane Katrina was on a direct collision course with New Orleans. We knew things were going to be bad; we just didn't have a precise measure of how bad it would be. As I drove back to NOPD Headquarters for our mandatory meeting with the city commanders and specialized units, I couldn't help but observe the city's scenery. The clear and sunny sky gave no hint of the impending fury of nature. With the windows of my SUV partially rolled down, the humid August air flowed freely through the vehicle. However, the energy of the people told a different story.

There was a sense of organized urgency permeating the city. People moved at a much faster pace than usual, entering and exiting shops, likely gathering last-minute necessities before leaving the city. The usual pleasantries and casual conversations had been replaced by determined facial expressions of those on a mission to escape the impending storm. The drivers mirrored this urgency. Unlike the usual relaxed and hospitable driving in New Orleans, the streets now buzzed with honking horns and anxious driving. Cars weaved in and out of lanes restlessly, trying to reach their destinations. Gas stations were beginning to experience heavy traffic, with cars lining up to refuel for the journey out of the city.

As I passed a gas station, I noticed one of our police cars and an officer mediating a dispute between two individuals vying for the same pump. Given the circumstances, this situation had the potential to escalate into chaos. Mayor Nagin's warning of an impending mandatory evacuation in the early morning crossed my mind. We would undoubtedly need to station officers near gas stations to help citizens navigate obtaining the necessary fuel and safely leaving the city. I doubted Chief Compass was mentally prepared to remember all of this, so I made a mental note to remind him to direct all police commanders to position their officers near gas stations throughout the city.

And what in the world was going on with Chief Compass anyway? Lately, he seemed more than a little off. His demeanor at City Hall went beyond being distracted by the enormity of the situation. It appeared as if he were in a mental fog. Every fiber of my being wanted to ask him what was happening, but it didn't feel like the right time. I reflected on his previous comments about his strained relationship with Mayor Nagin over the past few months. Once we made it through this crisis, it was definitely time for a conversation.

As I made my way through the Garden District, I passed a strip mall area on Magazine Street that didn't seem excessively crowded. When I noticed Sergeant Manuel Curry and Reserve Officer Travis St. Pierre from the NOPD present, I understood why. Although I needed to reach NOPD Headquarters, I couldn't help but take a moment to pay homage to Sergeant Curry.

Sergeant Manuel Curry was believed to be the country's oldest active-duty police officer, serving even at the age of 80. A World War II veteran who served as a medic in the 29th Infantry Division during the invasion of Normandy, he had a long history of patrolling the Irish Channel and the Garden District since 1946. He was tough, composed, and practically a legend within the department and the city. Everyone admired and respected Sergeant Manuel Curry. Despite his age, he stood tall with a confident stride. His gray-white hair was slicked straight back, contrasting with his pale skin. He was like a revered grandfather, someone you deeply respected but knew better than to cross. His presence, along with Officer St. Pierre, helped maintain order in the area. Sergeant Curry had been one of my sergeants when I was a rookie cop, and he was always fair and an overall exceptional person.

"Are you ready for this storm, Chief?" Sergeant Curry asked lightheartedly as I approached him, Officer Tate, and several other officers after parking my car. "We have to be, Sergeant Curry," I replied, greeting both him and St. Pierre shaking their hands firmly. "It looks like this might be the one we've been avoiding all these years," St. Pierre said, looking up at the sky that still showed no signs of the impending disaster. Officer St. Pierre was a reliable and dedicated Reserve Cop, married with three kids, who always gave his all to his duty. He was a handsome Caucasian man, about five feet ten and physically fit. He worked in my office from time to time and was a genuinely good person. If Officer St. Pierre was involved, you could count on the task being completed successfully.

"Unfortunately, I think you may be right, Officer St. Pierre," I responded honestly. Sergeant Curry seemed unfazed by the conversation. "Sergeant Curry, you know you don't have to stay," I said respectfully. "You've served this city for years. You are free to evacuate as well if you want." Sergeant Curry laughed. "You leave, Chief! I'm not going anywhere," he replied. "I tried getting him to leave, Chief," St. Pierre chimed in. "It's useless."

"I've been a part of every storm that has hit this city in the last sixty years," Curry explained. "There's no way I'm leaving New Orleans now. Why would I miss the big one?" He smiled, displaying his unwavering commitment and spirit. It was that dedication that set men like Curry apart from the rest. Instead of seeking the easy way out or prioritizing personal comfort, his loyalty to his job, his people, and the city prevented him from opting out. I could only hope that the rest of us could tap into that spirit in the trying times ahead. Something told me we were going to need it.

"Well then, St. Pierre, you make sure to take care of our guy," I said, acknowledging Officer St. Pierre dedication to looking out for Sergeant Curry. It was an obvious choice, but I wanted to emphasize the importance of having an extra support system in case things became challenging. "You know it," Officer St. Pierre replied, patting one of Sergeant Curry's shoulders. "I'm not going to let him out of my sight." "Yeah, that's the only way he'll survive this!" Sergeant Curry added. We all shared a good-natured laugh at the irony of his statement.

As I got into my car, Sergeant Curry called something out to me, but I couldn't quite hear it with the windows rolled up. I rolled them down to ensure I could catch his words. "What did you say, Sergeant?" I asked. "I said, I hope you know how to swim," he said, chuckling alongside Officer St. Pierre. "I better know how," I responded, laughing as I drove off. As I distanced myself, I couldn't help but think that my own swimming skills were barely adequate, and if it came down to it, relying on them wouldn't be a pretty sight.

Nearly an hour later, NOPD Headquarters was bustling with activity. Even from my office, I could hear the organized commotion as officers moved throughout the building. While not chaotic, there was a sense of urgency permeating the air. I had spent much of my time finalizing the notes I had prepared for Superintendent Compass, which he would use to brief our commanders and assistant commanders during our Hurricane Preparedness meeting. I was grateful for the extensive review of the Hurricane Preparedness manual I had undertaken in recent days, as it provided crucial information for making tactical decisions during this critical time. I had diligently recorded relevant details that were vital for addressing our most pressing needs. There was no room for error. The lives of our citizens depended on us. Our own lives depended on it as well.

After one final review of the notes, I secured them together with a large paperclip and made my way toward the large conference room where the meeting would be held. It came as no surprise that the room was already quite full. Commanders, assistant commanders, and personnel from the eight districts, detective bureau, special operations, and other supporting units of the NOPD filled the room, standing shoulder to shoulder. Many of them juggled tasks, organizing their districts while collaborating with other commanders. I found solace in seeing everyone focused and prepared for the challenges ahead.

Superintendent Compass stood at the head of the conference table, accompanied by Deputy Chiefs Steve Nicholas, Daniel Lawless, and Lonnie Swain. I approached them and discreetly placed the notes on the table directly in front of Chief Compass. "Chief, these notes cover everything you need to address during this meeting," I informed him. "I highlighted the areas of particular importance that you should emphasize." Chief Nicholas seemed satisfied with the information I provided, but Superintendent Compass appeared distracted once again. "Oh, okay, thanks," he muttered absent mindedly, fumbling with the paperclip holding the notes together.

I, along with Superintendent Compass and the other deputy chiefs, sat at the head of the conference table. Chief Nicholas and I did a final scan of the room to ensure that all the commanders and assistants were present for the meeting. Once we confirmed that everyone was accounted for, the meeting began.

Superintendent Compass stood up and, disregarding the notes I had prepared for him, began addressing the attendees. Initially, I thought he would use the notes as a guide for his speech. However, as he distanced himself from the table and the notes, it became apparent that he had no intention of utilizing them at all.

"If you haven't already heard, let me confirm it for you now... Hurricane Katrina is now a Category 3 hurricane, and it has made a turn for New Orleans," he declared. "There are going to be some challenging days ahead of us," he continued, gesturing somewhat dramatically. "But you all know what to do. This isn't the first hurricane we've dealt with, and it won't be our last." We are warriors, we're gladiators we've been through hurricanes before.

What the hell was he saying? Were we police officers sworn to protect the citizens of New Orleans or gladiators in police uniforms? This was bizarre. Glancing at the other deputy chiefs, I could see the same expressions of confusion and embarrassment on their faces. I tried to convince myself that maybe this was just a prelude to sharing some strategic directives that would provide guidance and inform the officers in the coming days, but my embarrassment and annoyance persisted.

At one point, Chief Compass made eye contact with me while speaking, and I discreetly tapped on the notes that were still on the table. I hoped he would take that moment to refocus and start providing tactical information. However, he completely ignored my gesture and continued down the same path of motivational rhetoric. It was beyond frustrating; he was unprepared and it was evident. The commanders and assistant commanders seemed perplexed by his actions. The situation had become incredibly awkward and had dragged on for far too long.

What was going on? I knew Eddie had a fondness for books about warriors and gladiators, but this was taking it too far. It was as if he believed we were facing an ancient, fictional opponent that only required courage and bravery to defeat, rather than the formidable force of Mother Nature. Hurricane Katrina was no ordinary storm, and we had never encountered anything like it. We were in uncharted territory and desperately needed practical guidance, not a motivational speech!

Finally, after what felt like an eternity, Superintendent Compass stopped speaking and allowed us to address the commanders. Chief Nicholas and I seemed to be in sync, both realizing the need for a joint effort to provide situational awareness to the staff. We advised the commanders to secure water, sandbags, and flashlight batteries, as well as ensuring the proper functioning of station generators. I also instructed them to relocate non-essential vehicles to the third level of the Superdome parking garage, while essential vehicles should be positioned in elevated areas like overpasses or second and third level garages.

I'm not sure if hearing the tactical information woke something up in Superintendent Compass, but he finally picked up the notes I had prepared and began scanning through them.

Compass grabbed the notes I had prepared, and proceeded and directed Chief Nicholas to handle logistics, Deputy Chief Lonnie Swain to command the Louisiana Superdome, and Chief Daniel Lawless to be assigned to the Emergency Operation Center (EOC) located on the 9th floor of City Hall. I outlined the agencies that would have representatives in the EOC, including the National Guard, Coast Guard, Sheriff's Offices, Fire Department, dispatchers from both the police and fire departments, City Attorney's office, Mayor's staff, and CAO's staff. Additionally, representatives of the Street Department, Health Department, and Parks and Parkways would also be housed in the EOC.

The Emergency Operation Center (EOC) played a vital role in collecting, gathering, and analyzing data, making decisions to protect life and property, maintaining organizational continuity within the boundaries of applicable laws, and disseminating those decisions to all relevant agencies and individuals. Various agencies operated in the EOC, primarily focusing on coordinating activities at a higher level and determining incident priorities.

Chief Riley then instructed all commanders to establish rallying locations for their personnel in case their current facilities were destroyed or if communication systems failed. I emphasized the potential escalation of the hurricane to a Category 4 or 5 before landfall. Handing Chief Compass, a list of assignments for each district and unit, he proceeded to read them out loud.

"Recruitment - Superdome; Homicide - Superdome; Crime Prevention and Child Abuse - Superdome; Rape - Superdome, and all other essential personnel from the Detective Bureau - Superdome. The Administrative Support Bureau (ASB) Support Staff will secure New Orleans Police Department's Headquarters. Special Operations will be assigned to cover Canal Street, the primary shopping area in Downtown New Orleans, with a focus on minimizing looting. They were also to assist the Fire Department in search and water rescue operations in the event of major flooding."

During our meeting, Superintendent Compass received a call from Colonel Henry Whitehorn, Commander of the State Police, informing him that Governor Blanco had ordered contraflow to begin at 4:00 p.m. in the late afternoon. When the Traffic Commander was notified of the Governor's order, he confirmed that they were prepared for contraflow. Chief Compass emphasized that contraflow was a last resort and explained that traffic would flow east on Interstate 10 to the Slidell area, where Interstate 12, Interstate 59, and I-10 intersected. From there, individuals could choose their preferred route.

I also informed the Special Operations Division (SOD) that 500 National Guard Troops would assist them in anti-looting efforts in the Central Business District within 24 hours after landfall. All District Commanders were instructed to deploy anti-looting units to areas with shopping malls, major grocery stores, pharmacies, and similar establishments. Regular patrols were to be conducted, and deployment would commence once hurricane winds reduced to 55 miles per hour. Second shift officers were to report to their respective units when winds dropped below 55 miles per hour. Officers unable to reach their assigned districts were instructed to report to the nearest district.

During the meeting, Lieutenant Michael Rousell raised a valid concern about married couples who were both police officers. He questioned who would evacuate their families if both officers were on duty. After a brief discussion with Superintendent Compass, it was determined that at least one of the parents would be allowed to leave to ensure the safety of their loved ones. Ultimately, 19 officers were granted permission to depart and attend to their families.

As the meeting concluded, I felt more reassured than when it began. Most of the officers seemed comforted by the fact that we had comprehensive plans in place, positioning us to move forward strategically. Superintendent Compass's impassioned motivational speech had largely faded from our minds. Following the meeting with the commanders and assistant commanders, Superintendent Compass held another meeting with Chief Deputies Swain, Nicholas, Lawless, and myself to ensure we hadn't overlooked any important details. We also took the opportunity to review the Hurricane Preparedness Manual once again, strengthening our confidence in our preparedness.

While in the office, we learned through the television that President George W. Bush had declared a state of emergency for Louisiana and ordered federal aid to the state. Hearing this news provided a sense of relief, as I believed that New Orleans would receive immediate help since we were on the radar. Little did I know how wrong I was. Not only was New Orleans on a collision course with an immensely powerful hurricane, but our government was tragically ill-equipped to respond in a manner that would provide the much-needed support to our city's desperate citizens. The countdown to Hurricane Katrina's devastating impact on New Orleans was now just a little over 24 hours away.

Chapter 6:
Katrina on the Horizon

As I opened the door to my office at Headquarters, my cellphone began vibrating, alerting me to an incoming call. With the seriousness of the impending events within the city, I quickly placed the items in my hands onto my desk and retrieved my cellphone from my pocket. It was my fiancée, Tiffany, on the other end. "Hello?" I answered, glad to hear from her. "Good morning, babe," came her sleepy reply. "How are you?" "I'm doing fine, baby. What are you doing up at this hour?" It was around 6:45 in the morning, and I wanted to get a head start on the day by getting some much-needed paperwork done before the 10:00 a.m. meeting at City Hall for the Mayor's press conference.

Katrina's track was predicted to head straight for New Orleans as a Category 4 hurricane, and it seemed the mayor would call for a mandatory evacuation for the first time in the city's history. This meant an exceptional amount of work for the police department, and we needed to be ready. "I couldn't sleep much," Tiffany responded. "The thought of Katrina heading straight for New Orleans has me stressed... especially with you in the thick of it, Warren. I don't like it." "Babe, don't worry, I will be fine," I said, putting on a brave front. "I'm already at the office, getting some last-minute details together before I head to City Hall." Tiffany didn't respond immediately. "Baby, we have it under control," I reassured her.

"That's just it, Warren," Tiffany's voice was filled with emotion. "You can't control the weather. You can only respond to what happens, and that's what has me so afraid." Her voice trembled, and I could hear her begin to cry on the other end of the line, which immediately pulled at my heartstrings. Tiffany was not the type of woman to cry easily. One of the things that drew me to her was her measured and calm demeanor. As a communicator by trade, she was adept at conveying a multitude of ideas and situations while maintaining emotional government over herself. But today was different. On the other end of the phone, I could hear a woman genuinely fearful for the safety of her loved one.

In that moment, I wished I could guarantee that we would sail through this seamlessly, but I had to be responsible with my words. This was not the time to make empty promises. We were up against a historical storm, and we had no way of calculating the outcomes. I would do my best to make it back to her. I proceeded to tell Tiffany: "Baby, don't do that. Don't give up on me already," I said. "We are going to fight this thing with everything that we have. I just need you to have faith, okay?" There was a long pause. Knowing Tiffany, she was collecting herself so that her response would be supportive and affirming. "I believe in you, Warren," she replied with as much confidence as she could. "Thank you for that, Tiff," I said. We talked for a few more minutes before wrapping up the call and expressing our love for each other.

I then called my precious daughter Morgan and I talked, I reflected on the previous morning her mother picked her up from home and evacuated to Houston. She was my world, and I loved her like any real father loves their daughter, a love beyond words. I knew that Morgan loved me just as deeply. Before she left for school each morning, we had a special routine. As I hugged Morgan, we did our little love touches. We would touch our eyes with our index fingers, kiss our index fingers, and touch the tips of our noses, then join our index fingers together and hug each other as we said, "I love you."

This was the longest hug, a love like nothing in this world. She was my heartbeat, and I hated that she had to leave, but it was for her safety. I wouldn't see Morgan again for 28 days. Gathering my thoughts,

My staff, consisting of Captains Michael Pfeiffer and Lawrence Weathersby, Sergeants Cynthia Landry, Michael Levasseur, and Gervais Allison, Officer Derek Brumfield, and Sergeant Andre Menzies, arrived at headquarters at approximately 7:30 a.m. Many of them had just been informed of Katrina's upgrade to a Category 4 hurricane. Understandably, they were concerned as the "Big One" was headed for New Orleans. It was a frightening thought to consider the intensity of the storm headed our way.

Officers were watching news on their computers in their offices, and we had a television on in one of the conference rooms to stay updated. "Doesn't look like we're getting out of this one, Chief," Sergeant Gervais Allison said as he walked into my office with some papers, I'd asked for earlier. "Sergeant, we've got a challenging road ahead of us, it seems," I responded honestly. "But as we have always done, we will rise to the occasion."

As upsetting as the news concerning Katrina was, it was important for me to assure our officers that we would go into it giving our best. I wasn't about to sugarcoat anything. It wouldn't be easy, and we had a long road ahead full of uncharted territory, but we would traverse it with bravery and confidence.

"Oh shit!" I heard someone exclaim from the conference room. Without a second thought, Sgt. Allison and I made our way there, knowing that there was yet another development. I didn't even have to ask. As I walked into the room, I could see on the lower-third of the television screen the words "Hurricane Katrina Now a Category 5 Hurricane." It took everything in me to maintain a poker face, but on the inside, I was overwhelmed. A Cat. 5 hurricane had maximum sustained winds of up to 175 mph, with wind gusts as high as 190 mph and a central pressure of 902. In short, a Category 5 hurricane would literally destroy the city of New Orleans. There would be catastrophic destruction, devastating fatalities, and absolute annihilation of the levees, which would not stand up to a storm of this magnitude. The room fell into silence as the reporter began to run down facts and statistics, confirming what we already knew. New Orleans was in deep trouble, and it just kept getting worse.

One thing was certain - a mandatory evacuation was definitely going to happen, and we had to get everyone out of the city as soon as possible. I knew I couldn't wait until ten o'clock to head to City Hall; I had to get there now and get ahead of all of this, if at all possible. We had a lot to do and not a lot of time to do it in. I gave some last-minute instructions to the officers remaining at headquarters before heading out. Captain Lawrence Weathersby, Sergeant Gervais Allison, Sergeant Andre Menzies, and Officer Derek Brumfield rode along with me to City Hall. As we were en route, we heard on the radio that Governor Kathleen Blanco had given orders for contraflow to begin. The people of New Orleans needed every possible avenue to get out of the city.

"Some of y'all are too young to remember Hurricane Betsy and how devastating it was to New Orleans," Captain Weathersby said from the passenger seat of my SUV as we headed to City Hall. Sgt. Allison, Officer Brumfield, and Sergeant Menzies were seated in the back. "I can't forget it," I stated. "September 9, 1965. It is a date that will stand in my memory forever." "Your family didn't try to evacuate?" Menzies inquired. "Nah, my father worked for the New Orleans Public Service Incorporated," I answered. "So, he had to work. There was no evacuation for him or for us, for that matter." "Much like today, many families either didn't have the resources to leave or had lived through enough threats that leaving didn't seem warranted," Weathersby interjected. "Right," I agreed. I proceeded "It was me, my mama, my sister, and her fiancé Roland in our house on Broadway Street in Gert Town."

"We hunkered down at the house while Daddy was out serving the city. It was crazy." "I'll never forget that storm," Weathersby agreed. "It was just me and my mama in our home in the Ninth Ward when Betsy hit." I could tell by the faraway look in his eyes that it was something that still impacted him even today. "I remember the water rushing into our home so fast," he continued. "Mama and I went into the attic to get to higher ground and wait it out." "Damn," Menzies said from the backseat. "Yeah," Weathersby agreed. "I still don't remember how we got out of the attic and onto the roof, but we were there for two days before anyone came to rescue us." "I'll be honest with you," Weathersby continued. "My mama and I had a bird's-eye view of the water rising higher and higher from our rooftop. I just knew we were going to die."

The conviction with which Weathersby spoke captured the attention of all of us in the vehicle. Not sure if it was the intensity of his storytelling or if it was the irony of the situation as we were in preparation for Katrina that made the story as compelling as it was, but all voices were stilled as he spoke. "I've never been more fearful of anything in my life... and I have seen a lot," Weathersby stated. "My mama did a whole lot of praying and bargaining with God during those two days that we waited to be rescued." "And when we were finally rescued from the rooftop of our home, that was the greatest sense of relief that I have ever felt in my life," Weathersby concluded.

"Now I did hear the rumors of someone intentionally blowing up the levees with dynamite to breach the Industrial Canal so that the Lower Ninth Ward would flood, and the French Quarter, Uptown, and Garden District would be spared," Officer Derek Brumfield spoke up. "I don't know about that," Sergeant Gervais Allison responded. "Um... I'm somewhat divided on the issue," Captain Weathersby stated. "The entire rumor has its origin in the Great Mississippi Flood of 1927." "That's right," I concurred. "The Mississippi River had been swollen with historic amounts of rain and spring snowmelt, causing the river to overwhelm its levees and flood six states, including Louisiana." Weathersby recalled. "The flood had already done great damage to many other states, so it was bad news to hear that floodwater were barreling toward New Orleans." I interjected.

"Right," Weathersby agreed. "So, city leaders made the decision to set off tons of dynamite on the levee, about fifteen miles downriver from Canal Street."

"Why the hell would they do that?" Officer Menzies wanted to know.

"To ease the pressure on the levees at New Orleans by speeding the water past the city," I answered. "But the problem was that it flooded St. Bernard Parish in the worst way."

"That's messed up," Brumfield replied.

"Absolutely, but we don't necessarily know if they did it with that specific intention in mind," I reminded them.

"Needless to say, when Hurricane Betsy pushed storm surge over the Industrial Canal in 1965, many people were reminded of the prior intentional breaching of the levees that seemingly spared what many perceived to be more desirable portions of New Orleans at the expense of the Lower Ninth Ward," Weathersby said.

"Well, I don't necessarily disbelieve that wasn't the case," Officer Brumfield asserted.

"The investigations determined that nothing beyond Mother Nature caused the breaches, and that there was no insidious plot to undermine one neighborhood while saving another," Weathersby clarified. "But the truth is, none of us know for certain exactly what happened."

"Well, here is something that we do know," Officer Allison said, reading my mind. "If the Industrial Canal is overwhelmed, once again, the Ninth Ward will be at risk for major flooding.

"You read my mind, Officer," I acknowledged. "I need to check in with Captain Bryson to make sure that they are evacuating."

When it came to flooding, the Ninth Ward was always vulnerable. With the Industrial Street Canal east of it and the Mississippi River due west of it, it was an easy target for storm surge and disastrous flooding. I knew we had to get ahead of it, so I immediately phoned Captain John Bryson, Commander of the Fifth District.

Captain John Bryson was one of the most compassionate individuals in the department. He was so compassionate that I actually wondered if he had the wherewithal to handle this impending disaster. He was just such an incredibly nice guy, and oftentimes, I had to really push him to get his people to get things done that needed to be done. Bryson considered many of the department-wide mandates as dirty work, and being too ambitious and expeditious in our expectations of our officers was not something with which he necessarily agreed. Bryson was a nurturer, and although there was a time and a place for that in leadership, this was not the time.

We were about to experience a full-scale disaster with Mother Nature, and all congeniality had to go out the window. This was about moving people and saving lives. We could deal with tone and feelings later. To be clear, though, Captain John Bryson was one hell of a trooper. The only thing that outmatched his congeniality was his unwavering commitment to his district and his community. There was absolutely no doubt in my mind that John had the strength to handle this. It was his having to force himself to make strategic decisions over compassionate decisions that I knew would hit him hard.

"Captain Bryson," I said into my phone once he answered his line. "It's Chief Riley. How are you guys making out?"

"My troops and I are out and about making sure people get out of here, Chief," Bryson replied.

The fifth district was comprised of many areas, mostly very poor but equally captivating and historic. The Lower Ninth Ward was considered one of the poorest areas in the city. It also had some areas that were quite historic, such as the Marigny, Holy Cross, and Bywater. All three were beautiful areas, with great history and culture, and one of the few areas of New Orleans that was culturally diverse. Those communities also had a large population of citizens who were elderly. I feared that many would not get out of the city because many of them had ridden out other hurricanes in the past, and complacency and familiarity had settled in relative to hurricane systems. This type of laissez-faire attitude was well-known for New Orleanians, hence the moniker the BIG EASY. In this case, however, this attitude could be detrimental.

"Bryson, listen to me," I instructed. "I need you and your officers to get on bullhorns and start knocking on doors in the neighborhood and get people the hell out of here. Everybody has to go!"

"Understood, Chief," he stated, assuring me that his officers would comply with my orders. "It is essential that every citizen is clear that they have to leave," I reiterated. "Leave nothing to their imaginations. There is a great likelihood that if they do not leave, they will probably die! This storm is nothing to mess with."

I was passionate in my assertions with Bryson, firstly because I knew he needed to hear the severity of the need for the people in his district, especially in the Lower Ninth Ward, to evacuate. Secondly, I fully expected that Governor Blanco and Mayor Nagin would be calling for the city's first-ever mandatory evacuation at the press conference this morning. We had to get the people out of the Ninth Ward immediately. It was literally an issue of life and death.

"We definitely have it covered, Chief," Captain Bryson assured me. "My troops and I will go door-to-door and make sure that everyone who can evacuates."

"You already know how much this area means to me, and I know how risky trying to hunker down in a storm like this is for people in this area," he added.

Bryson spoke with a determination that I needed to hear to feel good about our officers doing everything in their power to make sure the people in the Ninth Ward were given priority. Too many times in situations like this, it was perceived that they took the brunt of things. I wanted to ensure that we minimized whatever losses possible for people who already were having a hard time. We pulled up to City Hall not too long after I wrapped up my conversation with Captain Bryson. It was like a scene out of one of those end-of-days movies we have all seen.

There were news trucks and staff and reporters all over the place. The news trucks were parked on the sidewalks and illegally parked on the lawns and in no-parking zones, blocking pathways and setting up shop for remote reporting wherever they could find space. Cable and television wires were strewn across the sidewalks and the lawn of City Hall as they stretched into the building from blocks away. It took us a minute or two before we could find a viable space to park and exit our vehicle.

When we stepped outside of the vehicle, our ears were assaulted with a cacophony (a harsh mixture of sounds) of auditory iterations of reporters and cameramen trying to grab the right angle and pitch for what they perceived was going to be the inevitable eventuality of a historic hurricane for the city of New Orleans. As we wove our way through the labyrinth (a path difficult to get through) of people, reporters, and photographers, upon recognition of who many of us were, they began to ask a barrage of questions about whether or not Mayor Nagin was about to issue the city's first-ever mandatory evacuation. None of us were rookies to these kinds of moments, so we simply side-stepped their questions and made our way into City Hall.

In stark contrast to the palpable frenetic (fast, energetic, wild) energy and electricity outside of City Hall, once we entered and walked into the first-floor lobby, it was like a ghost town. Only a couple of civil sheriffs who provided building security could be seen on the first floor, which was usually the most active area of City Hall, with city employees and citizens needing building permits, business permits, homestead exemptions, birth certificates, wedding licenses, and such all over the place. Not today! As we walked through the halls, you could hear the echoes of our hard shoes reverberating off of the walls of the empty hallways of the building. I silently hoped that the emptiness of the building meant that people were getting the hell out of New Orleans!

We proceeded to the second floor to the Mayor's Office. As we entered the mayor's suite on the second floor and proceeded to the media room, the City's Chief Administrative Officer, Dr. Brenda Hatfield, Homeland Security Director Terry Ebbert, Maria St. Martin, the Director of Sewage and Water, Reginald Zeno, the Finance Director, and many other members of the mayor's executive staff were gathered there wrapping up what appeared to be a strategic tactical session. I remember hearing that, with the exception of Terry Ebbert, they should head to Baton Rouge immediately after the press conference and that, depending on how damaged New Orleans was by Katrina, they needed to be prepared to run the city government from Baton Rouge.

Just then, Mayor Nagin and one of his most trusted staff members stepped out of the room to handle what I assumed was mission-critical business. As Mayor Nagin stepped out, Superintendent Compass made his way into the room. Unlike the days prior, Chief seemed to be focused and in a good headspace. He immediately made his way over to where I was, acknowledging the staff with me before addressing me individually. "As you probably already know, they are going to announce a mandatory evacuation at this press conference this morning," he said to me. I wasn't surprised. Shit was about to get very real in New Orleans, and people needed to get the hell out of town.

"Yeah, once I heard the hurricane status this morning, I pretty much figured that would be the case," I answered. "That's why we made our way over here."

"You and I will need to address certain matters during the press conference," he advised. I figured that would be the case, so I'd written some notes for Chief and myself concerning contraflow as well as police coverage of the various districts that would enable us to mitigate and manage any potential looting. "Copy that," I replied. "I have some notes about coverage and police presence throughout the districts so that people recognize a sense of law and order even throughout the hurricane."

"I think you should handle disseminating that information, given your role as Chief of Police," I added.

"No problem," Compass agreed. "These motherfuckers gotta know we'll still lock their asses up if they start that looting shit." "I'll cover logistical information regarding contraflow and what getting out of New Orleans looks like from a vehicular position," I stated.

"That'll work," Compass said, taking the notes he needed from me. I figured it would be a few minutes before the press conference started, so I stepped out of the media room into the hallway to review some of my notes in a quieter area. I found what appeared to be an empty office not too far away and made my way over to it. Once inside, I took out my notes and began reviewing the contraflow process and what that was presently looking like for our citizens. A few minutes later, I could hear conversation in the distance. As the speakers drew closer to my location, I was able to make out the voices of Mayor Nagin and his staff member. The cadence of the conversation, though initially indistinct, bespoke of something that was both serious and critical. And then there was the voice of a third party whom I did not recognize. I went back to my notes, determined to mind my own damn business and become proficient in articulating this contraflow process to an already agitated community of people.

"If you're as smart as I think you are, you'll make sure that our interests are protected," I heard the unrecognized voice say. It wasn't the volume or even the words of what was said that arrested my attention. It was the command of the voice that gave me pause. This was a person who was not new to power but spoke with an authority of one who was well-seasoned in wielding it.

"If I didn't know any better, I would take that as a threat," I heard Mayor Nagin say, seemingly undaunted. "Calling a mandatory evacuation impacts the bottom line of important businesses and people in this city," the unknown voice said with a coldness that made the hairs on the back of my neck stand at attention. "Don't consider this a threat; but rather, consider it a reminder that you serve this city at our pleasure, and if at any moment it becomes too unpleasant, there will be consequences. I hope you understand that your service is no longer necessary." I wondered who the fuck these motherfuckers were.

Who the fuck was this, and what the fuck was going on? The cop in me wanted to come out and put this person in their place, but the strategist and good common sense in me restrained me, advising me to get more intelligence on this situation before reacting. This person was clearly not a low-level player, and he was obviously attached to an entity that had great reach within the city of New Orleans. Everyone with any real knowledge of NOLA knew that old money, generational money control NOLA and most of its politicians. They destroyed anyone in their path that dared to challenge them. If they could not control you, convince you to do what they wanted, convict you somehow, and definitely destroy your name.

"Mayor, we have to prepare for the press conference," the mayor's staff member said hurriedly, with an edge of nervousness that you could hear just under the surface of his speech. "I gotta go," Mayor Nagin said, his voice indicating no fear at all. "The mandatory evacuation is taking place immediately. You can go tell your people that!"

"You better hope this is the right move, Nagin," the voice replied. "I'd hate for things to get unpleasant between us at this juncture." "Yeah, right," Nagin said before he could be heard walking off. "We'll be in touch," the voice called after him.

I waited for another minute after I heard what I knew to be the footsteps of the unknown voice leave before I stepped out of the office. While I wasn't spying on anyone, I had clearly overheard a conversation that wasn't intended for me to hear.

Even in the face of the monstrous hurricane hurtling toward New Orleans, there was something so unsettling and disturbing about the conversation I'd just heard that pissed me the fuck off. I did not exactly know who they were, but I knew it was some rich motherfuckers, who put dollars over lives. It almost made me physically ill. Who was that talking to Mayor Nagin? What interest group did he represent? And why did it seem like they were the ones actually running things in New Orleans and not those of us who were actually elected to do so? No matter what, Mayor Nagin sounded as cool as he always was.

Chapter 7:
The "Calm" Before the Storm

Mayor Nagin, flanked by Governor Kathleen Blanco on his right and Councilwoman Cynthia Willard on his left, stood behind the podium before a room filled with reporters and media, prepared to give the press conference that he never wanted to give. Standing along with them were Superintendent of the Louisiana State Police, Colonel Henry Whitehorn, President of Entergy New Orleans, Dan Packard, Councilman Oliver Thomas, Superintendent Edwin Compass, City CAO, Dr. Brenda Hatfield, General Bennett Landreneau of the Louisiana National Guard, and a few other leading city, state, and national officials. Each of them, while projecting a sense of confidence and authority, couldn't obscure the gravity of the situation from their visages (facial expressions). The press was respectfully waiting for Nagin to begin. Like most of us, many of them knew what was coming, but in order to accurately report the news, there was nothing like getting it straight from the horse's mouth.

I stood off to the side of the platform where the mayor and leaders were gathered, as I would need to be prepared to speak to pertinent items at a moment's notice. Overhearing that conversation between the mayor and the unknown power group representative had fucked my brain up, but I knew better than to lose my shit. Besides, he'd seemed to be quite unbothered by the entire episode.

"As you all know, the storm is intensifying, and it is still pointed towards New Orleans, and there is not a meteorologist that I have spoken to that has not indicated that this storm will impact New Orleans in a major way," Mayor Nagin said, opening up the press conference. "As a result of that, I am this morning declaring that we will be having a mandatory evacuation."

To know Mayor Nagin was to know that he was a man of great confidence and swag mixed with just enough humility not to be construed as arrogant. Looking at him dressed in a simple white polo shirt with a light blue collar, I could see that his eyes bespoke the weight that all of this was having on him. He by no means appeared beaten, but the weight and gravity of the situation were definitely resting upon him heavily.

Taking what was the official written order for the mandatory evacuation, Mayor Nagin began to read from it. "Whereas the national weather service has indicated that Hurricane Katrina will likely affect the Louisiana coast with tropical force winds and heavy rainfall by late this evening," he began reading. "Whereas because of anticipated high lakes and marsh tides due to the tidal surge combined with the possibility of intense thunderstorms, hurricane-force winds, and widespread severe flooding, Governor Blanco and I, Mayor C. Ray Nagin, have each declared a state of emergency."

We all knew that it was coming, but hearing the words coming from him, you couldn't help but sense that New Orleans was in real trouble. "Now therefore I, as mayor of the city of New Orleans, pursuant to the authority granted by LA Rev Stat 29-727 do hereby promulgate and issue the following orders which will be effective immediately and which will remain in effect until the earlier of five days following the date of this issuance or the declaration by the Governor that the state of emergency no longer exists," he continued.

Governor Blanco and the others standing beside him looked out into the cameras with united visages of confidence, yet you could see that each one of them was concerned about the welfare of the city and its citizens. "Point one, a mandatory evacuation order is hereby called for all of the Parish of Orleans with only the following exceptions: Essential personnel of the United States of America, State of Louisiana, and City of New Orleans. Essential personnel of regulated utilities and mass transportation services. Essential personnel of hospitals and their patients. Essential personnel of the media. Essential personnel of the Orleans Parish Criminal Sheriff's Office and its inmates. Essential personnel of operating hotels and their patrons," Nagin detailed.

"Unless covered by one of the aforementioned exceptions, every person is hereby ordered to immediately evacuate the City of New Orleans. If no other alternative is available, please immediately move to one of the facilities in the city that will be designated as a refuge of last resort," he added.

Cameramen and women that were with reporters were intensely focusing and aiming cameras to ensure that the message was captured, while reporters and journalists were furiously drafting notes to ensure that no detail was missed.

There were a few reporters in the room who legitimately looked frightened. "Point two," Nagin continued. "In order to effectuate the mandatory evacuation at the direction of the mayor, the city, the Chief Administrative Officer, the Director of Homeland Security for the City of New Orleans, or any member of the New Orleans Police Department, the city may commandeer any private property including but not limited to buildings that may be designated as refuges of last resort and vehicles that may be used to transport people out of the area."

"The city's attorney has been directed to file this declaration promptly in the Office of the Clerk of Court and with the Secretary of State. Signed by the Mayor of the City of New Orleans," he finished reading the evacuation order.

Nagin paused briefly, allowing the weight of his words to sink in before speaking again. "Ladies and gentlemen, I wish I had better news for you, but we are facing a storm that most of us have feared. I don't want to create panic, but I do want the citizens to understand that this is very serious, and that's why we are taking this unprecedented move," he said after what was probably a pause of only a fraction of a second but seemed to last forever. "The storm is now a Cat 5 with sustained winds of 150 miles per hour and wind gusts of 190 miles per hour. The storm surge most likely will topple our levee system, so we are preparing to deal with that also. This is why we are ordering a mandatory evacuation."

"This morning, the Superdome is already open for people with special needs. If you have a medical condition, if you are on dialysis or some other condition, we want you to expeditiously move to the Superdome," he continued. "At noon today, the Superdome will then be opened up as a refuge of last resort where we will start to take citizens that cannot evacuate, but let me emphasize that the first choice for every citizen is to figure out a way to leave the city."

"New Orleans, this is a major opportunity for us to come together. Make sure that you check on your neighbors. It's very important. Particularly, I would ask that you check on the senior citizens. Let's make sure that they are okay and not too frightened by what's happening and that we assist them in any way that we can," Nagin said positively, noting New Orleanians' capacity to come together when necessary. "This is a way for us to come together in ways that we never have before to face a threat that we have not faced before. If we galvanize our forces together, I am sure that we will get through this. God bless us." Mayor Nagin then stepped aside, allowing Governor Kathleen Blanco to speak. Clad in a simple red blazer, Governor Blanco's face shared the same resilient yet beleaguered look as Nagin's.

"Thank you, Mayor Nagin," Governor Blanco said, assuming her position behind the podium microphones. "I want to reiterate what the mayor has said. This is a very dangerous time. Just before we walked into this room, President Bush called and told me to share with all of you that he is very concerned about the citizens." Hearing that President Bush was already aware and responsive to what was happening here gave me a sense of relief and security. That feeling of security and admiration would shift dramatically over the course of the next few days.

"He is concerned about the impact that this hurricane will have on our people, and he asked me to please ensure that there would be a mandatory evacuation of New Orleans. Leaders at the highest ranks of our nation have recognized the destructive forces and the possible awesome danger that we are in, and I just want to say that we need to get as many people out of here as possible," Blanco continued.

"The shelters will likely end up without electricity or with minimal electricity from generators in the end. There may be intense flooding that will be beyond our control, which would ultimately court the most dangerous situations that our people could find themselves in."

"Water could be as high as 15 to 20 feet according to the National Hurricane Center. That, of course, would be one of the worst situations, and we are hoping that it doesn't come to that. We need to pray very strongly that the hurricane force would diminish, but just remember even if it diminishes to a Cat 1, that there were six people lost in Florida when it was a Category 1 hurricane, so there is still imminent danger," Governor Blanco stated directly.

Admittedly, her words were hard to take. Hearing that it was an inevitable eventuality that the storm was going to overwhelm our levee system was alarming, but I was cognizant that at this point making sure that our citizens were motivated to get out of the city was paramount. The reality is that the nature of the city was for citizens to ride out the storms. Historically that was the general consensus in New Orleans. Why waste time and money for a storm that was never as bad as they predicted it to be? Standing in this press room today, however, there wasn't a person who didn't think that it was time to get the hell out.

"There seems to be no real relief in sight, and it has been startling to see how accurate the path of this hurricane has been predicted. It is literally following the predicted path, so we have no reason to believe that it will alter its path. We would be blessed if it did alter its path, but right now it is important for everyone to get out as expeditiously as possible," Blanco said, seemingly reading my thoughts.

"Now we just flew over here and viewed the situation on the interstates. I-10 in the interior of the city is gridlocked. It is total gridlock. I am asking people to look at alternate routes, if possible," she continued. "We are ready and prepared to do all that we can. We have our people deployed. Citizens on the Westbank, if they need to go west, you need to take Highway 90 as opposed to trying to get onto I-10 – and we are seeing cars coming in from the Westbank getting on to I-10, which is only creating more gridlock. Right now, driving on I-10 in the city itself is minimally progressive at this point. If you can take alternate routes to get out of the city, please do so."

"I have Colonel Henry Whitehorn here who can speak to that more specifically to the traffic situation as well as General Landreneau with the National Guard," she indicated, yielding to Superintendent of the Louisiana State Police, Colonel Henry Whitehorn. Colonel Whitehorn, dressed in State Police uniform, stepped up to the podium, replacing Governor Blanco at the microphones. Colonel Whitehorn spoke about navigating traffic for the purposes of evacuation and referred to utilization of the evacuation guides, which gives details of alternate routes available to citizens. Because it appeared that the utilization of alternate routes was key and critical to the evacuation, he gave the website address where a map and guide could be found.

"Finally," he said, wrapping up his talking points. "We are noting that there are many minor crashes along the interstates that are causing choke points and blocking traffic. We encourage you to move your vehicles to the side to prevent blockages and allow the passage of other cars who need to move out of the area."

As Colonel Whitehorn was finishing up, one reporter raised a question regarding traffic and additional gridlock as a result of the mandatory evacuation. "Unfortunately, a lot of people have waited to leave, and upon hearing this, most of them will rush out to leave, which could cause some additional delays," Mayor Nagin stepped in, fielding the question. "We have to think beyond getting on I-10 and heading to Houston and maybe consider alternate routes where possible so that we don't have complete gridlock and shut down."

General Bennett Landreneau of the National Guard then assumed the position behind the podium to address the conference. "At the directive of the Governor, all state resources are available to the local parishes to support the evacuation and to support any needs that they might have," he began. "All of our state emergency operation centers are ready and manned by state and federal agencies. The Governor has directed that we mobilize 4000 Louisiana National guardsmen to support the parishes, Mayor Nagin, Colonel Ebbert and his team, and whatever support we can offer. We are coordinating with FEMA to make Federal assets available, and we are ready and able to support whatever missions that the City of New Orleans has."

Once again, I felt a sense of confidence wash over me upon hearing the preparedness with which aid beyond the local level was postured to be engaged should we need them. After General Landreneau finished speaking, another reporter inquired about the fate of prisoners housed in the city of New Orleans. The question involved the capacity for them to remain in place throughout the life of the storm. Orleans Parish Criminal Sheriff Marlon Guzman was called to the podium to give further insight on that question.

"The prison has backup generators designed to accommodate any power loss," Sheriff Guzman responded. "Prisoners in Orleans Parish will remain where they are along with those assigned to guard them in accordance with our Emergency Operations Plan."

The remainder of the press conference detailed additional traffic concerns, some of which I was called upon to give the local perspective. I identified the logistical information of what contraflow looked like as well as concerns regarding backups at local gas stations. As planned, Superintendent Compass spoke of police presence during the storm, advising those who chose to ride out the storm that we'd do our best to keep them safe and giving a stern warning to potential looters that they would not be tolerated in any way whatsoever.

The press conference wrapped with a final encouraging word from Mayor Nagin and the need for all the citizens in New Orleans who could physically remove themselves from the city to do so. "God bless us all," Mayor Nagin said as he ended the press conference, ushering in a symphony of camera shutter clicks and reporters collecting soundbites. As the consortium of officials dispersed from the platform, Chief Compass made his way over to where Deputy Chief Nicholas and I were standing.

"Well, shit is about to get really chaotic," he said to us a little more loudly than I would have liked. "We have to make sure our men are on top of things and that everyone is stationed and in place."

I resisted the urge to point out that we'd already handled those logistics. I replied, "It's done, Chief!"

"Oh yeah," he added before I could say anything. "Nagin wants us to hunker down at the Hyatt with the other city officials that are staying in town."

"Chief, with Riley running Operations out of Base 9 and me running Technical Support and Logistics, don't you think we would be better suited to hunker down at headquarters?" Chief Nicholas asked. I completely agreed with him on this. It was an absolute clusterfuck of an idea for us to be in one space while our officers and staff were in another. What if we lost the ability to communicate with them? You'd have the executive command staff of the NOPD in one area while their operatives were in another.

"The mayor wants us at the Hyatt, and that's where we are going to be," Compass said directly to both of us. Perhaps he sensed our absolute disagreement with this direction and wanted to be clear that this was an order and not a request.

"We'll be there, Chief Compass," I said, diffusing the situation. "We are going to head to the east to check things out and work our way back through the Lower Ninth Ward and then through the French Quarter and uptown, check things out at the Superdome, and then we'll meet everyone at the Hyatt."

Seemingly satisfied with this answer, Compass walked away to handle whatever pending business he had.

"Riley, what the fuck was that?" Nicholas queried.

"Man, I don't know," I responded. "It makes no sense for us to be split up like that, but I can tell that he is hellbent on having it that way."

"Alright then, man," Nicholas acquiesced. "I need to wrap some things up, and then I'll meet you at the Hyatt." "Chief Nicholas, there is no way in hell we will follow that dumb ass directive" Riley added as they left the press conference.

It took me roughly about an hour to round up my team and get back to our vehicle. Captain Weathersby, Sgt. Allison, and Officers Menzies and Brumfield piled back into my large SUV, and we made our slow navigation around the city as we headed towards New Orleans East. As we drove throughout the city, we could see people hurrying and gathering belongings, bringing in lawn and porch furniture, loading their cars with luggage and food supplies. We could see folks that were hustling trying to get the hell out of NOLA as quickly as they could. However, many were boarding up their homes, trying to protect their property as best as they could, they covered doors and windows with plywood, two by four boards and whatever they could protect their property with. There was a sense of overwhelming fear in the air as we drove through Eastern New Orleans, the Lower and Upper Ninth ward and Gentilly. People were getting out of the city.

However, when we returned to the downtown area of the city and entered the French Quarter, we drove down Chartres Street, passing by Jax Brewery, Jackson Square, and numerous drinking establishments.

People, tourists, and locals were blasting music, dancing in the street, second-lining, some with rhythm and some in a drunken freelancing kind of way having a good old time. Partying was the only thing on their minds. We stepped out of the vehicle, and people came up to us, hugging us and saying thanks, officers, for your service. Drunken women were trying to kiss a couple of us and shouting, "You want to join our Hurricane Katrina Party?" and showing us their tits. There was no fear, no effort, or intent on leaving New Orleans. There is no place like the Big Easy. Officers were driving in cars with their blue lights on and shouting on the bullhorns that there was a mandatory evacuation; it seemed to fall on deaf ears. After hours of trying to people in the quarter to leave or prepare for the storm, it seemed as if alcohol and music rule. I admired their fearlessness, even if alcohol induced. Realizing that our efforts to influence the majority citizens and tourists to leave were useless, we reentered our vehicles. Using side streets in concert with the flashing blue lights from my vehicle allowed us to navigate traffic faster than the average citizen.

Traffic was at a standstill along the interstate in certain spots. Just as it had been reported at the press conferences, some vehicles were breaking down or even running out of gas along the way and causing additional traffic problems. We did our best to assist with moving the vehicles that we could off to the side to free up traffic and keep things at least moving in a progressive direction. The sky was now filled with gray clouds, and the wind had begun to pick up noticeably. If this was the "calm before the storm," I sure as hell didn't want to experience the actual storm.

"Please tell me why the fuck everybody would wait this long to evacuate?" Officer Brumfield asked.

"That's typical New Orleans, Brumfield," I answered. "We've been through this drill so many times that it is hard for many of them to take it seriously when there is a real threat."

"Yeah," Weathersby agreed. "Think of all the times when we've been under a stern warning and at the last possible minute, the trajectory of the storm shifted in a beneficial way."

My mind couldn't help but wander to the conversation that I overheard with Mayor Nagin and the unknown person representing some power group. I wondered how many times the decision to evacuate or not to evacuate had been influenced by this group before. I wondered how long they had been influencing movement within our municipal government and if their reach was even greater than that.

"We have to also consider that there are some people who actually can't evacuate," Sergeant Allison added. "For example, the medically infirmed or even those who don't have the financial means to do so."

"This whole thing is just fucked up," I heard Officer Menzies say more to himself than the rest of us in the vehicle. Menzies added I hope they are getting the senior citizens out of these nursing homes.

I had to agree with him. As we patrolled the area, I saw so many people doing their best to get out of the city. Their eyes were uncertain and fearful. Many of them weren't sure how long they were going to be gone. Others were agonizing because they failed to convince loved ones to leave. It literally seemed unreal that this was even happening. But it was happening. Ready or not, Katrina was headed to New Orleans.

Superintendent Compass had scheduled a final briefing for 2:00 p.m. that afternoon with all the commanders. The meeting was brief. He relayed the information from the mayor that Katrina was a Category 5, which everyone in the city knew already at this point. We confirmed that all commanders had secured their hunkering down locations and that their officers were traversing the areas, advising citizens of the mandatory evacuation. I called the traffic commander for an update on the contraflow, and he advised that it was still slow, five to ten miles per hour, but that the movement was constant.

After the briefings, I advised all commanders to make sure that they were visible to their personnel and gave guidance and encouragement through this difficult time. The commanders were also instructed to ensure that all the shopping areas and pharmacies had police presence because those where the first places potential looters would hit. And with that, our final briefing was adjourned.

It was about 6:00 p.m. and the city suddenly had an eerie darkness and winds had picked up significantly as we arrived at the Superdome for our final check-in of the day. It had been an amazingly long day filled with routing traffic and assisting officers with helping as many people evacuate the city as possible. We'd hit just about every district within the city of New

Orleans, ensuring that we were all clear on assignments and the line of communication that we would use should traditional communication systems become unavailable. Despite the gridlock that was still in progress as people were leaving New Orleans, it was estimated that approximately 450,000 people would successfully evacuate the city. That's 450,000 lives that I knew would be spared as a result of them leaving New Orleans.

The scene at the Superdome was intense, to say the least. The skies were cloudy and overcast, and the evening was rolling in, giving a menacing look to the already gray sky. There was a humid and tropical smell in the air, foretelling Katrina's arrival. The wind was steady, with the occasional gust or two, indicating that something wicked was in the air, manifesting its fury through the wind.

At 12 noon, Deputy Chief Lonnie Swain oversaw the opening of the Superdome's doors as a refuge of last resort for citizens unable to effectively evacuate from the city. The Louisiana National Guard delivered three truckloads of water and seven truckloads of meals ready to eat (MREs), enough to supply 15,000 people for three days.

Lines stretched from outside the Superdome to the streets, filled with people checking in for refuge. People brought their kids' toys, pets, ice chests, and anything else they could gather together. The types of people seeking refuge ranged widely. Some lacked the financial means to evacuate, while others were physically unable to do so due to medical conditions. There were those who appeared homeless, alongside others with colostomy bags, breathing apparatuses, and various medical supplies. People arrived in taxicabs, on bicycles, and using every mode of transportation available. Notably, some who appeared affluent had waited too long and were now forced to seek refuge at the Superdome.

During our final briefing, Chief Swain was instructed to ensure that each person entering the dome had to be searched to ensure no weapons or drugs were brought inside. Numerous barrels were placed at the entryway to collect weapons. Initially, an announcement was made that anyone voluntarily placing their guns, knives, or any other weapons in the barrels wouldn't be arrested. However, anyone found with a weapon during the search would be arrested and placed in the prison population. Depending on the damage caused by Katrina, they could be in jail for months. This tactic surprisingly worked, as over 150 guns were dropped in the barrels. Only God knew how many crimes and acts of violence were prevented by this collection.

As we entered the Superdome, it was no surprise that affluent individuals and people with money approached us, willing to pay almost anything to find a way out of the city. However, flights were no longer an option, and it was impossible to extricate them. Like everyone else, they would have to ride out the storm here.

By the time we made it inside the Superdome, over 14,000 people had checked in, which was admirable, to say the least. The concourses of the dome had been opened, allowing those inside to walk around the arena and connect with others. It wasn't long before we located Deputy Chief Swain and Captain Ernie Demma. Both of these veterans were working in tandem with the National Guard leadership team assigned to the Superdome and seemed to be in good spirits, considering the circumstances. One concern they expressed was the ratio of limited officers at the dome to the growing crowd of citizens checking in. As if on cue, they were greeted by over 400 National Guardsmen who were there to assist. We confirmed a few details with Lonnie as they set up their command post on the Terrace Level and walked the space one final time before we departed.

At about 8:30 p.m., Weathersby dropped off Sergeant Allison and Officers Menzies and Brumfield at NOPD Headquarters, where they were to hunker down for the night with the rest of the staff and some of their family members. Captain Weathersby and I then proceeded to the Communications Center within headquarters to request a weather update. I was advised that all news stations were reporting winds approaching 50 miles per hour. I instructed the Communication Commander to inform all personnel that the winds were now approaching 55 miles per hour and to head to their locations for the night. Communications Commander Captain Steven Gordon immediately ordered all NOPD personnel to stop all operations and proceed to their locations to settle in for the night, ensuring that they parked all vehicles and equipment in high and safe locations. After one final check of HQ, Captain Weathersby and I left and headed to the Hyatt Hotel to settle in for the night.

The conditions outside had definitely changed. Even though it was dark outside, you could hear the winds blowing intermittently and see the light mist of precipitation in the air. The winds had picked up dramatically, blowing debris into the air. It was obvious that a dramatic change was on the horizon. "You don't feel good about us being here and our men at headquarters, huh?" Weathersby asked me, though I was certain it wasn't a question. I had just settled my truck into a parking space at the Hyatt. I pondered his question thoughtfully before answering, "Not at all. It's not what leadership looks like in my opinion."

As we were getting out of the car, Chief Nicholas pulled his vehicle into the spot adjacent to mine. As he got out of his vehicle, I noted that he wore the same conflicted expression that I did. Like me, both Weathersby and Nicholas had small overnight bags for our luggage. These small "go-packs" contained three days of food, water, and a change of clothes. In cases like this, the luxury of overpacking was certainly not an option. We entered the hotel from Poydras Street and were immediately instructed to check-in. After checking in, one of the managers gave us three separate keys to rooms on the 11th floor. As we arrived on the 11th floor, we had to pass the ballroom, which was also on the same floor. Inside the ballroom, we saw Chief Compass, Mayor Nagin, Dan Packard, the President of the Entergy utility company, Sally Foreman, the Director of Public Information for the City of New Orleans, the General Manager of the Hyatt Hotel, Michael Smith, and at least another 60 people. Under other circumstances, I would have thought it was an official party of some sort because the "Who's Who" of the city were gathered in one place, but this was definitely no party. I knew I had to say something about us being here to Chief Compass, so I stepped inside to address him. I couldn't shake the overwhelming sense of duty I felt that we should be at Headquarters with the 200 plus dispatchers, 911 operators, and dozens of officers there who looked to us as leaders. I walked up to Chief Compass and pulled him aside. I advised him that I thought it would be a good idea for myself and Chief Nicholas to return to headquarters, considering that our command-and-control center and all of our major communication systems were there. I also recommended that he return as well to show strong leadership to those who were probably looking for us. "Riley," he answered, shaking his head no. "The mayor wants us here, and this is where we are going to be until tomorrow morning at the least."

As he was rude and brash, he was very emphatic in his response. It was enough to convince me that there would be no changing his mind on this issue. "Yes, sir," was the only response that I could give. At that moment, Chief Compass was approached by several people, so I utilized that moment to slip back into the hallway, reconnecting with Weathersby and Nicholas. "Let's get settled in," I said, indicating that any hopes of not staying were overridden. Without any further dialogue, we each headed to our rooms.

When I went into my hotel room, I immediately looked out of the window and watched the wind blow lightweight debris around the city. Some items were much higher than the 11th floor, and from the looks of it, light rain had begun. As I looked out of the window, guilt began to eat at my conscience. There was just something bothersome about the leadership of the police being here in this luxury hotel while our staff members were toughing it out all over the city. I laid down in bed to think as I continued to look out of the window. The moon was shining very brightly, peeking through the clouds every chance that it could. I stared at this mesmerizing scene until I drifted off into uncomfortable sleep. As I watched the clouds move slowly, it dawn on me that I'm in a room with all glass, if a tornado hits, that my ass.

My thoughts were interrupted by the sound of an alarm and an urgent voice over the hotel intercom system. "Please bring your pillows and blankets and report immediately to the 11th-floor ballroom," the voice said over the intercom. "We are expecting possible contact with severe weather and tornadoes, and strong winds could blow out the windows causing serious injuries. Please exit your rooms immediately and head to the hotel ballroom on the 11th floor." "Well damn!" I thought. My cellphone rang with a number that I wasn't necessarily familiar with, but I answered anyway. It turned out to be Michael Smith, the General Manager of the Hyatt. "Hey Chief Riley," he said urgently. "I need your help with Stacy Morgan." Stacy Morgan was a dear friend of mine who had worked several years for City Hall. Her last position with the city was in the Mayor's Office as the Director of Community Affairs & Special Events under the Nagin Administration. She'd left City Hall only a few years ago, but was still a dear friend. "What's going on with Stacy? Where is she?" I asked as I pulled my things together and quickly headed to the conference room. In that moment, I'd decided that there was no way I was staying at the Hyatt while my staff was in imminent danger.

It went against my core values, and I just couldn't do it. "Listen, Stacy is staying here at the hotel on the 24th floor," Michael answered. "She and her family didn't have time to evacuate, so I put them up here." "Her family has already reported to the ballroom on the 11th floor as we have instructed," he continued. "But from what they tell me, Stacy refuses to come down and isn't taking this notice very seriously. Can you help me with that?" "Ofcourse I can," I answered. Stacy was strong-willed and stubborn as hell, but she wasn't completely unreasonable. I called Weathersby and Nicholas to let them know that I had to make a quick stop to get one of the persons staying here to report to the ballroom, and then I was leaving heading to headquarters. If they were interested in joining me, I advised that they could meet me in the lobby in about twenty minutes.

It took me almost a full ten minutes to convince Stacy to come to the ballroom, and that was only after I threatened to carry her ass down to the ballroom myself. I made it to the conference room with about five minutes to spare before I had to meet Nicholas and Weathersby in the lobby to head back to headquarters. There were people everywhere selecting areas that they thought were cozy enough for them to spend the night. They were laying out their blankets and pillows all over the place. I saw Mayor Nagin and Chief Compass and several others talking.

I went over and engaged with them for a few moments as we talked about various things like if the levees gave way, how severe it would be. Mayor Nagin stated that there could be as many as 10,000 deaths based on projections and depending on where the levees would break. Several other people who were in admiration of the mayor came up to us, some for his autograph and some wanted to take pictures. Maximizing the moment, I used that time to leave and not say anything to Chief Compass or the Mayor. It was never my intent to be deceitful or insubordinate, but I did not want them to tell me that I had to stay at the Hyatt. My conscience would not allow me to stay there and not be at headquarters. I fully understood that the mayor and his staff staying at the hotel was just across the street from the City Hall, a mere 50 yards.

Chief Nicholas and Captain Weathersby were waiting for me in the lobby when I arrived. We didn't have to say much of anything. It was unspoken— let's go to HQ," Captain Weathersby said. "Did you tell Chief Compass?" I replied, "I mean no disrespect, but he'll figure it out." As we walked out of the lobby, outside, the strong winds were already blowing fiercely. It was hard to maintain our balance as we made our way to our vehicles. The wind was a harbinger (a person or thing that announces the approach of another) of the danger that was to come—yet and still, I was comforted by the fact that we were headed to headquarters where we belonged. As we drove to headquarters, which was only about one mile away, the wind was above 65 miles per hour, at the point where it was too dangerous to drive. As we drove, Chief Nicolas was in his vehicle, and we followed.

We left the Hyatt Hotel a little bit after 11:00 p.m. headed for N.O.P.D. Headquarters. Captain Weathersby was riding with me in my SUV as we followed closely behind Chief Nicholas. The light from our headlights showed the rain coming down in waves, being driven fiercely by the wind. There were hardly any cars on the streets at this point, and for good reason. The wind was simply too strong to drive without a major risk. The howling of the wind was audible even inside our truck as we battled to make headway on the streets.

I watched as Chief Nicholas's car swayed left to right in the battle against the wind. Seconds later, my vehicle would move in protest against those same winds as we continued to make our way forward through the sheets of wind and rain. Thankfully, we only had about a one-mile drive to headquarters as we could feel the wind gusts getting stronger as we arrived at headquarters.

For a moment, I thought about the possibility of us getting stranded en route to headquarters and how dangerous our decision to leave the Hyatt had been. They were literally gathering in the ballroom of the Hyatt, preparing for impending dangerous weather, and we decided to brave said weather so that we could ride it out at police headquarters. In principle, it absolutely made sense, but in this moment of intense driving, I honestly thought of the possibility that it may not have been the best move.

Suddenly, the wind gust would hit us every 15 or 20 seconds, pushing and causing our vehicles to sway from side to side. That was the bumpiest 5-minute drive of my life. As I stated, "what the fuck" on more than one occasion, I had to apologize to Weathersby, who was also a pastor. We rode in silence mostly, with the occasional sound of the wind cutting across the contours of my vehicle. I have no doubt that he and I were thinking of previous storms we had survived and comparing the similarities and dissimilarities of this one in particular.

We pulled into HQ and prepared to deal with the mother of all storms. Hurricane Katrina was barreling toward our fair city with a vengeance, but we would be among our troops to meet her when she arrived! Katrina was indeed upon us. If the pre-storm winds of Katrina were literally pushing us around, one could only imagine the strength of the winds to come. Despite our sincerest efforts, I couldn't help but think through what we could have done to better prepare for what was certain to be a landmark storm in our city's history. Our northbound journey on Poydras Street had been an intense one, and I knew full well that it would pale in comparison to the venom Katrina was about to spit.

The ride to police headquarters seemed to take an eternity, and when we finally arrived, I exhaled a breath I didn't even realize I had been holding. While we were still at the Hyatt, I had already made a decision that when we got to headquarters, we would walk the entire space to give the physical reassurance of the presence of leadership in the building.

Although I'm certain that Chief Compass would be pissed about my decision to leave, I knew that our presence among those whom we led was more important than political optics. He'd likely cuss our asses out, but serving our employees took precedence over any desire to avoid those repercussions.

As we entered the building, one of the first people I noticed was the Deputy Chief of Finance, Courtney Bagneris, with her husband and two small children heading to the elevator. Many of the officers' spouses, children, and other relatives were in the building along with some of the creature comforts of homes. Young children with their toys and even a few of their pets were moving throughout the building, likely accompanying an officer to whom they were connected.

There were roughly around one hundred civilians hunkering down with us in the form of husbands, wives, mothers, and children. We typically didn't allow civilians in police headquarters like this, but these were special circumstances, and some simply had no other option. Everyone seemed to be doing their best to maintain whatever sense of normalcy they would be able to hold on to over the next few days.

I felt a sense of gratefulness when I saw the smiles of relief and reassurance from the various officers who greeted us throughout the building. Even though we all knew we were in imminent danger, my encouraging statements that we would be okay, even as I greeted and shook hands with them, seemed to have a positive effect. This is why we needed to be here! This is what leadership does! Even in the face of looming adversity, leadership reassures those who are following.

We walked around the main floor for a few moments before heading to the 2nd floor where our Communications Center was located. There were about fifty dispatchers and 911 operators who were working in our Communications Center. Even as we got off the elevator, you could hear the symphony of voices, telephone lines ringing, and background noise of news stations. Organized and professional chaos, but chaos, nonetheless. Down the hallway from the Comm Center "Base Nine" was our Communication Special Event & Critical Incident Command Center known as Base 9. Only our best and most experienced dispatchers worked Base 9, and with the onset of Katrina as an inevitable eventuality, we certainly needed them. Three of our best, including Mary Knight and Levette Joseph, were staffed for Base 9 this night.

Chief Nicholas and I walked into the Communications Center, which was the literal epicenter of the sudden urgency that seemed to characterize the Metro New Orleans area. Call after call after call of New Orleans residents who had failed to heed the evacuation call and tried to hunker down in their homes was coming in, trying to broker a deal for transportation to the Superdome. Unfortunately, with winds now around 65-70 miles per hour, it was simply unsafe for first responders and the like to even attempt to transport them from their location. I could only imagine that the howling winds and storms were beginning to affect their confidence, and many were now regretting that they had not left their homes.

Our best-case advice in these scenarios was simply to hunker down. Even before entering the "Base 9" I could hear dispatchers and operators advising residents to fill their bathtubs with water in the event that post-Katrina they needed to flush their toilets and had no running water. They also advised them to make preparations for cases of rising water by keeping hammers, saws, and axes readily available if they needed to go to higher ground, and if they needed to vertically evacuate and make their way out of their attics onto their rooftops. I could even hear operators explaining the importance of storing nonperishable food in the attics in the event that residents needed to retreat to their attics for an extended period of time due to flooding.

The voices of the 911 operators and dispatchers were overlapping each other as they gave these instructions to multiple citizens who were now flooding the lines with questions and concerns regarding their safety. To their credit, the operators and dispatchers were exemplary in their professionalism and decorum as they swiftly but calmly dispensed this vital information to the residents. I couldn't help thinking how sad it was that these last-minute survival instructions had to be given.

Chapter 8:
Katrina is Upon Us

Once we made it inside the room housing our Communications Center, the visual picture of the organized chaos we had heard about came to life. Nearly forty-five calling stations and desks were organized in an almost perfect square shape, fitting the width and length of the room. The space was alive with energy and activity.

Most of the operators and dispatchers were sitting at desk stations with headsets on their phones, fielding and navigating the deluge of nonstop calls. The incessant ringing of multiple telephone lines served as the background noise of the room. At the moment, nobody seemed overwhelmed; instead, there was a focused professionalism with which they were handling the seemingly unending calls.

I immediately spotted Police Communications Supervisor, Andrea Skipper, at the desk of one of the dispatchers, flipping through a chart and giving instructions. I immediately felt better about the situation knowing that "Skipper," as those of us who had a relationship with Andrea often called her, was overseeing the operators and dispatchers. Andrea had well over twenty years of experience with the department and had been through multiple hurricanes with us. She was definitely the person for the job.

I headed over to Andrea for a quick debrief while Chief Nicholas, who was actually in charge of Communications during this stint, went over to discuss details with another supervisor. "Hello Chief Riley," Andrea greeted me warmly. "It's so good to see you and Chief Nicholas here." Once again, I was reminded that I had made the right decision in leaving the Hyatt Hotel. "Of course," I said lightheartedly. "It's good to see you here as well. How long has it been like this?" "Well," Andrea stated as she began looking through her notes.

"It was your typical stuff with petty robberies, shoplifters, a few domestic calls, trespassers, and things of that nature until around eight or so when the storm actually picked up." As Andrea said this, she pointed to a section of the room where three large television monitors were set up, showing actual satellite images of Katrina. The images were absolutely awe-inspiring. At this point now, Katrina's outer bands of wind and rain were covering the three states of Louisiana, Mississippi, and Alabama. In my many years and many hurricanes, I had never seen an image that was so terrifying. I thought to myself, "Oh my God."

"Once the rain and storms came in, a lot of the residents realized that they should've evacuated their homes, and so now many of them are afraid," Andrea added. "I know many of them couldn't afford to leave, but I wish that they would have at least come to some of the shelters of last resort." "You're right, Skip," I unfortunately had to concur. "If the projections are right, the next couple of days could prove very tough for them." I knew that my statement was an understatement, but I didn't want to even put that into the atmosphere. Hell, if the projections were correct, many of these people who failed to evacuate might actually lose their lives. I think that reality, though unsaid, was beginning to hit everyone.

"So how are the operators and dispatchers holding up?" I inquired. "We have our best here, and they are doing a great job," Andrea said, extending her hand in the direction of the operators and dispatchers. "Many of them have been through multiple hurricanes with us before, so this isn't their first time at the rodeo." "They're already doing an amazing job handling all of these calls." I noted. "Yes, they are," Skip agreed. "Me and some of the other supervisors are stepping in to give them breaks as needed because at this point there really isn't a break in the calls." "You guys seem to have everything under control thus far," I stated. "Yeah, we do," Skipper replied. "Many of us know the drill for these kinds of situations.

You pack up for about three days or so with enough clothes and extra snacks to last you, and you just ride it out. We will be fine." Andrea's ability to convey confidence and calm in circumstances like this was one of the many reasons why she had progressed so well in this department. I knew that she knew that Katrina was an extraordinary storm and that we were all in for one hell of a ride, but her resolve that all would be well was inspiring to say the least. Once again, I was grateful that she was present among us.

After talking with Andrea for a few more minutes, I made my way over to Chief Nicholas and Captain Weathersby as they conversed near a few of the television monitors at the opposite end of the room. The closer I got to them, I noticed that the local news stations, WWL, WDSU, WGNO, and WVUE, were all reporting from what appeared to be makeshift studios. Contrary to the first-class studios from which they normally reported, subpar backdrops and mediocre lighting comprised these remote studios, allowing the news anchors to continue reporting but from a safe distance from New Orleans. Even the news stations had a sense that New Orleans was in some deep shit.

"So, I see the local stations got the hell out of New Orleans," I said to both Nicholas and Weathersby. "Yeah, right," Nicholas said with a chuckle. "I only wish that more citizens would have taken Nagin's and Blanco's advice. These calls are coming in like crazy." "Yeah, I was just talking to Skip about that," I responded. "Unfortunately, at this point, they are just going to have to hunker down where they are until the winds die down." "Which might not be for a while," Weathersby chimed in. "The challenge is that some of our dispatchers and operators have family members who didn't evacuate because they thought they could ride out the storm," Nicholas stated.

"And now with them seeing how quickly this storm is escalating, many of them are rightly concerned for their loved ones as well." "Damn," I said out loud, but more to myself. In that moment, I was once again grateful that Morgan and Tiffany evacuated and were a safe distance away from the city. I could not imagine what it would be like to have to worry about them not being out of harm's way or not being able to get to them. I applauded the many workers who were able to continue to do the work with the thoughts of their loved ones in the back of their minds.

My mind also went to those whom we saw just a few hours earlier, laughing and dancing in the streets of the French Quarter as if nothing major was about to ensue. I wondered where those persons were taking refuge now and what was their condition? Were they inside a safe space? What would become of them? We went through such extraordinary lengths to get the message out that Katrina was not going to be an average hurricane, but somehow and for some reason, that message just did not resonate with everyone.

According to the weather reports on television, we were about seven hours from anticipated impact with Katrina. Given the pre-storm winds and weather that Katrina was bringing, unless a miracle occurred and the storm shifted, this was going to be disastrous. Admittedly, I began to consider how many persons would die in their homes over the next 48 hours and what our rescue efforts would look like.

My eyes drifted to the satellite image of Katrina shown on one of the television screens as the weatherman reported on its impending arrival. I had never seen imagery that was so horrific. It was now a Category 5 hurricane churning through the Gulf, covering three states, and slated to make impact within a matter of hours. At this point, it was understandable that so many calls were coming into our Communications Center, asking to be transported to the Superdome.

I imagined that fear and desperation were sinking in at this point, recognizing that barring some extraordinary scientific occurrence, this would likely be the big hurricane that all New Orleanians had feared. Again, the thought of navigating rescue efforts for so many citizens who did not evacuate gripped my mind.

"I think we should leave the staff with some words of encouragement," I said to Chief Nicholas and then added to Captain Weathersby, "And it would really be helpful to them if you could pray over us all." Captain Weathersby was the Pastor of Living the Word Church in Slidell, Louisiana. Aside from being an amazing officer and captain, he was an excellent minister who had an uncanny ability to inspire and encourage those with whom he came in contact. We could certainly use some of that inspiration tonight.

"Great idea, Riley," Nicholas agreed. It took Chief Nicholas about fifteen minutes to rally together in one room his staff, my staff, and the dispatchers and operators who were currently not on shift. We spoke honestly about the severity of the situation we were facing in the person of Hurricane Katrina. This was no ordinary storm, and though we were never going to communicate panic and fear, we wanted to be real with our people while inspiring hope that we would get through this together.

The central theme of our encouragement to them was that though we were facing a storm unlike any that we'd encountered before, we were facing it together, and our unity was our strength. While it was scary to think that we would have to navigate waters unknown to us, we could get through it if we stuck together and relied on each other for strength when we became weary.

We expressed to them that we would follow every protocol and contingency in place for addressing matters like this and that when and if we exhausted those contingencies, we would rely on our instincts and collective wisdom to guide us forward. And when we went as far as we could go in our strength, we would rely on the goodness and strength of our Heavenly Father to do for us what we could not do for ourselves.

At this point, Captain Weathersby prepared to lead us in prayer. Not all of us were aligned in our religious beliefs, but in this moment, we were all aligned with our need for a greater power to intervene on our behalf and on behalf of our great city. Most of us simply bowed our heads as a sign of respect, while others held hands to demonstrate their unity in faith and petition.

"Heavenly Father, we come to you in the name of Jesus," Weathersby began praying. "If ever there was a time that we needed you to hear our cry and move on our behalf, it is now." "Father, we ask that you bless the city of New Orleans," he continued. "Bless those who did not have the means to evacuate from the city and please protect them from all hurt, harm, and danger."

"Bless those of us who remain in the city as the first responders and the first line of defense," he continued. "May we find grace to guide us through the terrain of the days ahead of us." "We say a special prayer for our neighboring states of Mississippi and Alabama and the families and lives that are being impacted by this horrific storm," Weathersby prayed earnestly. "We need your hand of mercy and protection to be upon all of us, Lord." "Lastly, Lord, we ask that you grant wisdom, courage, and strength to the leadership of our city. Grant them the grace that they need to guide us through what may be one of the toughest storms of our lives. This day we ask for your mercy, strength, and protection. In the name of Jesus Christ, we pray. Amen."

"Amen." Everyone echoed their agreement with the sentiments of the prayer, and then everyone dispersed back to their respective assignments. I made it back to my office on the fifth floor around 1:00 a.m. I'd had a brief meeting with my immediate staff just before that to go over last-minute protocols and any other items that we may have missed.

Truthfully, even in that meeting, we mostly joked around about random things because at this point, there was no more preparation left to do...there was nothing left to do at all but wait and pray and wait and pray some more.

It was just around 1:00 a.m., and we all set up military cots in our offices, setting out to get the best amount of sleep that would be possible in these circumstances. At this point, sleep was critical, as our minds would need to be fresh and alert to fully engage with what was ahead. Mental presence and sharpness would be just as important as the strength in our physical bodies, so sleep was essential. I took one final look outside before laying down on my cot.

The wind was blowing pretty intensely. There were moments when I could see paper and trash flying high into the air, tossed about in indiscriminate directions. I lay on my cot as Katrina was making her entrance to the city of New Orleans, continuing to look up and out of my window, my exhaustion overpowering my anxiety, and I finally fell asleep.

3.5 Hours Later...

"Chief, so far none of the office windows have been blown out," Captain Michael Pfeiffer said as he walked up to me, flanked by another member of my staff, Sergeant Cynthia Landry. My heart was still racing as we had just taken shelter in the hallway of our office suite due to the tornadoes that had torn through our area. The time between me waking up from the water dripping onto me, watching as the windows in my office nearly imploded from the pressure shifts in the atmosphere outside, and retreating to the hallway due to the tornadic activity heralded by the deafening freight train sounds from outside, and now had seemed like an eternity when in actuality it had been little more than half of an hour.

As I glanced back inside my office, I could still see the impact of the strong winds outside through my office windows. Garbage, tree limbs, and tires were still being tossed throughout the air and over our building as if they were weightless. Trees were bent at impossible angles as they fought to remain upright against the onslaught of the raging winds. Katrina was here and she seemed mad as hell!

My cellphone vibrated in my pocket, alerting me to a call. When I looked down, I could see that it was Chief Nicholas. "Riley," I said, answering the phone. "Everything okay, Nicholas?" "So far yes, but I think we need to get a status report from the dispatchers," he answered. "Meet us down there," I replied. "We're going to head down there now." "Have we received any status reports from our Comm Center?" I asked Michael, referencing our 911 operators, dispatchers, supervisors, and even Base 9 Special Event Center. "Nothing so far," Pfeiffer replied. "We need to get a status check," I said, making my way toward the elevators with Landry, Menzies, and Pfeiffer following closely behind me. "This will help us better figure out what the fuck is going on and discern what's happening in the city."

As the elevator doors opened to the second floor, which housed our Communications Center and Base 9 Special Event Center, we were immediately accosted by a nearly tangible atmosphere of anxiety, tempered by sadness and depression. As we walked into the center where our 911 operators and dispatchers were located, I noticed the most confusing sight I'd ever seen.

If I were to close my eyes, I could hear the calm voices of dispatchers giving instructions and routing calls, not necessarily dissimilar to what we'd observed nearly 7 hours earlier. Advisement was disseminated with the tactful prowess with which they had been trained. It was the visual of what we could clearly see of the operators and dispatchers, however, that was the challenge and utterly confusing.

Dozens of dispatchers, outfitted with headsets, were manning their stations, taking and routing calls. Nearly every single dispatcher, male and female, was crying. Some were even sobbing silently. They were poised, professional, and calm when speaking on the phones, but most of them were unable to hold back their tears. Before I could voice my confusion, Andrea Skipper was making her way toward us. Even before she arrived, I could see that her eyes were puffy and red as well. The Police Communications Supervisor was crying. This was not a good sign.

"Chief..." Andrea managed to get out and then stopped speaking in order to remain composed. "Chief, it's really bad," Skip managed to say after taking a deep breath.

When she returned, she had a dispatcher's headset. "Chief, plug into one of the dispatch stations and just listen," she directed. I quickly walked over to a dispatch station and plugged into the Fifth District channel, which covered the Lower and Upper 9th Ward sections of the city. I will never be able to forget what I heard. Children were screaming in the background, and you could hear the magnified sound of splashing water as a mother did her best to protect and comfort her children.

"David, grab your brother," the anguish in her voice was indescribable. "Do not let him go under." "Mama, I'm trying, but the water is too high," I could hear the reply of the child come back to his mother.

"Ma'am, I'm still here with you," the calm voice of a male dispatcher came over. "We need you to get to the highest point possible in your home." "Somebody please, help us!" the voice of a frantic woman crackled into my ears. "We're trapped in the attic, and the water is getting higher."

The utter terror in that mother's voice touched the core of my soul. "Ma'am, we're sending someone as soon as possible," the dispatcher responded. "Do you have any tools that you can use to cut through the roof of your attic?" "No, I don't!" the mother's anguished voice shouted back.

"You have to send someone right now," the mother shouted hysterically. "My babies are drowning!" "We're going to get to you as soon as we can," he answered. My heart sank as I scanned the room and located the dispatcher who was speaking with the desperate mother on the other end. He was a well-built man who appeared to be in his late thirties. As he spoke, he held his head with both hands, and tears were free-falling from his eyes. With winds outside at hurricane force, it would be impossible to send any rescue vehicles out.

Winds greater than 60 miles per hour could easily turn over SUVs and other emergency vehicles. In this horrific moment, the dispatchers were in an impossible situation. All they could do was provide comfort and a listening ear. Screams, prayers, and sounds of people fighting for their lives and then an eerie silence had become customary for many. I pulled the earpiece out of my ear and just stood there looking at Andrea for a moment as an unspoken understanding solidified between us.

"Chief, I didn't have the language to verbalize what's going on here," she explained. "I had to let you see for yourself." I was literally almost unable to speak. My throat was locked. In truth, I wanted to burst out crying, but as the guy in charge, I realized that my first responsibility was to maintain a sense of order and control among those whom I had oversight. This shit was hard though, and in a moment, I felt like I lost a piece of my soul.

"At this rate, we are switching out operators and dispatchers every ten minutes because the severity of the calls is too much for them to handle emotionally," Andrea explained. "Especially knowing that many of these people aren't going to make it out alive." "How are you handling it?" I asked. I knew Skipper was tough and she was a professional. I wanted to break down after listening to one call, but they had been doing this for hours on end. I could not imagine the pain they were feeling. And with Andrea leading the way, I knew it was doubly hard for her.

I needed her to know that she was supported. Tears immediately filled her eyes. "One of the captains told me that I was wrong to tell the people that help is coming," she said, choking back a sob. "But Chief, the only thing we can give these people right now is hope. Hope that help is coming. Hope that may push them to find the strength to cut through their rooftops or whatever to save their lives rather than just accept death. I will not take hope from these people. So, if that means I have to be dealt with after this is all over with, so be it, but I'm not going to stop giving these people hope! It's all they have right now!"

"Skipper, you're right and you will provide hope and save many lives by giving them hope. Keep it going." Skipper was shaking with passion as she said this, and I couldn't have agreed with her more. For some of these individuals, the difference between life and death was whether or not they could will themselves into survival mode. Once again, I placed the headset back on to listen to another call. I didn't want to do it, but if those whom I had oversight were resilient enough to listen and endure those calls, I needed to be able to do the same. I wanted them to know that I was standing in solidarity with them. That's what leadership does.

As I switched from call to call, I heard women, men, and children calling for help. Their voices were filled with fear and terror as the waters from the storm overtook their homes. In the background, you could hear men and women using tools and blunt objects in their homes to break through their attics to escape the rising water. You could hear the panic of those who could not swim but were now faced with rising water in their homes that was surpassing the capacities of the highest elevated points in their homes.

"I can't find my mama. She went downstairs, and now she's gone," the frightened voice of a little girl came over the headset. "I'm so scared." The little girl was sobbing into the phone. "F**K!" I yelled repeatedly in my mind, only I could hear it but anyone who saw knew what I was thinking. Why was this happening to this baby???!!!! A female dispatcher was doing her best to comfort the young girl with words of encouragement. Turns out the young girl was in her room, and water was beginning to fill her room as well. At her young age, she wasn't sure if they had an attic or not and didn't know how to get to it. Without her mother, she was all alone.

"Listen sweetie, I want you to get on the highest thing in your room and stay there," the dispatcher directed. "I'm not going to leave you." The girl said there was a dresser, and the dispatcher said, "Yes, get on the dresser." "I'm so scared. Can somebody please come and get me?" she pleaded. There was a moment of silence. I spotted the dispatcher at her station sobbing into her hand to muffle the sound and continue to convey strength to this little girl. "Baby, we're going to get to you as soon as we can as her voice trembled. Are you on the dresser?" "Yes, ma'am," she finally answered.

I listened to a few more calls ranging in degrees of severity but all of them with some sort of life-or-death threat. This was an absolute clusterfuck of a situation! I feel like hearing those calls literally rearranged my DNA on a cellular level...they were that intense. This level of disaster was far worse than what we had projected or feared, and at this point, I was unsure if it would get better or if it was possible that things would degenerate from here. How did we miss this? Could we have been more prepared? Should we have evacuated the city earlier?

How would we navigate the days to come? What would the body count be? Would we even make it out of this alive? How in the fuck did we get here? I stepped outside of the room to take a breather, and when I was certain that no one could see me, I exhaled the breath that I'd been holding since I'd heard that first emergency call. I could feel the sting of tears that I

refused to let fall pool in my eyes. I probably needed to release those emotions, but I needed to save that for later because something told me that this
was only the beginning of Katrina's fury unleashed upon New Orleans!

Chapter 9:
Rescue Me!

August 29, 2005, would definitely mark one of the saddest and most traumatic days in recent American history for me, I thought as I went to another dispatcher station and plugged into the Fifth District channel, which covered the lower and upper Ninth Ward sections of the city. The human mind and psyche have an amazing ability to protect us from trauma by cloaking our emotions in numbness until such time as we are able to handle the mental weight of the trauma that we've experienced.

Either I am far more mentally robust than I have given myself credit for, or my numbing switch was broken because the emotional and psychic backlash of hearing the kind of human suffering that I had heard over the course of the last few hours was nearly suffocating me. There was no emotional distance. I felt an emotional connection to every single caller that I heard. Words will never be able to capture what it is like to hear someone begging you for help in the last moments of their life, and you can't do a damn thing about it.

It was now around 8:00 a.m., and the winds were still as high as 130 to 140 mph, with the expectation that it would be at least another 6 hours before winds would be under 60 mph. This meant we wouldn't be able to send help or search and rescue for at least another 5 or 6 hours! And this, of course, meant another 6 hours of trying to encourage people to live through and survive impossible circumstances, knowing that many of them would not live through it.

I looked around the Communications Center, taking inventory of all the courageous and professional dispatchers and 911 operators, and marveled at the depth of their internal fortitude. Many of them were in emotional distress, handling the deluge of calls that were coming in back-to-back. They had tissues at their desks, were wiping away tears, and silently sobbing into their shirt sleeves. But to hear them speak, you would never know it. Their voices were calm, professional, and as reassuring as humanly possible in these unbelievable circumstances.

I was overwhelmed after an inconsistent couple of hours of patching in every now and then to get an assessment of the situation out there, but they had consistently been taking calls throughout the night and into the morning. I knew that there would be a great need for psychological evaluation and assistance after this. There is just no way to process that kind of turmoil and not need professional guidance.

"Y'all have to get somebody here to get us," the terrified voice of a woman came over the channel I'd plugged into. The dispatcher responded compassionately and calmly, advising the woman those winds were still too high for us to send someone out, but once the winds let up, someone would be there as soon as possible. "My husband tore a hole in our attic ceiling," the woman said.

"The water's rising in our attic, and he's trying to make sure me and the kids can get out onto the rooftop if it gets too high in here." "Where are you and your kids right now?" the dispatcher asked calmly. "We're in the attic right now," the woman responded anxiously. "The water is up to our knees right now, but I can't tell, it's dark, I can't see a fucking thing, this fucking water is rising fast."

I scanned the room and located the dispatcher who was speaking with this woman. She appeared to be in her late thirties or early forties at most. She wore an expression of concern on her face. I figured that she was also a mother who could identify with this woman's anguish. She had just taken down the woman's name and address. Her name was Deanna, and she, her husband, and three children attempted to evacuate, but car trouble en route to Houston the day before forced them to hunker down at their home, which proved to be a disastrous move. Rising water in their one-story home forced them to move to the highest point in their house, which was the attic.

"Is the hole that your husband made wide enough for you to fit through?" the dispatcher asked. In the background, you could hear a hammering sound and the fearful chatter of children. "He used a hammer and saw to make the hole, and I think it's going to be large enough for us to fit through," she answered. "But it would be better if you all could bring us to a shelter or something because it's pretty bad outside."

"I'm glad that he was able to make a --" the dispatcher began but was cut off by a loud crashing sound and screams on the other end. "OH SHIT!" the woman exclaimed. "The wind is so strong it almost knocked my husband off of the ladder." With wind gusts as strong as 140 mph, I wasn't surprised by that at all. "Ma'am, are you all okay?" the dispatcher asked. "Yeah, we're alright," the woman answered. "The wind made him lose his balance, and he dropped the saw that he's using to try to make the hole a little bigger in case we have to escape through it."

A light tap on my shoulder arrested my attention, as I turned to see Andrea Skipper standing behind me with one of our communications radios in hand. I quickly took off the headset and placed it on the desk so that I could see what information she had for me. Skip was the consummate professional, and her twenty-plus years of experience as a dispatcher and calm demeanor allowed her to remain solid in circumstances where most individuals would completely lose their shit. She was a badass extraordinaire, to be sure, but the hours of nonstop mental and emotional catharsis were beginning to take their toll on her. The average person wouldn't see it, but her eyes betrayed her physical, emotional, and mental exhaustion. "Hey, Skip," I greeted her. "How are you doing?"

I knew there were pressing issues, but it was important for me for those I led to know that I cared about them individually. Skipper exhaled thoughtfully, choosing her words. "Chief, I'm not gonna lie. At worst, most of us prepared for two or three days of this," she answered, looking directly at me. "But from what I'm seeing and hearing, we haven't even begun to see just how bad it is." Her words resonated with me immediately. We anticipated wind damage from the storm. We even anticipated some secondary damage from minor flooding, but we did not calculate just how bad shit would kick off and how fast things would go from bad to even worse. "Yeah, Skip," I said, hating to agree with her.

"We've got some challenges ahead of us, but we have to believe we will, that we are going to get through this together." "Yep, that's what I keep telling the team," she said. "It's hard for some of us though because we've lost communication with our family members." Many of the dispatchers and 911 operators were in the precarious position of having to navigate strangers through impossible circumstances all while wondering what was happening with family members who had either evacuated or some who had to hunker down because they either refused to leave or waited too late to leave.

I knew it was a tough position to be in. I was blessed in that Tiffany and Morgan were safe in Houston, but with cell towers damaged by the storm, communication with them was all but impossible. I couldn't imagine if they were still here in the city not being able to confirm that they were safe.

At the mention of family, Skipper's eyes became a little distant. I knew that she still had family members that she was thinking about - her mother and grandmother had evacuated, but due to leaving at a later time, they had encountered an inordinate amount of traffic en route to their final destination, so she wasn't absolutely certain when or if they'd made it yet. I was certain that hearing individuals begging for help and knowing that sometimes she probably heard an individual take their last breath was beyond difficult and exacerbated by the fact that she was not 100% certain about the safety and whereabouts of her own loved ones.

FUCK! Katrina was already whipping our asses! I gave Skip a reassuring hug and a high five that hopefully conveyed what words could not. She received the embrace, and being the professional that she was, she shifted to the business at hand. "Ok Chief," Skipper said, shifting into professional mode. "We're still waiting on all the status reports from our District Commanders at their various hunker down locations to come in." "I was able to connect with District Five Fifth District Commander, Captain John Bryson, not too long ago," Andrea continued. "He stepped away for just a second but should be back any moment. He has an active situation going on at his location." Captain John Bryson and the Fifth District relocated to the St. Claude General Hospital as the hunker down location.

Although that area was about six feet below sea level, it was a six-story building and would allow for a vertical evacuation if things got bad. Operations of that district would be based out of St. Claude General until such time as they would be able to return to their normal headquarters. I was particularly interested in their update in that the Fifth District comprised the Ninth Ward, and most of our distress calls at the moment were coming from this area. We, of course, were not surprised that the distress calls were coming from the Ninth Ward. The area was at least 6 feet below sea level and vulnerable to storm surges.

This is why we practically begged the people of that area to evacuate because flooding would be life-threatening. I took the earpiece from Skipper that was connected to the radio and placed it in my ear and then held the radio at the ready so that when Captain Bryson came back over, I wouldn't miss him. "The Ninth Ward is in bad shape, Chief," Skip advised, gesturing her hands toward the room of dispatchers who were actively taking emergency calls.

"The majority of the calls we are getting are coming from the Ninth Ward. Chief, the callers are terrified, they are scared, they're desperate." I silently nodded in agreement as I listened for Captain Bryson to get an update. "It's a crazy dance because people are trying to escape the rising waters that are flooding their homes, but it's so dangerous outside right now." She added. "Yeah, I'll launch SWAT, I'll give SWAT the green light - as soon as Commander Jeff Winn feels it safe enough to go.

Keep a log of the addresses of the callers as I give in with SWAT Commander Jeffrey Winn to see when we can begin our search and rescue efforts, but right now, I already know that the winds are too high," I advised. The crackle of the radio, and then Captain Bryson's voice coming over the radio, interrupted our conversation. I pressed the earpiece deeper into my ear. "Chief," Captain Bryson said once he realized he'd reached me.

"It's pretty goddamn intense around here, man, Chief." "What's going on?" I wanted to know. Each time he patched into our line to communicate, I could hear those scrambled sounds in the background of people talking and orders and directives being passed between officers and medical staff who were at the hospital. "At this exact moment, Chief, the hospital is surrounded by at least 6 feet of water outside," Bryson said. "We've moved everything and everyone up to the third floor to get away from the water that's already flooding the first two floors." SHIT! I thought to myself. "Do you all have things under control within the hospital?" I barked. "What's the situation in the hospital? Are things under control?" "Yes," he answered. "Between our officers and the hospital staff, we were able to quickly get things moved and keep everyone relatively calm in the process." "Good," I responded.

"Do you have any eyes into what's going on outside?" "Chief, I'm looking out the window right now from the third floor." Bryson replied. There was a note in his voice that I didn't understand. I couldn't quite discern the mood of his voice, but something was off. I couldn't tell if it was exhaustion that I was hearing or if this was something else. "Bryson—" I started, but was cut off by his response.

"Chief, I just saw my first body floating in the water." Bryson said in a lowered but measured voice. There was a level of sadness and helplessness that was now explained by what he just said. If I'd understood him correctly, I believe he just told me that he saw a dead body floating in the water. "Bryson, did you just say that you saw a dead body?" I inquired. "Chief, I am looking at the dead body of a woman floating face down in the water moving past the hospital." He confirmed.

When he said the words, he seemed to be saying them more to himself than me. It was as if he was trying to convince himself that what he was seeing was real. "Fuck!" I couldn't help but exclaim. Suddenly, loud shuffling noises at one of the stations of one of the dispatchers caught my ear and my peripheral vision. I looked over to see Andrea walking over to the dispatcher who was handling the call that I had patched into earlier.

The woman was visibly upset but still issuing instructions to whomever she was on the line with. Andrea seemed to be giving her additional instructions to give to the caller. "Bryson, hold tight one second." I said, removing the earpiece and picking up the headset that was patched into the dispatcher's call. When I placed the headset back on, my ears were immediately assaulted by the blood-curdling screams of children and the distressed sobbing of a woman.

Even through the sobbing, I recognized the voice to still be that of the woman that the dispatcher had been speaking to earlier, Deanna Lewis. "I can barely understand you, Mrs. Lewis," I heard the dispatcher say. "Can you please tell me clearly what happened?" "MY HUSBAND! MY HUSBAND! OH GOD, MY HUSBAND!" Deanna's sobs pierced our ears.

"Mrs. Lewis, please tell me what happened." The dispatcher pled. Deanna continued to sob, and the children continued to scream and cry in the background. It was the perfect backdrop to whatever cataclysmic incident had just occurred. I will never forget that sound as long as I live. After a few moments, Mrs. Lewis composed herself enough to speak.

"My husband made it to our rooftop to confirm if we could get through the hole and get on the roof, that if we needed to evacuate there, that we could," she said against the background of crying and screaming children. "While he was trying to climb back down into the attic, the winds started blowing really hard and—". She started crying again. "The winds blew him off of our roof," she sobbed. "I think my husband just got blown off of our roof of our house and into the water."

She screamed at the top of her lungs. "My husband can't be dead! Please help him, GOD, please help him. What are we going to do!?" I listened with bated breath as the dispatcher, with Andrea's assistance, skillfully confirmed Mrs. Lewis's account that her husband had indeed been blown off of their roof and into the flood waters that surrounded their home. This was a literal fucking nightmare. "I can't do this," Deanna exclaimed through tears. "I can't do this by myself! What am I going to tell these kids? How can I do this? He was our everything!" she shouted hysterically.

There is nothing more heartbreaking than the sound of a strong woman assessing an impossible situation that she is faced with, fearing that she lacks the ability to navigate it on her own, but knowing that even though she is terrified to do it, she must do it anyway. This woman's cry seemed to echo the cry of generations of women who were forced to overcome unbearable circumstances, and in my heart, I cried for her too. Damn.

I took off the headset and tried to allow myself a brief moment to reset. On the one hand, I'd just learned that there was a dead woman's body floating down St. Claude Street and that my officers in the area were powerless to do anything about it. On the other hand, I just heard a family's entire world crumble at the loss of their husband and father, all the while wondering if they would come out of their situation with their own lives.

Fuck Katrina! I became angrier; fury surged inside me. I usually remain cool under pressure, but I don't tolerate being messed with. I don't take shit from anyone. The fury within wanted to lash out, to retaliate against Katrina in my own way. Retaliation was the norm for me, even if most of my attacks on my political nemesis were below the radar. Now, in the midst of a real-life nightmare, a battle, I was perplexed; I couldn't do a damn thing to help. People were dying, and I was used to helping, going after assholes, taking risks. Fuck Katrina! It had only just begun to kick our asses; people were dying, and we were facing an unbeatable foe. But giving up was not an option.

"Bryson, I'm back," I announced once again, pressing the earpiece into my ear. Bryson gave additional updates concerning the Fifth District's status and how they were faring. The Ninth Ward was taking a major beating. Flood waters in the area were at least 6 feet deep outside, and people's homes were flooding as high as their attics. The depth and height of the water were not the only issues at hand. The gale-force winds turned the moving water into a destructive force that was ripping apart homes and sweeping dangerous debris throughout the area. It would be virtually impossible for them to help anyone outside, even if they tried.

"It's so fucking frustrating, Chief," Bryson said. "I know there are people out there who need help, but there's no way we could even get to them."

"I understand, Bryson," I said. "But in these moments, as hard as it is, we have to be more tactical than emotional. We are going to get our opportunity to help them very soon."

There was a brief pause on Bryson's end. "Chief," he said slowly. "There's my second body floating down the fucking street. Goddamn!"

"Is it coming from the same direction as the first one?" I asked.

"Yep," he answered. "It's a black man who appears to be in his late thirties or early forties, floating in the goddamn street."

My thoughts immediately went to Mrs. Lewis and her family. The address she had given the dispatcher was not too far from St. Claude General Hospital. Her husband had just been blown off their roof into the water. I couldn't help but wonder if Captain Bryson was looking at Mr. Lewis floating in the water at this very moment.

"Chief," Bryson said, interrupting my thoughts. "I see a small baby floating in the water."

Skipper came over. "Chief, we have callers saying their houses are floating in the streets," she said. "What did you say? The callers are saying that their houses are floating." As she gave me the headset, Captain Weathersby and Chief Nicholas joined us, their faces displaying astonishment. I listened in and thought, "What the fuck is going on?" One caller said, "Our fucking house is floating, we must be in ten feet of water, I can't fucking swim, I need help." Another caller said, "All the houses are passing my house, the houses are floating by my house," then later he would state, "No, it's my fucking house that's floating, oh shit, please help me."

Skipper, Captain Weathersby, Chief Nicholas, and I all looked at each other with the most perplexed look imaginable. The dispatchers were continuing to try and keep the callers calm, asking their locations, how many people were in the house, and urging them to get to the highest point in their house. My disbelief was interrupted as I heard Captain Bryson saying, "Chief, are you there?" "Yes, John," I replied, and then silence.

"More bodies are floating, chief," he said. Neither of us said anything for what seemed like a long time. I knew that what he was seeing and what we were hearing was the manifestation of the brutality that is Mother Nature. Nature's fury did not discriminate between young and old, infants or adults, good or bad. Her brutality was objective and fucked up all at the same time.

In that moment, I knew that New Orleans would never be the same after Katrina. It was at this moment that I knew that the loss of life was going to be far greater than what we had projected and what was predicted. I knew that families were literally being ripped apart in this storm and that the collective mental repair of our city would take years. How many bodies would we find? How many bodies would we never find? Would we have to leave people behind? How many people at this very moment were dying as we waited for the winds to die down to help them?

There are no words to describe the level of helplessness you feel when you are a "helper," but circumstances beyond your control don't allow you to function in your ability. The citizens of our city needed us, and Katrina had us in a fucking chokehold, preventing us from getting to them. I could have literally punched a hole in the wall; I was so fucking mad.

I talked with Bryson for an additional five minutes, helping him to process and navigate the moment. He saw additional bodies floating down St. Claude, which informed my gut feeling that our initial rescue efforts had to be centered around the Ninth Ward. Captain Bryson kept me informed. "Captain Bryson there are several high-water deuces and half trucks that will be headed your way as soon as the winds subsides" I said. Captain Bryson interrupted me with a super sadden spirit as he stated in a depressed and seemingly defeated murmur "there are mother fucking houses floating down the street." Silence befell both of us as our phones disconnected.

I advised my staff that Bryson said that houses are floating down St. Claude Ave. My staff looked as shocked as I was. I regathered my composure and I was advised by my staff that around 7:55 a.m. the Industrial Canal levee had been breached, and water was flowing into the Ninth Ward like a linear waterfall. It was reported that a barge carried in by the storm had slammed into the levee, causing a breach at least 150 feet wide. This explained the catastrophic flooding and calls that we were getting from our Ninth Ward residents juxtaposed against the calmer calls that we were getting from our Lakeview, Gentilly, and Uptown residents.

Not too long after, I decided to go to the parking garage of our police headquarters so I could look out over South White Street and see what things looked like in our area. We were in mid-city and at least two-and-a-half miles from the nearest canal. The rain had stopped for a moment, giving me a moment to not only take in the sight but also the sound of what was happening.

Looking out over South White Street, you could see the water moving quietly in an east to west direction. The water was at least two feet high, so we hadn't experienced the level of flooding that those in the Ninth Ward were facing. Around 9:05 a.m., an interesting phenomenon occurred right before my eyes—the eye of Hurricane Katrina was passing over the southeast part of the greater New Orleans area. At that moment, as it passed, the water rose slightly, maybe two-and-a-half to three feet.

Suddenly, an inexplicable vision of serenity and peace emerged, one that I can't explain to this very day. Standing at the edge of the parking lot under the sky, looking down over the city below, the sun peeped through the clouds, painting the sky a bright orange and yellow and illuminating the clouds with iridescent hues. The winds died down, as if paying homage to this picturesque scene that seemed like the work of the Lord God Almighty Himself.

The scene was so peaceful and serene that I honestly questioned if I had died and gone to Heaven. There was an overwhelming sense of peace and serenity that made it hard to believe that just moments earlier, the sky was gray and the winds were raging. While I had always considered myself moderately God-conscious, this moment solidified my belief in God in ways I still can't describe. It was as if, in response to all the chaos I had witnessed, God offered this vision of peace and serenity to assure me that, somehow, everything would be okay.

Moments later, along with Captain Weathersby, and Officer Menzies, I watched in awe from the garage as the water on South White Street experienced a tide shift. We observed in silence as the water stopped flowing east to west, stood still momentarily, and then began flowing west to east! I had never seen anything like it before in my life. This confirmed for me that the eye of the storm had passed over New Orleans, and despite the craziness and chaos, this moment was quite amazing to witness.

I can't say that all fear was immediately replaced with hope because that would be a lie. We were still in deep trouble in New Orleans, and I knew that we didn't have the foggiest idea of just how dire the situation was yet. But it reaffirmed that God Almighty was there with us, and we would be alright. It was a sign of hope, strength, and determination. What I did know was that, just like the sun made its appearance in the middle of an epic storm, the indomitable and courageous spirit of our NOPD officers and the people of our city would show up and fight to survive. We would fight. Not all of us would win, but if we were going down, we would go down swinging.

Along with the hope and inspiration we had just received, the winds came again, this time in the opposite direction. The winds seemed to have slowly increased over the next 40-plus minutes, not to the level it was before, but it had to be at least 90-plus miles per hour. It began to push us around as if we weighed merely a few pounds. Myself, and Captain Weathersby immediately headed to base 9 on the second floor of headquarters to get a status check and prepare to run operations once the winds dropped below 60 miles per hour.

Chapter 10:
I Can't Die Like This

"My house is completely flooded, and I'm stuck in my attic," the woman's anxious voice buzzed through NOPD Dispatcher Levette Joseph's headset. With over twenty years of experience with the New Orleans Police Department, Levette had endured challenging calls, from police officer shootings to violent crimes and deaths. She had even handled the chaos of more than a dozen years of the greatest free show on earth, Mardi Gras. As a seasoned dispatcher, her role involved sitting behind a wall of computer monitors, intently listening to the phone, police radio, and officers who might stop by with updates. The job demanded thick skin, discipline, multi-tasking skills, and a well-trained ear to process constant auditory data.

"What's your address, ma'am?" Levette inquired calmly yet empathetically.

"4700 Citrus Drive," she responded.

A swell of emotion surged within Levette as she processed the information. The caller lived on the same street, perhaps only separated by one block. Levette's home address with her husband in New Orleans East was 4827 Citrus Drive. If the woman was in the 4700 block of Citrus Drive, her home was likely underwater. Everything lost.

So not only was Levette left to process whether or not this woman would make it out of her attic alive, but now she also carried the weight of knowing that her home was lost due to Katrina's destructive force. The last 72 hours had been a never-ending nightmare from which she couldn't awaken! She and George had built their lives with their family together in that home, and just knowing that was a painful game of tug-of-war with her emotions.

On one end, she was heartbroken and devastated. Her family's heirlooms and memories that a million dollars couldn't replace were washed away in Katrina's angry floodwaters. On the other end of her emotional spectrum, she was irate. She wasn't exactly sure whom her anger was directed towards, but it was there – hot and fiery with a barrage of questions.

Mary Knight, one of four NOPD Dispatch Supervisors on duty in Base 9, sensed a shift in Levette's temperament and approached her station to inquire about what was happening. "Vette, you alright?" Mary asked.

"I'm fine, Mary," Levette answered, briefly removing her headset. "It's just additional stuff on top of what's already happening out there."

Mary scrutinized Levette's face briefly, trying to discern what she was saying without prying. With over 33 years of experience with the NOPD and management, Mary knew how to offer the requisite emotional support an employee needed while allowing them the space to compartmentalize and stay task-driven if that was their desire.

Knowing Levette as she did, Mary was clear that this wasn't the time to push her for an emotional debrief. The lines in Base 9 had been lit up for hours before and after Katrina made landfall. In addition to getting rollover calls from citizens trapped in their homes with rising water, officers called in on their radios because many of the officers assigned to come in on the second shift were trapped in their homes or couldn't make it out of their neighborhoods.

Base 9, a special event unit, was typically staffed with the best of the best, and the Katrina event was no exception. There were six senior dispatchers assigned to Base 9. Base 9 was in a separate area from the communication center on the fifth floor.

Thirty-two dispatchers worked twelve-hour shifts, with 16 assigned to each change working in the communication center. Two dispatchers were assigned to each channel to provide support to the districts.

In addition to Mary Knight, Levette Joseph, Stepanie Briscoe, Jennifer McDonald, and Annie Rogers were the four other NOPD Dispatch Supervisors working in Base 9 to ensure that things went as smoothly as possible during this unprecedented event. Mary, Stepanie, and Levette were the three supervisors on duty, while Jennifer and Annie rested in preparation for the next shift. The mixed sound of telephone calls and radio communication notifications emanating from the room filled with dispatchers hunkered over their monitors with headsets reminded Levette and Mary that there was no calm in their immediate future.

As Chief Warren Riley, Chief Steven Nicholas, and Captain Lawrence Weathersby entered Base 9 for a status update from around the city, Mary began to quickly organize details in her mind to relay to them.

Meanwhile, NOPD Officer Chris Abbott stood in the middle of his New Orleans East home on Primrose Street, exclaiming, "Mother Fucker!" Despite being divorced with no kids, the circumstances were still shitty. Water pooled around his ankles, confirming that his one-story home was flooding. The lukewarm water sent a chill through his soul, and looking outside, he saw the entire street flooded with water rushing at a moderate pace, gently pushing against parked vehicles.

With the rain coming down in sheets and the wind blowing steadily, visibility was significantly decreased during this unprecedented storm.

He ran one hand quickly through his short blond hair as he tried to sort out the situation. Despite being assigned to NOPD's Crime Prevention Unit, he had been redirected to report to Methodist Hospital in New Orleans East, where the 7th District was hunkering down under the command of District Commander Robert Bardy. His home was about a ten-minute drive from Methodist, so in theory, getting there shouldn't be that difficult.

The timing was critical. If water continued filling his home at this pace, he might be in trouble in a few hours. In his gut, however, Chris believed that the flooding would abate, and while he'd have to deal with some troublesome cleanup, it wouldn't be anything he hadn't experienced in the past. With Chris, things always seemed to work out. It didn't matter how crazy or dangerous the circumstances were; he always seemed to come out on top. Many within the Department chided him about being the cop with nine lives. To date, Chris has been shot five times in two separate shootings. In 1998, he was shot in the chest and survived thanks to the bulletproof vest he was wearing.

A few years later, in 2001, he was shot twice in his upper torso and twice in the back of the head by a gunman determined to end his life. Though the recovery from both shooting instances was painstaking, he survived and continued to grow as an officer. Chris firmly believed that if God allowed him to live through those shootings, which could have easily ended his life, it must mean that a purpose for his life remained.

"Bark! Bark! Bark! Bark!" The frightened barks of his miniature schnauzer, Trevor, alerted him that the dog was in his bedroom, likely sheltering on top of his bed to avoid the water. At this exact moment, Trevor was probably in the safest place he could be – sheltered inside and above ground. Hopefully, the same could be said about Mrs. Epstein. Just yesterday, he had checked on his elderly next-door neighbor, Mrs. Epstein, to make sure she had everything she needed.

A lively and vital widow around 85 years old, Mrs. Epstein was the neighborhood grandmother to most of the block. She was fiercely independent and singularly ensured that her yard work and everything else in her household was taken care of.

She prided herself on her ability to fully function without the aid of anyone else, including her children, who lived out of state. No one had been able to convince Mrs. Epstein to evacuate her home, but yesterday, Chris figured he'd give it one more try with a different approach.

"I have to work at Methodist Hospital over the next few days," he had shared with her yesterday. "Why don't you come in to work with me and maybe cheer up some of the patients on the floors who could use some encouragement?"

"Nice try, son," she chuckled, shaking her head no. "I'm going to be just fine here. I've seen these things come and go over the years. I'm not worried at all."

He thought of trying to convince her one final time but quickly dismissed the idea, knowing how determined she was to stay in place. A noise that sounded like running water caught Chris's attention, bringing him out of his thoughts. He followed the sound to the kitchen and noticed that the water coming in from the door in the back of the kitchen, which led outside, had increased in intensity and seemed to be coming in twice as fast and in greater volume than before.

As much as Chris hated to think of it, he had to leave his home. He'd get to Methodist earlier than his required clock-in time, but he knew that if he was going to leave, he needed to do so sooner rather than later.

He quickly went through his home, ensuring all the windows and doors were locked. He grabbed his go-pack and stopped by his room to see Trevor before leaving. "Hey, buddy," he said to the dog. "Daddy's going to step out for just a few minutes to make sure that everything is okay at the hospital where he's going to work. As soon as I know everything is okay, I will come right back and get you."

He placed Trevor's food and water dish on the bed for him to eat in case he got hungry while he was gone, but Chris estimated that he'd be back for Trevor in less than two hours. With one final look around, Chris saw that Trevor was unusually excited, actually a little nervous. It was almost as if he wanted to tell him something, maybe even warn Chris. Chris looked at Trevor and said, "Buddy, I promise I'll be back," before heading out the door.

Back at Base 9, Mary Knight watched as Chief Riley and Chief Nicholas processed all the information, she'd relayed to them regarding updates from the eight districts and several specialized units. They were hunkered down at elevated locations all around the city. Ms. Knight also provided several locations where they'd made radio calls to officers, providing guidance and instructions.

While it would have been easy for Chiefs Riley and Nicholas to call in and dictate orders to those who worked under them, she admired their ability to get in the trenches and do the job with them. Base 9 received calls that St. Bernard Parish, not far from the Lower 9th Ward, was completely underwater. In addition to an uptick in calls from the 9th Ward, reports were coming in that New Orleans East was experiencing heavy flooding. Flooding appeared to be widespread and growing. They knew the Industrial Canal levee had been breached in three areas, causing massive flooding in St. Bernard Parish and the Lower 9th Ward.

Reports were coming in about the 17th Street Canal levee, which divided the Gentilly and Lakeview area of New Orleans and Jefferson Parish, having several breaches and massive overtopping by the floodwaters on the west side of New Orleans. There were also rumors of the London Avenue Canal in the Gentilly area being breached on both sides and the 17th Street Canal on the west side of New Orleans. Things were going to hell. Everything that could go wrong was happening. The room was abuzz with dispatchers handling citizens' calls while simultaneously navigating the police radio with officers either asking for backup where they were stationed or reporting that they could not report for duty because they were trapped in their homes.

"If you can't get in, that's fine," Mary heard Chief Riley saying over the radio to one of the officers attempting to report in. "Just get to the district station that is closest to your home as soon as possible and stay safe." With worsening conditions, Mary didn't know if that would be likely for some time. It might only be a matter of time before cops started popping up on the rescue list. "Have you all heard from any other officers who are having difficulty making it in for their shifts?" Chief Riley asked Mary as he and Chief Nicholas made their way closer to her desk space.

"We've had a few here and there, Chief," Mary answered. "But I think we could see an upsurge depending on the types of flooding we may have." "Yeah," Riley agreed. "We won't know how bad it is out there until the winds die down, and we can begin search and rescue efforts." "Well, our initial critical calls for help were coming from St. Bernard Parish and the Lower and Upper Ninth Wards," Mary stated. "But now the urgency in calls is increasing in the east."

"If we follow the path of the emergency calls, then we can make an educated guess as to the path of the flooding and severe weather," Chief Nicholas said as he walked over to a large map of the city of New Orleans that covered most of the west wall of the office space. "Yeah, I know," Riley agreed. "We've got reports of breaches all over the damn city." "It may take us some time to receive official confirmation of the breaches," Mary interjected. "True enough," Nicholas said, making his way back over to them. "But even still, you get a sense that you don't know how crazy it is out there right now."

Meanwhile, Chris carefully applied pressure with his foot to the accelerator of his car as he slowly drove up the street en route to Methodist Hospital. The rain was still coming down in sheets, and the wind gusts were rocking his car back and forth a bit. New Orleans East was essentially a ghost town. Houses were precariously boarded up where owners had made last-minute decisions to evacuate. The streets looked haunted as bushes and trees protested against the strong gusts sweeping through.

Strewn debris of garbage, tree limbs, and the occasional piece of lawn furniture inappropriately littered areas as if they'd been dropped there with no sense of intentionality. Due to the high water, Chris had only made it a little more than a block in his vehicle. He had to proceed slowly. Chris couldn't risk flooding his engine, and he, for damn sure, couldn't get stuck in this mess. He was negotiating a right turn onto Morrison Road when he saw something in the corner of his eye to the left.

Chris's heart sank into his stomach. An entire wall of water at least ten feet high rushed toward him, overtaking everything in its path. In split seconds, Chris could see tires and tree limbs swept up by this mud-colored wall of water headed straight for his car. "Oh shit!" he exclaimed. His first instinct was to gun his accelerator, but he knew there was no way he would outdrive this water wall. Bracing himself for impact, Chris steeled himself as the water cascaded over the top of his vehicle. His ears were assaulted by the sound of the rushing water and debris bumping against his truck.

The force of the wave began to push the car eastward on Morrison Road, and for a moment, Chris expected the vehicle to overturn. Initially, all Chris could see was water; for a moment, he'd begun to think that his vehicle was fully submerged. Water was leaking into the car through the windows and the doors. After what seemed like an eternity, however, the rush of water had fully passed over his vehicle, and he could now see out of the windows of his car.

A massive deluge of water had just inundated the streets, filling them with even more water. Chris's vehicle was floating in water up to its windows. "Jesus Christ," he exhaled. He would have to leave his truck here and return to the house for higher ground. "Get it together, Abbott," he said to himself. The prospects were unfavorable, but he knew what to do. He was about a block from his house.

He would have to walk/swim back home. Having been shot multiple times before this, including two shots to the head, Chris refused to die on the streets and drowned in his car. He could not die like this. He would not die like this. He summoned the mental wherewithal to roll down the windows of his truck and, using a great portion of his upper body strength, pulled himself through the driver's window into the water on the street. Chris found himself in chest-high, murky, lukewarm water.

He looked around, trying to get his bearings and location. He would have to swim at least a block to get to his house. Commanding all the willpower he could muster, Chris launched forward into the water, taking a deep breath before cutting the water with his body.

Utilizing the butterfly stroke, Chris propelled himself through the water at a moderate pace. He refused to consider that he was swimming on the street outside that was flooded due to a catastrophic hurricane, as that would likely overwhelm him and cost him momentum. The physical task of swimming was exhausting. His breath was ragged as he inhaled and splashed through the water.

He wanted to take account of how quickly he was progressing but didn't take inventory for fear he hadn't made it as far as he perceived. Occasionally, he could feel his arms hit against foreign objects in the street, or he would have to shift further right or left to avoid debris. That was a mind screw that perhaps made this swimming journey seem longer than it was. He stopped swimming to take a break, using his feet to balance himself.

His body was fatigued from the demand of swimming through the water. His breathing was still ragged and required deep inhalations to adequately get the oxygen he needed to fuel him for the journey ahead. It took him roughly twenty minutes to get to his house. He could no longer see his lawn and barely see his porch, now wading in a pool of water that came up to a quarter of the height of his door. He'd made it home. Now, all he had to do was not die!

Back at Base 9, the room remained abuzz with movement and activity. "That doesn't surprise me at all," Mary Knight said with a chuckle as she disconnected her headset, walking over to Chief Riley and Chief Nicholas, who was still with her in Base 9, assessing their position and developing strategies. "What doesn't surprise you, Mary?" Chief Riley asked, hearing her words and noticing her chuckle.

Any news that made someone smile on a day like today was worth repeating. "Sergeant Manuel Curry with the 6th District is schooling the younger officers on handling a storm like Katrina," she answered, still smiling. Chief Nicholas and Chief Riley both chuckled with her. Their laughter had everything to do with admiration and nothing to do with derision.

As an eighty-year-old World War II Veteran and longest-serving active-duty police officer, Manuel Curry had a way about him that made you feel like everything was going to be all right and that there was nothing that couldn't be overcome. "If anyone was qualified to school them, it is Manny," Chief Riley said. "They better listen up."

"Ms. Knight!" Levette Joseph's voice rang out, catching their attention as she motioned for them to join her at her desk. Upon their arrival, she quickly switched the audio from the police radio call from her headset to the computer speaker. "Officer Abbott," Levette said. "I've patched in Chiefs Riley, Nicholas, and Ms. Mary Knight." "Chief," Chris's strained voice came over the speaker. "I'm in big trouble here." "Tell us what's going on, Chris," Chief Riley said, motioning for Levette to turn up the volume of the call. "He's already given us his address," Levette advised as she turned up the volume of the call. "Okay, water is filling up my house," Chris began.

"I'm in the attic now with my dog. I had to tie him to one of the beams because he's small, and the water is already up to my knees." "Chris, you are saying that you are in your attic and the water is up to your knees?" Chief Riley asked for clarity. "Yes, sir," Chris replied. Chief Riley didn't like the entire feel of this moment. "Are you in a one-story house, Officer Abbott?" Riley asked. "Yes, sir," Abbott answered. "The water is rising fast; Chief and I don't see a way out."

Riley exhaled to maintain his composure. "Chris, do you have any tools with you? Is there anything you can use to break out of the attic?" "No, sir," came Chris's resigned response. The entire moment felt like life and death were hanging in the balance, and everyone was grasping at straws to meet this moment with all the strength they could muster. Just then, First District Commander Jimmy Scott came over the radio at that moment. Riley couldn't help thinking that it was almost providential that Commander Scott had come on the radio at this moment. Jimmy Scott was a 25-year decorated veteran and a former SWAT Commander. They could use his assistance.

While Chief Nicholas continued to speak to Chris, Riley updated Scott on his condition. "I'm trying to get out of here," Chris said with an edge to his voice. "Do you see any windows?" Chief Nicholas asked. "No," he responded. "You are sure you don't see any tools or anything that you can use to cut open a hole or something in the roof?" "No." By this time, the call had caught the attention of the entire Communications Department, and officers all over the city were intently listening to their radios.

They'd dealt with citizens trapped and needing help, and now one of their own found themselves in the same predicament. Would it end the same way as so many other calls? All eyes were fixed on the group at Levette's station, and all ears tuned in to the call. They could hear the water moving around and Trevor barking vehemently. "Officer Abbott, can you tell us what's happening right now?" Mary Knight asked.

"The water is rising so fast," Chris said. "I'm doing my best to get out of here, but I don't see a way out." "But nothing!" Commander Scott interjected passionately over the radio. "Chris, where is your gun? Do you have your gun with you?" "Yes, I have it right here with me," he answered.

"How many rounds do you have?" Jimmy asked. "It's full, and I have two clips, about 45 rounds."

"Do you see an A/C vent anywhere around you? There has to be one," Jimmy said emphatically. Looking around the roof, Chris spots an A/C vent. "Yes, I see it," Chris answered.

"Is it big enough for you to fit through?" Commander Scott inquired. "Yes, but the water is up to my chest now," Chris answered dejectedly. The tone of resignation in his voice did not sit well with Chief Riley. As the man in charge, he could not even remotely convey how scared for Chris he was at this moment, but his mind was completely overwhelmed at this point. He could not lose an officer like this. Not now.

"Chris, you can't give up, man," Riley pleaded with him. "You've been through too damn much, man! You can't give up." It was as if the air had been sucked out of the room, and nobody could breathe. You could hear light sobs. Some of the dispatchers were praying. And some individuals struggled to breathe.

"I would like to thank everyone for everything they've done for me," Chris said with a sob in his voice. "I've survived so much due to the efforts of so many people in the Department, and I am grateful for what you've done for me then and even for what you've done for me today."

"CHRIS!" Jimmy Scott yelled, trying to get his attention. No response from Chris's end except for Trevor's incessant barking could be heard.

"CHRIS!" Jimmy yelled again. "I appreciate every one of you," Chris said softly.

"Fuck that!" Jimmy yelled. "CHRIS, TAKE YOUR GUN AND SHOOT OUT THE GODDAMN A/C VENTILATOR NOW!" Chris did not respond, but you could intermittently hear Trevor barking his ass off.

"I dropped the damn radio," Chris said after what seemed to be an eternity of silence, except for Trevor's loud barking.

"Shoot around the edges of the A/C vent!" Scott commanded. There was another long period of silence.

"Do it now, Chris! Shoot out the fucking ventilator!" Jimmy Scott ordered, breaking the silence. "Get out of there! Shoot it out and punch through it! Do it now!"

"Water is up to my neck," Chris said.

"Chris, I said do it NOW!!!!"

"Okay," Chris said. "I'm trying. I'm trying." They listened intently, waiting to hear the sound of Chris's weapon firing, but instead, they only listened to the sound of the dog barking.

Seconds later, there was the sound of several gunshots being fired, and then an unnatural and haunting silence followed that could be felt. No gunshots. No dog. No Chris. Silence. Everything went silent in the Communications Department as well. Everyone held their breaths, hoping against hope for any word from Chris. No one dared to say a word as if speaking might weaken the possibility of his escape.

"Chris?" Jimmy Scott inquired over the radio, breaking the silence. "Chris?" "Chris?"

Silence.

"God, no," Levette breathed out. A small tear trailed down her cheek. Slowly, you began to hear the muffled cries of dispatchers and other officers in the room. Mary Knight, Chief Riley, and Chief Nicholas exchanged looks with each other. Their hearts were hurting, and their eyes were filled with tears that they refused to allow to fall.

After a few minutes of silence, I left Base Nine and went to my office. Tears I fought to hold in finally flowed down my face as I walked into my office, ensuring no one saw my tears.

The weight of hearing dozens of citizens stuck in their attics, fighting with all they had to survive, and many, I believed, I'd heard them take their last breaths. The haunting sounds of terrified children begging to be saved and the might of Katrina daring us to take a chance on rescues against her might, inviting us to become another victim, left us paralyzed to do nothing but wait for her fury to subside. Now, I had to process Officer Chris Abbott's circumstances. Was he alive or not?

Sitting at my desk, I reflected on the two years Chris worked with me in the COPS for Kids Program in the Housing Developments of New Orleans, which provided needed services to underprivileged kids. The kids and the community Chris served loved him. Chris was their go-to guy. I process the loss of many citizens, children, and now one of my best officers.

As I tried to process the might and bullying blows of Katrina and dealt with the unimaginable potential loss of life, my thoughts, and my Pitti party were interrupted by my true inner self, my natural-born leadership skills, and my leadership training kicked back in. I prayed to GOD the Almighty to give me more strength and more wisdom to push forward because I knew that I was amid Katrina; at this time for a reason, it was not a coincidence. As my mind recalibrated to the true leader that I am, there was a knock at the door. It redirected my focus:

My chief of staff, Captain Michael Pfeiffer, poked his head in my office as I sat silently behind my desk." Chief Riley, Ms. Knight needs you in Communications ASAP," "

I'll be there," I replied from my desk, looking down at the notes I'd written. I imagined that with my pen in hand, to the casual observer, it probably appeared that I was documenting a strategy or signing off on some critical executive action. That couldn't be further from the truth. The truth was, I just needed a few minutes to process these horrifying events.

After a moment, I regained my focus.

I realized things were going to shit, and Mother Nature was shaking the city like a Pitbull on a fucking ragdoll, literally. I needed a minute, just a minute. I'd never have felt more powerless if I were honest with myself. Being second in command of the New Orleans Police Department didn't mean shit when it came to controlling Mother Nature. Katrina had rolled into New Orleans like a venomous, angry bitch with a vendetta to execute.

Her rage was merciless and indiscriminate. She poured out her wrath equally upon all she encountered, whether they were old or young, good or bad, jaded or innocent, rich or poor. She instilled fear in all of us. Katrina was the great equalizer. And then there was Chris Abbott. Though one would be hard-pressed to prove it, I was pretty fucked up behind possibly losing Officer Abbott the way that we just did.

He didn't deserve to go out like that, and the Department didn't deserve to have to endure hearing that shit, either. I'd spent the last hour on the radio with various officers who'd listened to what happened with Chris. I spent most of that time rallying them together and encouraging them that we didn't know what happened with Chris but could keep pressing forward even if it was in his honor.

Whether we liked it or not, this was the job. Even when you felt powerless, you had to summon the courage to show up and do the work.

As I walked back to Base Nine, I stopped in the communication division and walked the floor. I wanted them to see me. I wanted them to know that leadership was with them; during these troubling times, they needed to know that leadership was in it with them. As I looked across the room full of dispatchers navigating call after call from citizens and officers needing assistance, the dispatchers and 911 operators were still focused, diligent, and determined as they answered call after call. Their resiliency was more motivation for me; I thought to myself as I headed back to Base Nine. "Hold on New Orleans... help is on the way!”

But even beyond our officers, I intended to save as many people as possible. Anyone and everyone that I encountered en route to the Eastbank of Eastern New Orleans would be a candidate for rescue as long as it was in my power. Yes, I had officers assigned to specific areas to rescue citizens, but there was no way in hell that I could see a person in need and bypass them, whether it was my assigned area or not.

I knew that the search and rescue ahead of us would likely change our lives in ways we couldn't anticipate. We would likely see things that we couldn't "unsee." We would probably encounter circumstances for which there was no human way to prepare. We would be forced to make choices that would stretch the elasticity of our conscience in ways that we couldn't even imagine. Yet, somehow, I felt gratification at the thought of finally pushing back against Katrina. These searches and rescues would be our way of beginning to undo the damage Katrina had inflicted upon our city and our beloved people.

As I looked across the room full of dispatchers navigating call after call from citizens and officers needing assistance, I thought, just another couple of hours. We can help our people's search and rescue begin.

Chapter 11:
Chaos & Fear

Approximately 2 pm, August 29th

"CHRIS, SHOOT OUT THE VENTILATOR NOW!!" Commander Jimmy Scott's voice boomed.

BARK!

BARK!

BARK!

"I appreciate everything all of you have done for me," Chris Abbott's voice was resigned and dejected.

BARK!

Bark!

"CHRIS, DON'T YOU DARE FUCKING GIVE UP!" Scott yelled.

BARK!

BARK!

BARK!

BARK!

BARK,

BARK,

BARK,

BARK,

BARK!

I must have replayed the scene with Officer Abbott's barking terrified dog and him struggling to get out of the attic a million times in my head.

There was a whirlwind of activity going on around me as I stood in the middle of communication center. The chaos level was at a ten, and just when it seemed that it couldn't go any higher, I would hear someone saying to me, "Chief Riley, we have a situation," and shit would go even further left. Mary Knight, Levette Joseph, and Stephanie Brisco were furiously fielding police radio calls and assisting officers, while me, Captain Weathersby, and Chief Nicholas were beginning to execute a strategy for search and rescues.

"Chief Nicholas," I said, turning to him and Captain Weathersby. "Contact Chief Compass ASAP. He needs to know what happened with Chris Abbott and advise him of the situation." As fucked up as what may have happened with Officer Abbott was, we needed to notify Chief Compass to keep him abreast of it. There was no way for us to know for certain whether or not Chris had made it out of his attic, so we had to move forward until we knew differently.

"Ok, I'll reach out to him right now," Nicholas affirmed, stepping away. "Chief, we have another bad situation," Mary Knight said, walking up to me and Captain Weathersby.

"What is it?" I asked.

"Officer Cathy Cartier has called in on one of our channels stating that a wave of water just crashed through the doors and windows of her home in New Orleans East, she also with her elderly mother."

"She lives with her mother, right?" Captain Weathersby asked as we followed Mary to the dispatcher handling the call.

"Correct," Mary confirmed. "She's screaming that her home is under what appears to be six to seven feet of water, and it looks like it is getting higher."

"Officer Cartier, I have Chief Riley and Captain Weathersby here," the dispatcher said, placing the call on speaker when we arrived. "What's your situation?" Cathy Cartier's voice was bathed in absolute terror, but she managed to speak slowly. "I was walking down the steps of my house when I heard this rumbling sound, and I was going to look out the window when this 10-foot wave of water crashed through my living room door, flooding my house." From the slow measured way that Cathy was speaking, you could tell that she was intentionally being calm to govern any fear that threatened to take her over. "I just barely made it up the stairs to the second floor," she added.

"Are you injured?" Captain Weathersby asked.

"I'm ok, but that wave of water almost crushed me," she answered somewhat breathlessly. "I'm with my mom. Your mom is with you?" Weathersby followed up.

"Yes," Cathy answered. "Thankfully she was already on the second floor. With her being confined to a wheelchair, there is no way I would have been able to move her to the second floor fast enough."

Cathy was a dedicated officer who always gave 100% on the job and off. In addition to serving the city of New Orleans, she also provided care to her seventy-two-year-old mother who was confined to a wheelchair. "Officer Cartier, what's your address?" Weathersby inquired. As Officer Cartier provided the address to her home in New Orleans East, the dispatcher captured the details.

"Officer Cartier, stay safe. We have your address, and as soon as the wind dies down, we're headed your way to get you and your mom," Captain Weathersby assured her.

"Thank you, Captain Weathersby," Officer Cartier said in her customary gracious tone. "I really appreciate it."

"No problem, we got you covered—" Captain Weathersby started to respond but was cut off by the shrill sound of Officer Cartier's scream. "OH SHIIIIT!!!!!"

"Officer Cartier, what's going on? Are you ok?" I asked.

"Fuck no," she answered in a panic. "There are a bunch of goddamn snakes swimming in the water in my living room. I can see them from the second floor." Officer Cartier's voice was shaking with emotion. Those who knew Cathy knew that she was deathly afraid of snakes, so the fact that her home was flooded with water and snakes were swimming in that water was the perfect storm for an absolute shitshow.

"Where in your house are you located right now?" Captain Weathersby asked. Being a former SWAT Commander, Captain Weathersby was adept at navigating tense situations with a level head.

"I'm in the hallway of the second floor right now, trying to see how fucking high this water is getting with these damned snakes in it?" she answered, her voice tight with fear.

"Do you have your weapon with you?" Weathersby asked.

"No, it's downstairs on the sofa underwater at this point," Cathy answered. "The water seems to get higher every few minutes."

"Did you say that the water is getting higher?" I asked.

"Yes, waves of water keep pushing it higher and higher every few minutes," she replied.

"GODDAMMIT!" Officer Cartier screamed one of the most blood-curdling screams I've heard in my life. Before any of us could ask, she stated, "Some of the snakes are on my steps now. One of them looks like it's trying to come up the fucking stairs."

"Do you have anything long enough to knock it down?" Weathersby asked.

"No, everything is downstairs." Cathy screamed in full panic. "No! No! No! No!" Cathy screamed fearfully. We had to arrest Officer Cartier's emotions in this moment. Phobias could be downright debilitating, but we couldn't afford to let her be overtaken by this. It could be the difference between life and death.

"Officer Cartier, try your best to compose yourself; we're going to help you," I said. There was no response from Cathy, but we could hear her breathing heavily. She was clearly paralyzed by the moment.

"Officer Cartier!" I snapped into the radio to get her attention. "Yes sir," she finally replied. "I'm here."

"Listen Officer Cartier," Captain Weathersby said in a calm voice. "The snake is just as frightened as you are. He's just trying to find a safe space."

"Bullshit!" Officer Cartier screamed. "There are at least five or six fucking snakes down there."

"Officer Cartier, can you tell us what the snakes look like?" I asked, wanting to assess just how dangerous these snakes might be. It might be easier to calm her down if we could affirm that these snakes were non-poisonous.

"The motherfucker trying to come up the stairs is at least five feet long, and he's black and yellow," she answered. "Some of them look gold with black spots and some of them are black or gray—I can't be certain of shit right now." Oh shit, I thought to myself.

"Officer Cartier, whatever you do, stay away from those snakes," I cautioned. "One could be a water moccasin, and they are very poisonous."

"Shit! I knew THAT!" Officer Cartier screamed.

"Cathy, do you have any rooms or bedrooms on the second floor that you can go into?" Weathersby interjected.

"Yes," Cathy answered. "I'm standing in the doorway of one of the bedrooms right now."

"Where is your mother?" he inquired.

"She's in the bedroom with me," Cathy responded. "Officer Cartier, I need you to listen to me carefully, ok," Captain Weathersby stated. "I'm listening," she confirmed. "I need you to block the bottom of the door with anything that a snake wouldn't be able to move," Captain Weathersby advised. "Stuff blankets and sheets under the door and fortify those blankets with heavy items, like books, a nightstand to hold them in place."

"I can do that with what we have in this room," Officer Cartier stated.

"Great," Captain Weathersby said. "Once you do that, I want you to place something really heavy against the bottom of the door." Officer Cartier started gathering the items that Captain Weathersby told her to and then placed them to seal off any potential entrance that a snake might try to use.

"Cathy, I promise you that you are number one on our list to rescue when we go out," Captain Weathersby said.

"Chief Riley," I turned around to the female voice that was calling my name. It was Dispatcher Levette Joseph walking up to me with a handheld radio in hand.

"Hey, Ms. Joseph," I answered, meeting her halfway. "What is it?"

"Captain Demma has been trying to reach you on all channels," she replied. "He's saying that it is urgent." Levette handed me the handheld radio she'd been holding. Deputy Chief Lonnie Swain and Captain Ernie Demma were stationed at the Superdome, working in tandem with the National Guard assigned there. If Captain Demma was calling me on all channels, it was a serious matter.

I quickly connected with Captain Demma on one of the channels he'd been attempting to reach me on. I learned from him that a tornado had hit the Superdome some time earlier and tore a hole in the roof that appeared to be 20 by 30 feet wide and that rain was pouring into the dome.

"What the fuck?" I exclaimed after Captain Demma finished explaining about the tornado hitting the Superdome.

"Everybody's alright so far, but we've had to move citizens around due to the water coming in," Demma explained. I ask how many citizens are in the dome; Demma replied, "I'm guessing 20,000." As Captain Demma was outlining the details of the situation at the Superdome, he was going through-out various locations to provide situational updates by location. So far, things were still calm at the Superdome, and as long as they could keep citizens sheltering there dry, things should be ok.

"Oh shit, Chief," Demma's voice rang over the radio. "Captain Demma, what's going on?" I asked.

"The Hyatt hotel, Chief," he answered. "I'm looking at it right now through one of the windows here. It's ripped apart, Sir."

"What do you mean?" I asked.

"Chief, it looks like every goddamn window in that place has been ripped the fuck out," he responded. As if on cue, Chief Nicholas walked up to me and said, "Chief Compass is not answering. I've tried him on all channels and called his phone." I stood there for a moment processing the infor-mation. Chief Compass, Mayor Nagin, and a significant amount of the city's leadership team were all at the Hyatt Hotel. My mind even went to my friend Stacey Martin, who was there with her family. I could only pray that they were inside a safe space.

"Dammit, what the fuck is going on?" I said exasperated, before direct-ing Chief Nicholas, "Keep trying to reach Chief Compass." In that moment, I was affirmed in the decision I had made for me, Chief Nicholas, and Cap-tain Weathersby to shelter in at headquarters as opposed to the Hyatt Hotel. We would either have been cut off communicatively from those whom we lead or worse. Leaders should have been at Base 9, not a hotel, and the Emergency Operation Center at City Hall, not a fucking hotel.

"Captain Demma, we have been trying to contact Chief Compass for the past 10 minutes. How bad is the weather?" I asked.

"Chief, the wind is still super strong; debris is flying all over the place," Captain Demma responded. That comment suppressed my thought of hav-ing Captain Demma send officers to look for the Mayor and the Chief and make sure they all were safe. Captain Demma wrapped up his status report with me, and I ended the call just as Mary Knight was walking up to me.

"We have calls coming in with stranded officers and civilians, from New Orleans East, the Lower and Upper Ninth Wards, Lakeview, and reports that water is rising in some of the Uptown areas. The Fifth, Seventh, and Third District Police Stations are all underwater," Mary reported.

"Do we have any reports of officers drowning?" I asked.

"No sir," she answered. Mary stated that the Third District was taking shelter in the LSU Dentistry School, located in Gentilly at 1100 Florida Ave. She added that Captain Donald Paisant advised that their building was surrounded by at least six feet of water, and all of their vehicles were underwater. "God dammit," I stated collectively but pissed off.

"Mary," I said, turning specifically to her and Levette Joseph. "I need a report of all the officers and citizens that have called in for assistance. I need their addresses, how many people are in the house, how many are children, how many have special needs, and their ages as well."

"We have that info, Sir! You and the other dispatchers have already been compiling that information, right?" Mary inquired of Levette.

"Yes," Levette confirmed. Mary Knight stated, "Chief Riley, all landlines and cell phone services are down."

In my mind, I wondered what else could go wrong. I was pissed and scared, but I maintained my composure to not let anyone think it was a problem. "Never let them see you sweat," I thought, but the butterflies within me were having a fucking party. "Thank you, Ms. Knight. Knowing that that was beyond my control, I immediately returned back to Ms. Levette. Ms. Levette, tell me some good news."

"So, sir, we just need to isolate the time period for those that we know we weren't able to send any assistance to because of the storm, and that should give us a complete list," Mary stated.

"Great," I said, grateful that they were so efficient. "If you guys could have that ready for us ASAP, we will begin search and rescues as soon as this wind dies down just a little bit more."

"Off the top of my head, I know that Sergeant Michael LeVasseur and his family need help," Levette indicated. Her words immediately caught my attention. Michael LeVasseur was the Commander of the Crime Prevention Unit, who up until I made that appointment for him just three months ago, had served on my staff. But even more than that, Mike was my former partner when we worked in Vice & Narcotics together. We not only had a long history of working together, but on a personal level, Mike and his family were important to me. If he was in trouble, I definitely needed to know how we could help. I looked squarely at Levette.

"What's the word with Sergeant LeVasseur?" Levette stepped away to her desk and came back with a notepad from which she'd obviously captured details.

"Sergeant LeVasseur and his family are ok at this very moment," Levette began, much to my relief. "His home, however, was partially damaged by a tornado."

She flipped the page of her notepad, securing more details. "A portion of the roof of his home has been blown off by the tornado, and there is some rising water from what has been reported," Levette said. "He's currently stuck on the second floor of his home with his wife, his mother, and his daughter," Levette concluded.

I gave a silent prayer of thanksgiving to God that Mike and his family hadn't been hurt. It was still a high priority to get to them. Not everyone knew it, but not too long ago his wife Michelle had been released from the hospital following her second surgery connected to the cancer she was fighting.

"His home is in New Orleans East, right?" Mary queried.

"Yes, his home is actually located in the Lake Forest Estates subdivision," Levette answered.

"Ok great," I replied. "Make sure that his name is listed as a top priority when we get ready to head out."

"Will do, Chief," Levette said. "I'm going to go get started on it," Levette added as she walked away toward her desk. Mary seemed to be deep in thought with her eyebrows furrowed.

"That list is going to be pretty extensive, Chief." I knew she was right. There were literally hundreds, if not thousands, who needed rescuing in this exact moment. Some we would likely get to on time, and others we might not – but we had to do our level best to rescue as many as we could.

"You're right," I replied. "And we are going to save as many as we possibly can, and that will literally mean the difference between life and death for somebody."

Around twenty minutes later, Levette walked over to us with the requested reports of those who needed assistance. As I knew it would be, there were hundreds of names and addresses of citizens who needed rescuing. With Chief Nicholas assisting, Mary Knight, and the other Dispatch Supervisor, Danielle Briscoe, began dividing up the list into clusters of geographic locations so that we could respond to the most critical areas and immediate needs first.

I had already determined that I would take a group out with me to rescue Officers Doucette McReynolds, Officer David Davillier, Officer Cathy Cartier, and Commander Michael LeVasseur. These were some of our NOPD officers who were trapped in their homes and in need of immediate assistance. Each of their homes was located in New Orleans East, which would also allow me to assess, from a personal perspective, the damage that had occurred from Uptown to the East.

But even beyond our officers, it was my intent to save as many people as possible. Anyone and everyone that I encountered en route to the Eastbank of Eastern New Orleans would be a candidate for rescue as long as it was in my power. Yes, I had officers who would be assigned to specific areas to rescue citizens, but there was no way in hell that I could see a person in need and bypass them, whether it was my assigned area or not.

As I looked across the room full of dispatchers navigating call after call from citizens and officers needing assistance, I thought to myself, "Hold on New Orleans... help is on the way!"

Chapter 12:
Navigating the Deluge

August 30, 2005 – 3:00 p.m.

The hot and humid afternoon air greeted me as I stood on the front steps of the NOPD Headquarters. Despite the scene before me, I intentionally filled my lungs with air as I peered out over South Broad Street, flanked by Captain Lawrence Weathersby and Lieutenant Gervais Allison. In the immediate aftermath of Hurricane Katrina, New Orleans looked like it had been hit by a nuclear bomb. Trees were toppled about with broken branches and limbs strewn throughout the front area of Headquarters. Though the rain had stopped, the streets were flooded, and with each ebb and flow of the water, you could see that it was rising even higher. Even as we stood on the front steps, we could see the water lapping up over the streets and sidewalks, all the way up near the front entrance of headquarters. The intense winds and consistent deluge of water conspired to create the perfect storm for a city primed for flooding due to its low-lying areas and below sea level positioning.

"National Guardsman Corporal Phillip Emerson will be our contact and driver once we get to the courthouse," Captain Weathersby advised me. To facilitate our search and rescue efforts, we were collaborating with the National Guard, who had agreed to meet us just up the street at Tulane and Broad at the Criminal District Court. The National Guard was staged at the Criminal District Courthouse with a M35 truck know as a deuce and a half military truck and driver who would transport us throughout the city as we engaged in our mission to save as many stranded cops and citizens as we could. A deuce and a half is military slang for a 2 1/2-ton cargo truck with the ability to drive through water as high as 5 – 6 feet due to its height and placement of its specially designed exhaust pipes, so it would serve us well.

"Copy that," I replied. "We need to hurry because if things are looking this bad over here, I can only imagine what it is like everywhere else." My mind immediately went to Sergeant Mike LeVasseur, Officer Cathy Cartier, and their families, all of whom were depending on us to get to them. Because the streets were already flooded, we couldn't possibly drive any of our vehicles to the meet-up point with the National Guard. Even though Criminal District Court was just a little more than a block up the street, we were going to have to use motorized flatboats to get us there. Officer Derek Brumfield, Reserve Officer Andre Menzies, and Officer Mark Osborne had gone to retrieve the flatboats from the parking garage to secure our passage to the meet-up point and were waiting for us by the side ramp exit of Headquarters on Gravier Street.

Moments later, Captain Weathersby and I were making our way up South Broad Street on a flatboat guided by Officer Menzies, closely followed by another boat driven by Officer Brumfield and Officer Osborne. The boats easily sliced through the floodwaters as we made our way to our destination. The air flowing against our faces as the boats plowed up the street was a welcome relief from the hot air that seemed to hang over the city. Navigating through the city on a boat was absolutely surreal. Instead of seeing cars parked alongside the street, you saw the rooftops of cars barely peeking out from under the water as we passed by. On occasion, something would scrape underneath the bottom of the boat, and we'd later discover it to be the rooftop of a car. At various points, it was difficult to identify certain streets because instead of seeing concrete and sidewalk, all you could see was water. At other junctures, it was as if we were in the middle of our own personal swamp, with nothing but water all around us.

For a brief moment, I allowed my mind to think about Officer Cathy Cartier and the snakes she encountered in her home and couldn't help but wonder what wildlife was lurking beneath the water's surface that had literally spilled into seemingly every corner of the city.

Within a few minutes, our boats arrived at one of the side entrances of the Criminal District Courthouse. Just ahead of where we stopped our boats, I spotted the camouflage-painted M35 truck that was parked and waiting for us. Our driver and National Guardsman Corporal Phillip Emerson were standing in the exit doorway. Mary Knight and her team had already communicated to him the various rescue destination points to which we were headed, but I had also communicated that we needed to be flexible with our intended route. If we encountered ANYBODY along the way that required rescuing, we were going to make it happen!

"Man, this is like one of those fucking apocalypse movies or something," Officer Menzies said once he shut off the motor of the boat he was driving. Andre was a notorious jokester and often said whatever the hell he could think of, but in this moment, he was spot on. The streets were empty, and there was a palpable silence that could be felt in the eeriest of ways. The whole vibe was like some end-of-days movie kind of shit.

"Let's make sure that we have everything that we need to rescue as many people as humanly possible," I directed as we got out of the boats and onto the grounds of the ramp by the side entrance of the courthouse.

"We have everything that we need," Captain Weathersby replied.

"Good," I said, shaking the hands of our National Guard driver. "Your Special Operations Division indicated that they have the locations of Officers Davillier, and McReynolds and have already sent a team to retrieve them," National Guardsman Phillip Emerson said. "We will be heading primarily to New Orleans East to retrieve Sergeant Mike LeVasseur, Officer Cathy Cartier, and Officer Doucette."

After a few preliminary directives, we all started piling into the truck. I had just made it into my seat in the front next to Corporal Emerson when a voice crackled over my radio. Officer Osborne entered the front of the vehicle along with the rest who climbed into the bed of the truck.

"I'm out! I'm out! Can anybody hear me?" I turned my police radio up so that I could hear better over the sound of the truck engine. "I'm out! I made it out!"

Officer Christopher Abbott! Never in my life had I been so happy to hear a voice as I was this one. Officer Abbott continued to call out over the radio that he had made it out of his attic! I motioned for Corporal Emerson not to move just yet. "Officer Abbott?" I inquired over the radio to be sure. "Yes, Chief!" he responded. "I made it out!" Menzies, Brumfield, Allison, Osborne, and Weathersby erupted in excitement! This was the best news!

"Chris what happened, man?" I inquired unable to contain my excitement. "We thought we'd lost you."

"My radio got wet and shorted out, so I couldn't communicate," he replied. "I almost didn't make it, Chief, but thanks to you and Captain Scott, I fought my way out of that attic onto the roof." I could have wept tears of joy. Thinking that we'd lost Chris and now hearing him alive on the other end of the radio was beyond description! It felt like we were finally able to give a hard middle finger to Hurricane Katrina. I could not have been happier. "Officer Abbott, we are headed out to New Orleans East now, and we're coming for you, man," I stated happily. "I know the whole department is glad to hear that you are alive and well."

Just as Officer Brumfield was writing down Chris's address to give to Corporal Emerson, our SOD Unit came over the radio channel. "Chief Riley, you all can maintain your current course route; we are happy to pick up Officer Abbott," Special Operations Division Officer Sgt. Lajon Roberts stated over the radio. You could literally hear the smile in his words. It was clear that everyone was overjoyed that Officer Abbott had made it out alive. It was a major win in what had been a series of losses since Katrina hit New Orleans. "Copy that Sgt. Lajon Roberts," I responded. "Officer Abbott... Chris... we are glad that you're still with us." I exhaled, taking in the moment. "I'm glad to still be here," he replied. "I'll just be sitting on top of my roof, waiting until somebody gets here," he added with a chuckle.

I motioned for Emerson to move. This was just the jumpstart that we needed to begin our search and rescue. Before we could pull off, Officer Menzies shouted to Chris, "Where's your dog? Where's the pooch?" "He's okay," Chris stated over the radio. "He's right here with me." Another dose of positivity! An additional series of high fives went around inside the truck, along with a couple of fist pumps and all smiles. This moment had just given us a boost of positivity after all the negativity and tragedies we had experienced in the last 30 plus hours.

Later we learned from Officer Abbott that while he was on his roof, he saw through his neighbors' window, his elderly neighbors body floating in the water. She had apparently drowned.

Sitting high on the M35 truck, we easily navigated the water on Tulane Avenue as we made our way toward the Superdome. As we drove onto Poydras, there was only a few inches of water, which was nothing to be concerned about. As we passed the Superdome, however, we could not believe our eyes. "What the fuck?" Officer Menzies shouted. "Look at the Hyatt Hotel." We all looked in awe. As we drove closer, all we could see was massive destruction of this hotel, which was so iconic just 24 hours ago. Windows were completely blown out. It looked like every window on the North side of the hotel was gone. It looked like it had been hit by a barrage of missiles. As I looked to my right, there were cars lying on Poydras Street that were crushed, sitting on their sides and upside-down laying on the roof. "What the fuck happened here?" I thought aloud. "Chief, that had to be the tornadoes we heard last night," Officer Osborne said in response. "You're probably right Mark," I replied.

Knowing that our main radio system was down, but our barely adequate back up mutual aid system was working. I needed to connect with Chief Compass immediately. "Car 3 to Car 2," I spoke into my radio, calling for Superintendent Compass. Every officer had a radio call number. Mayor Nagin was Car 1, Superintendent Compass was Car 2, and I was Car 3. No response from Chief Compass. "Car 3 to Car 2," I said again, still trying to reach him. I tried multiple times but never got a response. I then decided to reach out to Captain Ernie Demma, who was at the Superdome, via my radio. "Captain Demma to Chief Riley," he responded much to my relief. "Captain Demma, what's the status in the dome?" I asked. Captain Demma responded, "Chief, rain is pouring into the dome from the hole that was ripped into the roof, and the generators went out this morning."

"There are no lights, and there is no air," he added. "The people are scared, but they are remaining pretty calm."

"We have to put together plans to get those people out of there as soon as possible," I replied. I then inquired about Chief Compass. "Do you have an update on Chief Compass and Mayor Nagin at the Hyatt?" "Yes," Captain Demma replied. "Chief Compass, Mayor Nagin, and staff are good. There are no injuries in the Hyatt Hotel that we know of. They were all in the ballrooms and protected by the interior walls of the ballrooms."

"Fortunately, they all got out of their rooms because the tornado sucked beds, dressers, and all kinds of stuff out of the Hyatt Hotel," he added. "If anyone stayed in those rooms, God be with them!" "They're getting a head count, but at this point, no serious injuries, and no one is known to be missing," he finished. "Great! That's really great," I replied. "Captain, please locate Chief Compass and get him on the radio with me. We have citizens and cops that are stuck in attics and rooftops all over the city. We are headed to New Orleans East to get as many people as we can." "10-4," Demma replied.

"Thanks," I responded. Our celebration of Officer Abbott being safe was short-lived once I saw the Hyatt Hotel and the cars in the street that were tossed around like toys. I did not know what the hell to think. We proceeded East with our rescue mission in mind.

As we turned onto the I-10 East on-ramp by the Superdome, Captain Weathersby spoke to me. "Chief, it could be worse," he stated. "Abbott is safe, no serious injuries in the dome or Hyatt, GOD is good." "All the time," I said. Suddenly, energy hit me with the knowledge that Chris Abbott had survived, and as Weathersby had stated, things could have been much worse. In spite of all that had gone wrong, I began to smile and took in the scene of the city from the interstate as we made our way toward New Orleans East.

The bowl-effect of New Orleans was having an interesting impact on the distribution of flooding throughout the city. Low-lying areas of New Orleans were prone to greater water retention and flooding as opposed to areas that were more elevated. This explained why certain areas looked like a swamp with large concentrations of water, while others appeared normal in comparison.

As we traveled on I-10 from Tulane, most of the areas on either side of the interstate appeared to have little to no flooding. This was actually a good thing as I had initially thought the entire damn city to be underwater. As we passed the Canal Street exit and I noticed that flooding was minimal, I thought to myself that maybe it wasn't as bad as we all thought. From the looks of things, there was obvious evidence of wind damage and some minor flooding, but nothing that seemed greater than a typical storm we'd encountered before in New Orleans.

As we continued to drive east on Interstate 10, passing the N Claiborne Avenue exit, I continued to examine and assess the layout of the city and the neighborhoods as I could view them from my aerial position. To be clear, there was definitely storm damage, but nothing like what we had in our minds based on the calls we were receiving.

However, as we began to pass the Elysian Fields exit, drawing closer to the Louisa Street exit, approaching the City's Ninth Ward, things took a hard shift. Whereas before there was minor flooding and a few downed trees, and roof damage, immediately to my right, there was absolute catastrophic flooding with water as high as the rooftops of many homes. "Ah shit," Menzies said almost on cue, you could hear the murmurs of everyone from OH MY GOD, to what the hell to What the Fuck! Interstate 10 running east through New Orleans is highly elevated at certain junctures, allowing you an aerial view of the city and neighborhoods on either side. From our vantage point, as we looked to the right of the interstate, we had a high-level view of the city, even the Lower Ninth Ward. It was apparent that the Industrial Canal had been breached by the floodwaters, and the result was disastrous flooding in the Lower Ninth Ward and further east. The sight of homes with water up to their rooftops literally took my breath away.

From our elevated view on the interstate, we caught sight of entire neighborhoods with homes nearly covered to the point of being underwater. It was as if someone had dumped an entire ocean in the middle of a residential area. Residents had positioned themselves on the tops of the roofs of their homes and were waving sheets and anything else they could to signal that they needed help. Several more "Oh MY GOD" came out of officers mouths some mumbling in disbelief as we looked at what could only be described as a living nightmare. We had just literally cross over into a twilight zone. It was mind blowing! Disheartening! This unbelievable scene broke our hearts and breached our souls with overwhelming dismay.

We could see many families on top of the roofs of their homes, who had done everything within their power to survive. We had literally driven from minor damage and moderate flooding to chaos in a matter of fifteen minutes. All I could think of was that I was in the twilight zone. What the fuck are we dealing with? How fucked up, unpredictable, and dangerous was all of this? This uncertainty of the damage and danger hit me like a ton of bricks, and the turmoil was evolving the further east we went. Every 100 yards we drove, we could see in the distance more houses underwater, more people on rooftops, and more people screaming and waving objects in the air desperately seeking help. Our citizens were in danger, and we were in a momentary state of shock, completely overwhelmed! It felt like someone was sticking needles in my brain, and the more destruction I saw, the more my head spun. Strategically, I knew I had to maintain my composure, but in truth, the challenges before us seemed insurmountable. I did not know what to do, but we would do all that we could.

As we looked over the right of the interstate, the complex interchange of railroad tracks that housed many of the train carts and tractors utilized for interstate commerce were in complete disarray, with many of them weighing almost three hundred thousand pounds flipped over as if they were toys. Derailed and mangled train carts and tractors had seemingly been thrown together by the angry force of this relentless storm. The sight of it all was both infuriating and awe-inspiring. Mother Nature's power was not to be messed with!

"Those are some of our officers in their own boats," Officer Brumfield stated. "I recognize them." Even in the middle of chaos, there is something about the fight of the human spirit that rails against defeat. Within many of these neighborhoods, we could see many of our officers, as well as other citizens, using their personal boats to extract people from their homes and bring them to higher ground. When we noticed what appeared to be the base of the makeshift rescue operations at the off-ramp exit for Louisa Street South, we pulled over and stopped our truck to confer with the team of officers and citizens and to see where we could lend our support.

With the interstate being empty in both directions, except for our military vehicle and a few police cars, emergency crews would be able to utilize both sides to get citizens to a space well elevated above the floodwaters. Just short of a dozen residents had already been rescued and positioned on the interstate, and they were now walking in the opposite direction towards higher ground.

As we came to a stop at the Louisa Street off-ramp, I immediately spotted some of our own officers: Officer Michael Rousell, Officer Joey Catalanotto, and a few others. I was not at all surprised at their ability to jump right into the chaos and begin helping people because that was the type of guys they were. They spotted our truck and made their way over to us as I stepped out of the deuce and a half.

"Chief Riley," Officer Rousell said as he shook my hand in greeting. "It's good to see you, sir."

"Thanks, Officer," I replied. "Good job on initiating and facilitating rescues here."

"We got out here as soon as we could," Officer Catalanotto stated. "Fortunately, each of us had boats of our own that we could use, so we've been able to get to the residents."

"We've also got a lot of good citizens here who came out to help within their own neighborhoods as soon as it was safe," Officer Rousell indicated. "There are several members of the Cajun Navy who are here as well" Russell added. "Who?" I replied. Officer Russell advised the Cajun Navy, see those men and women out there with coon skin hats, and those long beards and hunting dogs, they say they are with the Cajun Navy and they have rescued a lot of people. I was not familiar with them but I certainly welcome their help.

I looked out over the side of the interstate to one of the neighborhoods in time to witness two citizens and an officer helping an elderly woman and her family off their roof into the safety of a boat. It was surreal to see water almost as high as the roof of a home, and watch people, in some cases, literally step from their rooftop into a boat. I felt like I was watching a movie as many of the residents, guided by officers, made their way up and over the train tracks and gate that led onto the interstate. Once on the interstate, they walked westward toward the high point where they would wait for officers to transport them to safety.

I was filled with pride as I observed NOPD officers immediately taking initiative and using their own boats to rescue our citizens. At that moment, the stress in my brain seemed to disappear. I realized how resilient the men and women of NOPD were in the face of adversity. Within split seconds, my thoughts combed over the bravery of our dispatchers, the tenacity of Officer Abbott that allowed him to save himself and his dog, and the courage of so many NOPD officers who, on their own accord, were rescuing citizens. I was as proud as I could be.

I understood that I had to take the good with the bad, and in that moment, I knew that we would get through this somehow. In the flooded residential areas, you could hear shouts for help, and then see the corresponding officers and neighbors spring into action. Sometimes it was helping somebody through a hole in their roof, and other times it was assisting someone to swim to a boat if the boat was blocked from getting close enough to the house for them to step inside of it. At this point, we were all in survival mode. Whatever needed to be done to preserve and protect life, we would do it. Getting people out of their homes, off their rooftops, and onto higher ground was the immediate priority. We'd figure the rest of it out later.

I then called the Emergency Operation Center (EOC) located at City Hall and advised them that we needed the Air National Guard, and that we had hundreds of citizens stuck on rooftops in the Lower Ninth Ward with water as high as 10 to 14 feet.

"Repeat that, sir," the officer who answered the call at the EOC stated. I repeated what I had just said to him.

"Yes, sir," he answered, seemingly perplexed by what I'd just communicated. "I'll relay it to the Emergency Support Function for the Coast Guard."

"Sir, you did say that hundreds of people were stuck on their rooftops, and hundreds of homes were involved?" he asked, baffled and bewildered by what he'd just heard.

"Young man, you heard me correctly," I responded. "The Ninth Ward is under water!"

His response was filled with confusion, concern, and disbelief, "Yes, sir, I will relay the message."

"Most of the residents here couldn't afford to evacuate," Officer Catalanotto stated once I finished with the officer at the EOC. "And by the time the storm intensified, they were forced to shelter in place."

Looking at many of the homes now drowning in water made my heart sink. Not only were families literally losing everything they owned, but I knew for certain that there were some people who hadn't made it out of those homes. For many of those people, that home had become a watery grave.

"Chief, we are just getting everyone we can off the roofs," Officer Catalanotto added. "The water is continuing to rise. We are getting them to the interstate to dry ground and telling them to get on the interstate and stay dry and wait. We tell them that someone will be there to assist them, but we can't tell them exactly when."

Catalanotto quickly wrapped up his debrief to us. It was obvious he was on an adrenaline rush, and you could tell that all he wanted to do was get back on his boat as quickly as he could to save more people. He hopped in his boat and took off.

As Officer Catalanotto departed, Officer Mike Rousell arrived on his boat with five people. "Great job, Mike," I praised him. "Just keep getting them to walk up on the interstate, and we'll find a way to get to them as soon as we can."

I tried to contact Chief Compass and the Mayor via police radio, but still no response. My attempts to reach them by phone were futile due to the lack of signal. To explore an alternative approach, I asked if anyone on the air was near the Hyatt Regency Hotel. Sergeant Timothy Morris, a friend, responded, confirming he was outside the hotel.

"Sergeant Morris, I am trying to contact Chief Compass or Mayor Nagin," I explained. "Would you please go to the third-floor conference rooms and see if you can locate them?"

"Yes, sir," he replied.

Officer Rousell remarked that one positive aspect amidst the chaos was that many people had managed to evacuate their homes before the flooding occurred. Captain Weathersby agreed, acknowledging that despite this, many people had still lost everything, including loved ones.

As we continued to assist people onto the interstate, my attention was drawn to a man with four young children sobbing as they walked up the interstate. He attempted to turn back towards the flooded neighborhood several times, but officers and other residents guided him and the children towards the higher ground of the interstate. His heart-wrenching sobs echoed as he called out a woman's name. The young children were also crying, and the devastation on the man's face was overwhelming.

"He's one of the residents that we rescued," Officer Rousell informed us. "He lived next door to his sister and her four children," he added. "When the flood hit, his sister told him to get her four kids out first, and when he came back to pull her through the roof, she was lost to the water inside the home. We couldn't find her."

As the man and the four kids walked further up the interstate, I watched him comfort the children, ensuring their emotional well-being despite his own devastation. He was a good man, and I couldn't help but wonder what the future held for him and those kids once this disaster was over. The man and the four kids continued walking up the interstate, weighed down by grief. "Damn it!" I exclaimed, more to myself than anyone else. I was tired of witnessing such heartbreak. I fought to restrain my anger and profanity, but I fought harder to hold back my tears. Four kids had just lost their mother, who had saved their lives.

"Is this really just the beginning?" I questioned the officers around me, who seemed to share complex emotions of sadness, anger, and fear. As their leader, I knew I had to step up and provide direction. "Gentlemen, we have a job to do, so let's saddle up," I declared with determination, and I jumped onto the back of the deuce and a half truck, followed by the rest of the team. City Councilman Oliver Thompson pulled up in his FORD Crown Victoria. "Chief, what's happening?" he inquired.

"Councilman," I responded. "Chaos and more chaos! We're headed east to assist stranded officers and citizens." "Do you mind if I come?" he asked. "Sure," I answered, and he joined us on board as we proceeded east and his assistant Officer Wilbert Theodore drove behind us.

As we drove, the scenes and emotions were surreal. The interstate had no traffic, only citizens of various backgrounds—individuals, families, black people, white people, a few Asians, and Hispanics—wandering aimlessly. Despite their different stories, they were all New Orleanians. They appeared scattered, battered, and confused, resembling characters from an apocalyptic zombie movie. However, these were real people in desperate need of help.

Continuing eastward, we treated this as a triage mission to reach those who were still stranded and alive. Sergeant LeVasseur reached out to us, warning that coming this way might not be possible due to severe flooding.

"The water around my house has to be at least five or six feet." I assured Mike that we would do our best to reach him, and even if we couldn't, we would send forces that could help. We continued further up I-10, crossing the I-10 High Rise Bridge, which provided an expansive aerial view of the city. From my perspective, the areas immediately to the right of the bridge seemed less flooded than they were about a mile earlier, but given LeVasseur's status, I wasn't sure how much longer that would last.

As we approached the I-10 and Chef Highway exit, I noticed a man standing next to a small white car under the overpass that led onto Chef Menteur Highway. The car didn't appear to be in the best condition, and the man was standing outside of it, so I immediately wondered if his car had stalled during the storm, and he sought shelter here while waiting for assistance. "Let's pull over and see if this guy needs some help," I told our driver. We stopped about ten feet in front of his vehicle. He seemed relieved that we were there to help. "Hey there, do you need any help?" I asked as Captain Weathersby and I approached him. "We need help," he answered with a thick Spanish accent. Before we could respond, a pregnant woman slowly got out of the car and made her way toward us. She was about eight or nine months pregnant, appearing ready to give birth at any moment. "My name is Mario Rodriguez, and this is my wife Camille," he stated, gesturing to the pleasant pregnant woman who joined us. I chuckled to myself as I observed his gentle nonverbal overtures to get Camille to return to the car. Of course, she ignored his gestures and engaged us in conversation, nonetheless. Regardless of culture and background, some relational dynamics are universal, I thought to myself with a smile.

"We were attempting to leave town to get away from the storm, but the winds and rain were too strong and heavy," Mario explained to us. "We ended up taking shelter under this bridge for protection, and we stayed through the night," he added. "You all stayed here throughout the night through the hurricane?" I asked. "Yes," Mario answered. "GODDAMN!" I could hear Officer Menzies exclaim in the background. The couple shared their story of hunkering down in their car under the bridge as the winds and water beat against it. They described watching debris flying in the air around their car and how at one point, their car moved a couple of feet due to the force of the winds.

"I had to use the emergency brake to keep us steady, but even then, we were still moving," Mario recalled. He told us how he saw a tornado moving in the eastern part of New Orleans. "Trash and debris were flying everywhere," Mario recollected. "Did the tornado get close to you?" Captain Weathersby inquired. "No sir. It was at least a mile straight ahead," he replied, pointing east. "I thought we were going to be sucked right out from under the bridge," Camille said with a nervous laugh.

"I'm glad you all were safe, especially with your wife being pregnant," Captain Weathersby said. "Yes, she is due very soon," Mario said, and for the first time, his calm demeanor was replaced with a level of anxiety. "I don't want her to have the baby like this," he stated. "We're going to make sure that we get you all to safety," I said. "We have a couple located on the I-10 off-ramp to Chef Highway," I said, calling in to Dispatch. "A female is pregnant and in need of medical assistance right away." At that time, Councilman Oliver Thomas and his assistant Officer Wilbert Theodore, who was following us in a car, approached us.

"We'll get her to the hospital right away," Councilman Thomas offered, much to the couple's relief. Mario and Camille then entered the rear of the 2004 Crown Victoria with Councilman Thomas. Mary Knight responded over the radio. "Ochsner Hospital in Jefferson Parish is available to receive them," Mary said over the radio. Shortly after they left for Ochsner Hospital, we continued east on I-10 past Chef Highway, headed toward the homes of Sgt. Mike LeVasseur and Officer Cathy Cartier. "It looks like the water is getting higher the further east that we go," National Guardsman Private Emerson said to me, peering ahead as we drove. Given Mike's warning earlier, this was exactly what I was afraid of. No longer elevated by bridges and overpasses, I-10 further east leveled off and ran even with the surrounding areas and neighborhoods, which meant if those areas were flooded, the interstate would be as well.

We noticed the truck kicking up more water as we moved through the interstate, and the water level grew higher. "Sergeant LeVasseur's home is in Lake Forest Estates, so if we are able to make it to Bullard Road, we might still be able to get to him," Officer Brumfield said to me and Captain Weathersby. We were less than a mile away from the Morrison exit, only about three miles from Read Boulevard, but at the rate the water was rising around us, I began to doubt that we would make it that far. The water splashed into the truck through the open window areas, and our National Guard driver started to slow down, trying to progress with less water splashing.

Looking out over the side of the interstate, we could see that the businesses along the I-10 service roads on both sides were badly flooded, with water covering many cars and obscuring much of the buildings. The neighborhoods along the way were also severely flooded, similar to what we had seen along Louisa Street and Almonaster.

"Gentlemen, this is as far east as we are going to be able to go," Private Emerson announced as he brought the truck to a stop on the interstate. Though we hadn't quite made it to the Morrison Road exit, it was evident that the water was only getting higher as we looked in the distance and saw more extensive flooding. The amount of water around us made it feel as if we were driving in the middle of a lake. Captain Weathersby immediately notified the SWAT Division that we would be unable to get to East New Orleans due to the flooding, and advised them to send out their Special Operations unit to the addresses for Sgt. Mike LeVasseur, Officer Cathy Cartier, and the others on our rescue list in the East.

I informed Mary Knight via police radio that we were unable to reach Sgt. LeVasseur and the others who were further east. Furthermore, I asked Ms. Knight to provide locations in the Uptown area where citizens were stranded. She quickly provided information for the Carrollton area of Uptown New Orleans, identifying it as a place where citizens presently needed assistance. Mary gave us the names and addresses of officers and citizens in the Carrollton area who were stranded.

At the moment, the floodwaters were navigable with our deuce and a half truck. Since there was virtually no traffic on I-10, we easily turned around and headed in the opposite direction as Emerson drove toward Carrollton. We arrived in a Carrollton neighborhood on Dante Street, where a man named Darrell Livingston, who lived with his elderly parents, needed rescuing. The water reached the windows of many homes, covering at least half of the houses on the street. Some trees had been knocked down by the storm, and cars that had been moved onto lawns to avoid water damage were literally floating in water.

When we pulled up to the address Mary had given us, it was a blue brick-colored one-story home with a high and wide porch. A man in his early to mid-thirties stood between his elderly parents, who were both sitting in wheelchairs. The water was so high that it reached the windows on the lower part of the home, and the elderly couple's wheelchairs were submerged up to the seat levels. They were sitting in water. I couldn't fathom why this guy would have his parents sitting in water outside like this instead of inside.

"Goddamn..." Officer Menzies uttered as he, Officer Brumfield, and I stepped out of the truck into the warm water. Initially, the water was waist-deep, but at certain points where the ground level dipped, we found ourselves literally having to walk in water up to our necks reach the porch of their home.

Seeing this, the rest of our crew piled out of the truck as well, recognizing that extracting this elderly couple from their home in water this deep would require extra muscle. At this point in the afternoon, the heat was insufferable. New Orleans is known for its intense humidity, but on this day, the humidity level was off the charts. It was hard to tell the difference between sweat and water at this point.

"Mr. Livingston," Officer Menzies greeted Darrell with a smile as we reached the porch. "We're here to transport you and the elder Mr. Livingston and Mrs. Livingston to safety." "Thank God you all made it here," Darrell said with a sigh of relief. "I didn't even care about myself as much as I needed to make sure my mama and daddy were going to be taken care of." I looked down at the senior Livingstons, and they both returned my look with warm smiles combined with a quiet fear. My heart went out to them immediately. They were both clearly wearing adult diapers that had been soiled multiple times with urine, though it was barely noticeable because they were sitting in water. The faint smell of urine mixed with the water emanated from both of them. Given Darrell's limited ability to move them due to the flooding, there wasn't much he could have done.

"Mr. and Mrs. Livingston," I stated, looking at them warmly. "Don't worry; we're going to get you out of here and see to it that you get cleaned up." "Thank you, sir," Mrs. Livingston said in almost a whisper, but maintaining a warm smile. "Do they have any medications that need to be transported?" Officer Brumfield asked Darrell. "I have all of their meds in this bag hanging up over the porch," Darrell responded. "Why are you guys sitting out here instead of inside?" Menzies asked. "Believe it or not, once the power went out and the air stopped working, it was hotter inside," Darrell answered. And then it made perfect sense to me. It was less hot outside than inside their home, and the airflow allowed for the uncomfortable situation with the adult diapers not to be as obvious. Because the elder Livingstons were immobile, getting them from their porch to our truck proved to be quite challenging.

"Lieutenant, I'm going to hold her legs while you hold her upper body," Captain Weathersby said to Lieutenant Allison. With his arm around Mrs. Livingston for support, Lieutenant Gervais Allison began walking in chest-deep water from the front area of the Livingston home toward our truck. Captain Weathersby followed closely, wading through the water and giving support to Mrs. Livingston's legs. Working in teams of two, we were able to get both Mr. and Mrs. Livingston and Darrell safely loaded into the deuce and a half and transport them to the Convention Center before heading right back into the Carrollton neighborhoods.

The rescue efforts in the Carrollton area were strenuous on all of us. The streets were uneven and dipped in certain areas, requiring us to walk in water as high as our necks to reach residents. In many cases, we had to climb on rooftops to get to those waiting to be rescued. In most cases, we had to walk in water as high as our necks to get to them. Captain Weathersby and Lieutenant Allison had to literally swim to reach a female and her son who were stuck on a roof; they were either too weak to swim or didn't know how. Whether swimming, climbing, or any other means necessary to rescue and transport our citizens from their homes to safety, we were willing to do it.

As night slowly rolled in, we realized that power in the entire city had likely been lost, and it became necessary to use the lights from our truck to illuminate our way as we continued to save more citizens. We spent the next five hours rescuing and transporting Carrollton residents to the Superdome. We were physically spent, fatigued, and hungry, but every time we thought we were done, there was another person in need of our assistance. It was close to eleven o'clock at night when we finally wrapped up our rescues for the day. We had nothing left. It was time to head back to Headquarters.

On that final transport, we noticed that the water that was only a few inches in the area was now at least four to five feet high. At that point, we realized that something was really wrong. Now Uptown New Orleans was flooding at a dangerous level.

Throughout the evening, I had been trying to call Chief Compass to update him and ensure that he was okay, but I realized at some point that not only was power out in the city, but our cell towers were down as well. And now, our backup system was also down, and we had no means of communication. As we headed back to Headquarters, it was pitch-black as far as the eye could see. The only illumination came from the lights of our truck and the occasional building whose backup generators were powering some of their lights. Passing by the Superdome, I noticed that some water was coming into the truck, indicating that flooding had increased exponentially in the area. "The levees at Lakeview must be breached as well," Captain Weathersby stated as we drove by the Superdome. We would later learn that not only did the Lakeview levees breach, but every canal in the city was overflowing with water. Water was coming in from the Lower Ninth Ward, Lakeview, overtopping from New Orleans East, and in Gentilly. We were being attacked from the North, East, and West. The only direction that waters was not flowing in from was from the south, which was the Mississippi River. Thank God that the river levees held strong because if they had not, there would most likely not be a New Orleans.

Once we negotiated our way onto Tulane Avenue through the pitch-black darkness, small lights flickered off and on again on top of buildings and hotel's balconies that lined the street. "Those are people on top of those buildings," I stated. "You're right, Chief," Weathersby agreed. "They figure this is the best place to be seen to get help." We rode in silence the rest of the way, taking in the scene and all that was happening. At moments when it was completely quiet, you could hear the people on the rooftops calling out for help. It was probably one of the most eerie experiences I'd ever had. "Please help us!" one man's voice cried out. "Can you see us up here?" a female voice asked.

"We need your help!" another female voice implored. "We don't want to die!" "Please, please help us." The water was too high, and we could not see very well. The water continued to rise, reaching the point where it was now in the truck. When we arrived at Tulane and Broad Street, we had to get a boat to reach Headquarters. I then sent that boat back to the areas on Tulane Avenue to rescue the people and citizens who were begging for help. Those words, "please, please help us," hit me in my gut! We did a lot of good today, saving and rescuing people, but I knew for a fact that there were people out there whom we didn't get to, and there were some that we might not ever get to.

Hearing them say, "We don't want to die," stuck in my head. We would do our best to keep them from dying if at all possible.

Chapter 13:
Heartbreaking Choices

August 30, 2005 – 11:00 a.m.

The temperature on the flooded first floor of Methodist Hospital in eastern New Orleans had to be at least a hundred degrees, if not higher, Officer Lorenzo Carter thought to himself. He drew a deep breath before immersing himself in the murky, warm water that inundated the floor, aiming to move more swiftly than he could on foot.

Splash!

He sliced through the warm water, propelling himself forward with powerful leg kicks. He pushed as far as possible with the air he had inhaled until his lungs screamed for more oxygen. Using his arms to guide his ascent, Officer Carter emerged, quickly assessing his surroundings from the other side of the room. The flashing emergency hallway lights, which provided partial illumination of the completely flooded hospital floor, immediately caught his attention.

A jolt ran through him when he spotted the bloated body of a woman floating past him. Once again, he employed his legs to push away from the drifting corpse. Officer Carter acknowledged the truth of the reports about bodies from the morgue floating on the first floor. Surveying the scene, he realized the hospital was in dire straits. The flooding, which persisted throughout Monday and the night, had knocked out the generators. In many areas of the hospital, temperatures soared beyond 100 degrees. Family members of patients attempted to cool their loved ones by fanning them, struggling to maintain their comfort.

Toilets were backed up, food supplies had dwindled, and essential items were scarce. Operating critical equipment, such as dialysis machines, x-ray apparatus, and elevators, had become increasingly challenging, if not impossible. Lorenzo had heard two particularly troubling pieces of information: emergency surgeries were being conducted by flashlight, without anesthesia, and ventilator-dependent patients were being manually ventilated using bags, with staff rotating to keep patients alive.

Regardless of consensus, Lorenzo understood that the time had come to evacuate over 300 patients. With no power and a faltering sewage system, the stench within the hospital, stemming from the backed-up toilets and the now overflowing morgue, was becoming unbearable. The hospital's first floor, completely flooded, had become afloat with bodies from the morgue. With officers, patients' families, and children present, containing these bodies was imperative, as the sight could be traumatic, especially for children.

Lorenzo and his partner, Officer Lawrence Celestine, needed to devise a plan to confine these bodies to a specific area, as an emergency evacuation loomed. The main hallway, along with the corresponding waiting rooms and business offices on the first floor, were submerged under at least five feet of water. Less than 48 hours prior, Officer Carter, his partner Lawrence Celestine, and the officers of the 7th District had settled on the fifth floor of Methodist Hospital, ready to weather Hurricane Katrina.

Though the district station was just up the street from Methodist Hospital, the multiple levels and spacing of the hospital was thought to yield a better tactical space for the officers. Many of the officers started arriving at the hospital, some of whom had family members with them, early on Sunday morning. The fifth floor was designated as the spot for the 7th District officers. There were plenty of waiting room spaces, offices, and even a kitchen for the officers and their families to relax and watch television. The 7th District was under the leadership of Captain Robert Bardy, who had nearly thirty years of experience, Lieutenant Michael Lohman, and Sergeant Arthur Kaufman. Leadership occupied a different space from the officers in a room behind a door that bore a sign reading "SUPERVISORS ONLY."

Despite the expectation that Hurricane Katrina would hit New Orleans hard, the massive flooding that followed couldn't have been anticipated, even in their worst-case scenarios. When the storm began rolling in on Sunday evening and power was lost, the hospital's backup generators easily kicked in, and everyone moved forward with no thought for the looming catastrophe.

The following Monday morning, Officer Carter and many others knew things were different. Reports on the radio indicated widespread catastrophic flooding across the city. There were also reports of tornadoes and damaging winds. Officer Carter distinctly remembered a moment during the night where the building seemed to shake against the developed windy conditions outside.

Needless to say, when Officer Carter and the others encountered ankle-deep water on the first floor of the hospital on Monday morning, they knew it was time to prepare for the storm. "Lorenzo!" Officer Carter heard his partner, Lawrence Celestine, calling his name in the distance. Lorenzo looked eastward and saw Celestine walking through chest-high water towards him. It was quite a sight to witness Lawrence walking down the corridor, considering he was about 5'7". The fact that the water was up to his chest testified to the magnitude of the flooding at Methodist.

"Man, there are at least three bodies in that hallway alone, just floating," Celestine said to Lorenzo upon reaching him. Celestine was sweating profusely due to the heat, but Lorenzo sensed that something else was afoot. There was an edge of anxiety in his voice that Lorenzo hadn't heard before. With years of partnership and history between them, Lorenzo knew when Celestine wasn't telling him everything. They were more than friends; they were brothers.

When Lorenzo and Celestine became partners, they had both seen much within the intricate and thankless world of policing. Being a cop in a tough and corrupt city like New Orleans could wear at the fabric of your soul until you became something you never intended. They knew of excessive force, planting evidence, ripping off drug dealers, and even taking bribes. Modifying the rules in one of those moral and ethical areas could leave a negative imprint on one's soul.

The corruption had been part of New Orleans since the first police chief, David Hennessy, was killed just outside his home - allegedly by several Italians in 1890. When Officers Carter and Celestine became partners, they determined they would be better than that. They decided they would hold each other accountable and not allow the nature of the job to shift who they were. They used their integrity to bring about real change in their community. To hold themselves accountable, they operated by the mantra 'The wrong thing done even for the right reasons is still wrong.' This mantra informed their decisions and shaped how they would police their assigned areas, and it worked well for them.

A little more than five years ago, they received a commendation from the Department and the city for a major drug bust they coordinated and executed, seizing over eighty-one pounds of marijuana. They utilized a criminal informant (CI) who tipped them off about a dealer coming in from Texas with a significant number of drugs. Per the CI's information, the dealer was staying at a Motel 6 off of Chef Highway. Carter and Celestine set up surveillance in the area and conducted a routine traffic stop on the dealer, discovering drugs hidden in the speakers of his vehicle. This led to a warrant to search his hotel room, where they found large quantities of marijuana hidden in the ceiling. It was a proud moment that showcased their ability to uphold the law effectively.

With water now higher than their chests, Lorenzo pressed Celestine further, knowing his partner well. "Celestine," he addressed him directly, "What's the word?" Celestine, wiping his face with both hands, replied with urgency, "Man, bodies are floating out of that morgue like they're coming from every direction! And not just adults," he added, his tone heavy. "Some of those bodies are kids."

As evacuations began, Lorenzo recognized that all traffic would have to pass through the first floor. They couldn't afford to have dead bodies floating around, risking chaos. "Celestine, we need to move those bodies to a specific area where nobody will see them during the evacuation," Lorenzo instructed. Celestine nodded, wiping his face, and pointed to some rooms nearby. "There are a couple of rooms back there," he said. "We can move the bodies there and close the doors."

"Sounds good," Lorenzo agreed, spotting the first body not far from them. "Let's start with this one."

Although neither Celestine nor Carter relished handling bloated corpses, they knew the importance of controlling the situation to prevent evacuees from seeing an entire room filled with floating bodies.

Meanwhile, on the third floor of the hospital, Officer Denise Mercer found herself in a routine she could never have imagined. Sitting in a dimly lit room, illuminated by two flashlights, Officer Mercer and her partner, Officer Leon Baptiste, along with nurses Felicia Johnson and Nancy Rappaport, worked diligently to keep 80-year-old patient Langford Weston properly ventilated. Unlike at least eight other patients on the ICU floor of Methodist, Langford had a good chance of surviving the transport to another hospital. However, it was crucial to maintain his oxygen levels through manual ventilation using a Bag-Valve-Mask (BVM) unit until evacuation and transport could begin.

Hospital Administration, in coordination with the 7th District Officers, had determined that evacuating the hospital was imperative to save lives. Compromised by floodwaters and without power, Methodist Hospital was no longer safe. While the National Guard was on the way to assist with evacuations, some officers with personal boats had already begun moving patients and families to receiving hospitals in the Westbank and Jefferson Parish.

The chaotic noise from the hallway outside the room, as staff and officers rushed to evacuate patients, was audible. However, the mission within this room was singular: to focus on preserving the life in front of them. "You're doing great," Nurse Johnson reassured Officer Mercer, securing the mask around Langford's mouth to ensure the oxygen being manually pumped from the bag reached him effectively.

Denise and Felicia formed a two-person team on duty for the next half-hour. Denise operated the manual air pump while Felicia ensured a proper seal of the mask. They positioned Langford, who was sedated, on the floor with pillows under his head to maintain a clear airway. Officer Mercer's partner, Officer Leon Baptiste, and Nurse Nancy Rappaport were scheduled to relieve them after their shift to prevent exhaustion from setting in. Despite the impending shift change, Denise was already fatigued from the past two hours of effort, both physically and mentally.

As she continued pumping air into Langford, the weariness in her arms intensified, compounded by the stress of the last 48 hours. Hurricane Katrina had been anticipated as a major event, but nothing had prepared Denise for the current chaos. Frustration mixed with fatigue as she realized that none of their leadership, including Captain Bardy, could be located. A locked room on the 5th floor, assumed to be their base, only added to the mystery. Determining the necessity of evacuation, Denise and her fellow officers had made that decision without their superiors, and they planned to inform Captain Bardy as soon as they found him.

The uncertainty of leadership's whereabouts was aggravating. As she continued to operate the air pump, Denise looked down at Langford, his elderly face peaceful in sleep. Nurses had informed them that Langford's family was anxiously waiting on the same floor, concerned for his well-being. They assured the family that they were doing everything possible for his safe transport, promising to provide immediate updates on the receiving hospital and transport time. The challenge lay in the uncertainty of Langford's survival during transport, given the extreme temperatures and flooding.

Suddenly, the portable EKG monitor began beeping erratically. "He's going into cardiopulmonary distress," Nurse Johnson exclaimed, quickly switching places with Officer Mercer and taking over air pumping. Denise focused on Langford's chest, observing the rise and fall as she had been trained. Nurse Johnson assessed the situation and decided to bring in Nurse Rappaport for a thorough evaluation.

As Felicia left the room, Denise continued pumping air and monitoring Langford's chest movements. Nurses Felicia and Nancy returned with Officer Baptiste, who expressed encouragement for Nurse Johnson's efforts. Denise's arms were growing fatigued, and she knew she would soon need a replacement. Just as this thought crossed her mind, Langford's daughters entered the room, their arrival almost ironically timed.

"What's wrong?" the elder daughter asked, her concern evident. "Why are all three of you working on him?" questioned the other daughter. "Your father's pulse rate has dropped considerably and suddenly," Nurse Johnson responded. "We need to stabilize him!" The elder daughter's voice grew louder, bordering on panic. "Why is this happening??" "We don't know yet, but we're doing our best to figure it out," Nurse Rappaport reassured them, continuing her efforts.

The daughters became hysterical, tears streaming down their faces as they pleaded frantically for their father's life. Denise closed her eyes briefly, focusing on maintaining concentration and ensuring Langford received the necessary oxygen. You're not leaving us, Mr. Langford Weston, she thought fiercely, her gaze fixed on him, determined to will him to survive.

Meanwhile, Officer Lorenzo Carter and Officer Lawrence Celestine made their way out of the stairwell, stepping onto the third floor. During their ascent from the first floor, they encountered fellow officers and hospital staff relocating patients to more manageable floors for evacuation. Both officers understood the urgency of moving patients and their families, especially considering the dire state of the hospital and the ongoing crisis on the first floor. The past hour had been physically demanding as they worked tirelessly to corral the floating bodies from the morgue into a designated area. Lorenzo couldn't shake off the mental image of those bloated corpses, swollen from prolonged exposure to water. The nauseating blend of decaying flesh, stifling heat, sewage, and other odors ingrained itself in their senses, lingering even when they managed to escape its immediate vicinity.

Despite their physical exhaustion, they knew the road ahead allowed no room for fatigue. The entire hospital was engulfed in darkness due to the power outage. Emergency lighting at the base of the floors and a few operational lights, presumably powered by the last functional generator, provided minimal visibility. Word had just come in that the National Guard had arrived to assist with evacuations, which were now underway. Most patients were to be transferred to Ochsner Hospital in Jefferson Parish or other facilities on the Westbank, which had sustained less damage and had the capacity to accommodate them. Even with the National Guard's support, the hospital staff required the officers' assistance for the evacuation process.

The most heart-wrenching situation was unfolding on the very floor they were on, the ICU wing of the third floor. Many critically ill patients wouldn't survive the evacuation due to insufficient equipment or their unstable conditions. Families were being informed that their loved ones couldn't be evacuated and would be made as comfortable as possible until additional resources became available. In essence, they were being left behind to face the harsh conditions. The officers recognized the grim logic behind prioritizing those with a better chance of survival, yet the decision weighed heavily on them. It felt like a cruel, Darwinian approach to a dire situation.

The sounds of anger and desperation drew their attention to a heated exchange nearby. A man was protesting the decision to leave his loved one behind, his frustration evident in his words. "No! No! Fuck that!" he shouted, expressing his outrage at the news. A woman's voice joined the chorus of distress. "How the fuck are y'all just gonna leave him here?" she cried out. "We ain't going no damn where without our father, fuck that!" The officers instinctively moved in the direction of the commotion. It was clear that hospital staff might require police assistance to handle these emotionally charged situations.

Suddenly, a woman's anguished scream from across the hall diverted their attention to a different emergency. "WE HAVE A CODE BLUE!" a male nurse's voice rang out urgently. Celestine and Carter turned their focus toward the room from which the voice emanated, rushing to the scene. The rooms were dimly illuminated by small portable lights or flashlights, making it challenging to see inside. Without hesitation, they entered the room, finding a male nurse, a young boy in a hospital bed, and his distraught parents gathered around him. The nurse, identified as Gregory Furst, appeared to be in his early thirties and was athletically built.

"Officers, this patient is in cardiopulmonary arrest and we need to start rescue breathing immediately," Nurse Furst informed them urgently. He had already attached a breathing mask to the young boy's mouth and prepared the equipment for manual oxygen pumping. "Mrs. Arrington, the best thing you and Mr. Arrington can do for Tommy right now is to allow us to do our best to resuscitate him," Gregory said with a mix of gentleness and determination, urging them to give the medical team space to work.

Officer Celestine swiftly moved to the side of Mr. and Mrs. Arrington, offering them comfort while the medical team fought to save Tommy's life. Nurse Furst directed Officer Lorenzo to administer air to the young boy while he hurried to administer epinephrine. The constant, eerie tone of the flatline emanating from the EKG machine gripped Officer Lorenzo's senses, a chilling reminder that the young boy before him was no longer breathing.

"Please, God, don't take my boy," Jonathan Arrington whispered in a desperate prayer, his arm around his sobbing wife, Keisha. Celestine, a father himself, struggled to contain the emotional weight of the scene unfolding before him. The pain and helplessness of witnessing a child in distress resonated with him on a profound level, causing his shoulders to tense and his breath to catch.

"Why does it all have to happen at once," Celestine murmured, his voice laced with frustration. Tommy was the Arrington's' only child, a miracle after Keisha's previous belief that she couldn't conceive. His diagnosis of Chronic Bronchitis had significantly altered their lives, restricting the once-active boy's movements and filling their days with medical uncertainties. They hadn't evacuated the city due to Tommy's fragile health, and now, in a darkened hospital room, their worst nightmare was unfolding.

As Nurse Furst worked tirelessly on the young boy, Lorenzo observed Tommy's chest rise and fall with each pump of oxygen, yet his condition remained unchanged. "Come on, Tommy, breathe, baby! Breathe!" Keisha pleaded through tearful sobs. Officer Carter continued his rhythmic pumping, his own heart heavy as he silently beseeched for a positive outcome. He prayed that this child's life would be spared.

Further down the hallway, Officer Denise Mercer felt the strain in her arms slowly give way as she heard the words she had been yearning for. "His condition has stabilized," Nurse Felicia Johnson announced. A wave of relief washed over Officer Mercer as Mr. Weston's daughters expressed their joy and gratitude through tearful embraces. The EKG machine's tone had steadied, and Langford Weston was breathing on his own once more. It was the outcome they had all hoped for.

"What happened?" Officer Baptiste inquired. Nurse Rappaport explained that Mr. Weston had experienced a temporary pulmonary event that had obstructed his breathing. The nurses provided a comprehensive account of the medical situation to Mr. Weston's daughters, assuring them of their father's improved condition and his readiness for transport. They stayed with the Weston family until the evacuation team, comprising National Guardsmen, officers, and hospital staff, arrived to facilitate the patients' move.

As Officers Mercer and Baptiste prepared to leave, Nurse Johnson requested a moment of their time. "Officer Mercer, can I speak with you for a moment?" she asked. Denise approached her, sensing the emotion in Felicia's voice. "Firstly, thank you for your assistance today. Your support has been invaluable," Felicia expressed her gratitude. "I hate to ask this, but I need your help with a delicate matter," she added.

"Of course, I'm here to help. What do you need?" Officer Mercer offered.

"I need you to accompany me to see a patient," Felicia said. Even in the dimly lit room, her eyes glistened with tears. "What's going on, Nurse Johnson?" Denise inquired.

"We have an 86-year-old patient named Mrs. Thompson," Felicia began.

"She's the sweetest woman ever. Never complains. Always has a kind word." Nurse Johnson's voice trembled with emotion. "Given her medical condition, there's no way she would survive transportation. Her body is just too frail," she continued, her composure wavering. Officer Mercer's heart sank. The woman Nurse Johnson was referring to, Mrs. Thompson, was not going to be evacuated from the hospital. She would be among those left behind.

Meanwhile, in the ICU wing, Officer Lorenzo Carter stared down at the lifeless body of 10-year-old Thomas Arrington. Tommy's parents clung to each other, their sobs echoing through the room. The flatline tone from the EKG machine no longer pierced their ears; Tommy had been disconnected from it after over five minutes of unsuccessful resuscitation attempts. Tommy was gone. Officer Lawrence Celestine gazed into the distance, seemingly consumed by the weight of the moment, while Nurse Gregory Furst concluded his tasks in the room. Officer Carter's emotions swung from helplessness to seething anger.

How had they missed the scientific knowledge that could have guided their decisions during Hurricane Katrina and minimized the loss of life? Why hadn't the hospital been evacuated sooner? And where was Captain Bardy and the rest of the leadership team? These questions churned in his mind, threatening to overwhelm him. Just when he thought things couldn't get any worse, they were faced with the agonizing task of telling Tommy's parents that they had to evacuate immediately for their own safety. The hospital was no longer a safe place, and due to the ongoing emergency, they had been allowed to remain until the last possible moment. But now, they had to leave.

Yet leaving meant leaving behind Tommy. Technically, Tommy was already gone, no longer eligible for evacuation. But for parents who had just lost their child, leaving him behind felt like abandoning him to an unknown fate. No closure, no proper farewell.

Two additional officers from the 7th District arrived, accompanied by hospital staff, to assist with the evacuation. The Chief Resident, looking exhausted, did his best to explain the situation to the grieving parents. But at the mere mention of leaving, both parents broke down. The most heart-wrenching moment for Officer Carter was watching Tommy's parents being gently but firmly escorted out of the room where they had said their final goodbye to their son.

In Mrs. Thompson's room, Officer Mercer stood to the side as Nurse Felicia Johnson approached the patient's bedside. The hospital was a chaotic swirl of activity as evacuations were underway – patients heading to receiving hospitals and officers' families moving to the relatively safe Crystal Palace on Chef Highway, which, for the moment, remained unflooded. The air was thick with the sounds of weeping and sobbing family members, torn between the heartache of leaving their loved ones behind and the urgency of their own safety. It all felt surreal, and Officer Mercer half-hoped to awaken from what seemed like an incredibly detailed nightmare. But reality held its grip, and her purpose here was to provide strength for Felicia in a moment where strength seemed scarce.

"Is that my favorite nurse?" Mrs. Thompson's voice, soft as a whisper, carried a hint of a smile as she opened her eyes to see Felicia standing by her bed. "Yes, ma'am, it's me," Felicia replied tenderly. "There's a lot of commotion today. What's happening?" Mrs. Thompson inquired, her gaze steady despite the turmoil surrounding them. In the stifling room, Denise wondered if Mrs. Thompson could sense the oppressive heat in the air. "Well, as you know, we've been without power for over a day now, and so we're having to move patients," Felicia explained gently.

Denise could sense Felicia's struggle to find the right words to convey the difficult truth to Mrs. Thompson. Though she wanted to offer support, introducing another person into the situation might complicate matters. So, she simply nodded to encourage Felicia to continue.

"Mrs. Thompson, the issue is that not everyone is well enough for us to transport," Felicia began, her voice gentle. "Some patients will have to remain here until we can restore power," she continued, her gaze fixed on Mrs. Thompson. Tears welled in the elderly woman's eyes as she comprehended the situation. She knew she wouldn't be evacuated. The reality that her chances of survival were dwindling sank in.

"Mrs. Thompson," Felicia's voice trembled, "I'm so sorry, I—"

"I've lived over 86 years, dear," Mrs. Thompson interjected softly. "You have no need to apologize." Felicia knew she was departing from protocol, but it hardly mattered anymore. There was nothing just about this, and it pained her deeply to see such an extraordinary woman facing this fate.

"I'll make sure you're comfortable," Felicia managed, struggling to compose herself. "Sweetie, I spend more time asleep than awake. When my time comes, I'll be at rest," Mrs. Thompson assured. "Don't worry about me. You have a purpose to fulfill and many more lives to save." Denise felt a lump in her throat, moved by the selflessness and courage radiating from Mrs. Thompson's words.

"I'll go back to sleep now," Mrs. Thompson said, her tears flowing. "Thank you for being the best nurse I've ever had and for taking care of me," she added. Felicia leaned in, embracing Mrs. Thompson, and both women wept. After a few minutes, Mrs. Thompson gently patted her on the back, saying, "Now, go on, before we cause a scene." Amid their tears, they shared a chuckle.

Recognizing that Felicia might not be able to leave on her own, Denise approached and wrapped her arm around her, guiding her toward the door. Once they were outside Mrs. Thompson's room, Felicia collapsed to the floor, overcome by sobs, and Officer Mercer held her close, offering whatever comfort she could.

Chapter 14:
Chaos, Determination, and Hope

August 30, 2005 – 4:30 a.m.

I rubbed the temples of my head to relieve some of the tension threatening to set in from the ever-unfolding events of Hurricane Katrina as I sat in a chair at the head of the big table in our main conference room at NOPD Headquarters. Yesterday had been draining as hell with the beginning search and rescue missions. It not only put a physical demand on the body, but the mental pull was just as intense if not more. I still could not shake the visual of seeing those flashlights and cigarette lighters on the tops of buildings. I kept hearing those people cry out to us in the darkness for help, wondering if and how many people may have been killed or injured in the Hyatt Regency Hotel when the tornado hit it. I was concerned about if Sgt. LeVasseur and his family had been rescued and how many citizens did I hear take their last few breaths before Katrina's waters overwhelmed them while I was listening at the command desk and Base 9. How many are trapped in their attics? I haven't been able to contact Mayor Nagin or Chief Compass. The last time I spoke with or saw them they were in the Hyatt Hotel. I hoped and prayed that they were safe.

During my career with law enforcement, I had seen some ill shit before but the stuff I was witnessing and experiencing was definitely next level. It was like the many horrific crime scenes I had seen of the expanse of my career, but even greater. Damn near the whole city was one big massive crime scene and Katrina was the villain. We had to find a way to make sure that every single person was rescued. Little did I know at the time that 83% of the city was filling up with Katrina water. Was that even possible? And just when it seemed that things could not get any more intense, Katrina would gut punch my ass back to reality. About an hour earlier the night staff had awakened me with the news that the basement of Headquarters was now completely flooded and that flooding on the first floor had intensified. Dammit!

I immediately went downstairs and realized that the entire basement of headquarters was underwater. Central Property and Evidence, where all our evidence was maintained, was also underwater. Rape kits, drugs that were seized, and weapons were underwater. Our gym and workout facilities were underwater. As the water rose around headquarters, Chief Nicholas told me that the crime lab two blocks from headquarters was underwater. Our auto mechanic repair shop located in headquarters was under water. As the information came in it just kept getting worse. Chief Nicholas was in charge of the buildings so I inquired if there was any way we could get into the evidence room to save as much as possible. "Sir, it is eight feet under water," he responded. "What the fuck!" I said in a mumbled voice.

As I walked around the first floor of headquarters which was 8 feet above the basement, the water seemed to be rising at least an inch or two every 15 minutes or so and was now at my knees. I'm both pissed and momentarily confused, but with no time for pity or confusion I ordered an evacuation of the building. We were going to have to evacuate Headquarters and set up operations remotely. I quickly rounded up my staff so that we could have a quick strategy meeting and map out our evacuation plan.

In addition to Deputy Chief Steven Nicholas, seated around the table was my Chief of Staff, Captain Michael Pfeiffer, Captain Lawrence Weathersby, Sergeant Cynthia Landry, and Reserve Sgt. Andre Menzies, Lieutenant Gervais Allison and Dispatch Supervisor, Mary Knight. Each person had a variety of papers in front of them on which they'd mapped out tentative evacuation plans as well as tactical strategies aimed at efficiently setting up headquarters at remote locations for their staffs.

"So, we need to be prepared to evacuate in shifts," Captain Pfeiffer said as he looked over his notes. "We've already requested three M35s for transport to our remote locations."

"Our initial effort will have to be centered around getting the dispatchers to a place where they can set up communications," I responded. "They still have to be able to respond to citizens because 911 calls are not about to stop anytime soon. We also have to communicate with city leaders and maintain communication with leadership."

"Agreed," Chief Nicholas chimed in. "For the sake of getting everyone out of the building we can utilize the Broad Street Overpass and position everyone there before we route the dispatchers to their remote location."

"Right," Chief Nicholas stated. "This will give us a chance to get everyone out of the building quickly." Chief Nicholas stated, we have no backup radio system as you know. We discovered that the generator that provided fuel to the backup radio tower fuel line was cut by debris during the storm and all of the fuel leaked out and was not going into the tower. My guys had to walk up 44 flights of stairs to the roof of the Entergy building where the tower was. "We will have it repaired within the next 16 hours." Everyone at the table had looks of disbelief. When will the chaos slow down? Riley thought.

"Chief, we have portable systems that we can set up at the Emergency Operations Center in City Hall," Mary Knight stated.

"Great," I replied to her. "Take everything that you will need to function remotely."

"I'll advise Ms. Levette to prepare the equipment we need for transport sir," she answered.

"Great," I said satisfied.

The burgeoning plan for evacuating Headquarters was a solid one. The Broad Street Overpass was just up the street, but elevated enough to ensure that everyone was safe from the flood waters below. Given the number of staff and family members here it would take us a couple of hours to evacuate, but we could have everyone safely out of the building before noon if we started now.

I was in the midst of mapping out the intricate details of our evacuation plan when a dispatcher entered the conference room, motioning for Captain Weathersby to join her. He left the table, and within moments, they returned, gesturing for me to step outside with them.

"What's the situation?" I inquired as soon as I stepped into the corridor.

"We have Mrs. Boutin on the line," the dispatcher said, presenting a mobile device. "She's the wife of one of the Deputies at OPSO (Orleans Parish Sheriff's Office). She says she desperately needs to speak with you."

Without hesitation, I took the phone from her hand. "This is Chief Riley," I addressed the caller.

"Chief Riley, this is Karen Boutin. My husband, Oscar Boutin, is one of the deputies at the jail," Mrs. Boutin's voice, though calm, carried a tight undercurrent of anxiety.

"How can I assist you, Mrs. Boutin?" I asked.

"There's chaos at the prison," she disclosed. "The power is out, and the prisoners are rioting and attacking deputies. They need help."

"How do you have this information, Mrs. Boutin?" I inquired. "Have you heard from your husband?"

"Yes," she responded. "He called me about an hour ago."

"Amidst the commotion, he managed to convey that prisoner were assaulting officers and that the building is without power," she explained. I couldn't help but wonder where Sheriff Gusman, the head of the Orleans Parish Sheriff's Office, was in this situation. As a former City Chief Administrative Officer, he was an effective leader, but his limited experience in law enforcement concerned me. He surely must have reviewed disaster protocols by now. If riots were erupting at the prison, there had to be a plan in place.

"Rest assured, Mrs. Boutin, we will do our best to address this," I offered reassurance. "We will investigate, and a member of our team will follow up with you."

"My husband is terrified," Mrs. Boutin revealed. "He shared that he and the other deputies removed their uniforms because inmates were patting everyone down in the dark, trying to identify officers."

"He also mentioned that once an officer is recognized, they're subject to severe beatings," she added in a desperate tone.

"We'll do whatever is within our power," I affirmed. "Have you managed to reach Sheriff Gusman?" I asked the dispatcher and Weathersby after concluding the call with Mrs. Boutin.

"Not yet, Chief Riley," the dispatcher replied. "We're still attempting to establish contact."

"Keep trying, and inform me as soon as you do," I instructed. "For now, our priority remains evacuating our personnel before we can even think or remotely consider deploying anyone to the prison."

Meanwhile, within the confines of the Orleans Parish Prison, Deputy Oscar Boutin grunted as he struggled to pry two burly inmates off Deputy Lena Williams. The corridor of the prison's Administration Building had become an unexpected battleground, and Boutin was bewildered as to how the situation had escalated to this point.

Moments earlier, Boutin had traced the cacophony to an Administration room adjoining an inmate area. He had taken refuge in a side administrative office hallway, locking the door behind him, assuming he was finally safe from the chaotic turmoil.

CRASH!

Just as Deputy Boutin believed he had found a moment of safety; the sharp sound of office furniture shattering shattered the illusion. Uncertain of the situation, he initially stood beside the door, straining to hear the tumultuous events on the other side.

"Get off of me! Get the fuck off of me!" The voice, a female one he recognized as Deputy Lena Williams, pierced through the chaos. Without hesitation, he yanked open the door to a shocking sight. Two massive inmates, each easily six feet tall and weighing around 220 pounds, were pinning Deputy Williams to the floor. They struggled to wrestle her gun away and even seemed to be attempting to remove her pants.

Deputy Williams, though of average build at 5'7" and 135 pounds, was a fighter through and through. Fearless and scrappy, she fought back with every ounce of her being. Her adrenaline-fueled strength allowed her to hold onto her holster, a grip fortified by determination. The stakes were high; losing her gun would alter the dynamics dramatically.

Despite her fierce resistance, the assault was growing increasingly brutal. The larger of the two inmates began choking Deputy Williams, while the other, now on his feet, relentlessly kicked her side. Just as the situation teetered on the edge, Deputy Boutin stormed into the room, his anger ignited by the shocking scene.

Without a second thought, Deputy Boutin brandished his nightstick, delivering powerful blows to the backs of both inmates. The impact stunned them enough for him to wrench them away from Deputy Williams, his effort accompanied by a forceful grunt. Seizing the opportunity created by Deputy Boutin's intervention, Deputy Williams summoned all her strength. She fought through the pain and launched a kick squarely into the chest of the choking inmate. The kick's force propelled him backward, granting her a moment to retrieve her gun and draw it.

Deputy Boutin, using his nightstick, expertly swiped the legs of the second inmate, causing him to tumble clumsily to the floor. Swiftly recovering, Deputy Boutin followed up with a solid punch to the inmate's jaw, causing him to collide with the wall behind him with a resounding thud.

"Back the fuck back right now, or I'll blow both of your goddamn heads off!" Deputy Williams' voice was resolute and unyielding. In the dimly lit room, her firearm was pointed directly at the inmates, while Deputy Boutin stood by her side, nightstick poised for action.

"Are you okay, Boutin?" Deputy Williams queried, her grip on the situation reestablished.

"I'm fine," he affirmed. "Let's secure these two assholes somewhere."

Both deputies were acutely aware that securing the inmates could be a precarious endeavor given the current state of the jail. Two of the three prison buildings were engulfed in riots, adding further turmoil to the volatile situation. The entire prison system was grappling with power outages, enabling some inmates to escape restricted areas, unleash their fellow inmates, and turn against the guards and remaining staff.

The chaos had escalated to a point where guards had shed their uniforms to blend in with the prisoners, in the eerily dark hallways an attempt to evade attacks. In the aftermath of the riots, many guards sought refuge anywhere within the prison, desperate to remain undetected. Compounding the crisis, flooding was encroaching upon the facility, and the backup generators were faltering, casting nearly 80% of the buildings into pitch-black darkness.

"There's a holding room where we can confine these two," Deputy Boutin suggested, his focus shifting to the immediate tasks ahead. "Then we need to ascertain the progress of our prison evacuation plans."

Within a mere fifteen minutes, Deputies Boutin and Williams managed to secure the protesting inmates within a holding room, albeit with promises of eventual evacuation. After locking the door behind them, the deputies navigated their way back to the main corridor, where Deputy Williams, finally relieved of immediate danger, could release her pent-up emotions.

"I think my ribs might be broken," she sighed, gingerly easing herself onto a nearby seat.

"Those motherfuckers," Deputy Boutin responded, standing by her side and sharing her outrage.

"Yeah, they got me good," she responded. "Somehow, they must've managed to get one of the guards' keys and gained access to the admin area," she continued. "I heard something, but didn't see them until it was too late," she stated. "They jumped me from behind." "I was in the area, trying to see if there was any flooding over here and find a place away from the inmates," Boutin replied. "I just happened to hear the scuffle and was able to respond." "Glad you did," Williams said gratefully. "I think one of them was going to rape me." "Well, we've got to get you out of here now," Boutin said, looking Williams over.

Her face had a few cuts over her right eye, her lip was swollen and bleeding, and the way she was holding her side suggested that her ribs were likely broken. In this section of Templeman One, there was currently no flooding, but other parts of the building where the inmates were housed had been compromised, and evacuation was necessary.

The challenge that the leadership would face in evacuating the building was how to subdue the prisoners and get them out of the building while they were rioting. Boutin had already heard stories of some guards and deputies who had decided to leave rather than deal with the riots and attacks from prisoners.

While he could understand the frustration and even the anxiety that came with trying to rescue a group who viewed you as the enemy, he couldn't agree with those deputies who abandoned their posts. Regardless of the circumstances, they had taken an oath to protect and serve, and he took that oath seriously.

"The National Guard is supposed to help out with the evacuations," Deputy Williams stated. "And as I understand it, Sheriff Gusman is reaching out to NOPD for assistance in getting things under control here." Deputy Boutin thought back to the conversation he had had with his wife about an hour earlier. He had told her about the chaos that was unfolding at the jail and how they were overwhelmed trying to keep the prisoners in check.

She suggested that they reach out to a friend of theirs in Dispatch at NOPD who might be able to connect them with leadership there and get them some assistance. He figured that given the city's circumstances, getting in touch with NOPD leadership was a long shot, but he didn't have anything to lose. For all he knew, she might actually make contact with them. And even still, given Sheriff Gusman's gregarious nature, there was always the possibility that he would secure assistance from other sheriffs around the state.

Back at New Orleans Police Department Headquarters, we were already implementing a solid plan to evacuate our building and ensure the safety of our officers, staff members, and their families. Our Special Operations Division, led by Captain Jeff Wynn and Lieutenants LeJon Roberts and Duane Sherman, equipped with flatboats, zodiac boats, and multiple M35 trucks, was currently evacuating Dispatchers, women, children, and pets to the Broad Street Overpass.

Officers were present to watch over them and ensure their safety while the rest of the Special Ops Team returned to evacuate the rest of us. So far, the evacuation was proceeding smoothly. Similar to Officer Glenn Madison, some officers with personal boats were using them to assist with evacuations.

"Officer Madison," I radioed via the mutual add radio system "Can you confirm your ETA?" Officer Madison had a 20-foot towline fiberglass boat that he was using to transport people to the Broad Street Overpass. He had come from the New Orleans Crime Lab and had been tirelessly helping out since evacuations had begun around 6:00 a.m.

With the evacuations completed here, I had directed him to a specific home of a family that needed rescuing back in Carrollton. It wasn't a life-or-death situation, but we needed to ensure that they reached the Convention Center, and I knew that Madison would be the perfect person for the task.

He was a dependable officer and dedicated to his city. "We're en route back to Headquarters to pick up more people," he responded. "Do you need me to change my course, Chief?"

"No, that's fine," I replied. "Let's just make sure to connect once evacuations are complete." "Yes, sir," he responded. My staff and I were in the conference room, discussing details about maintaining operations and potential remote locations. We planned to send a portion of our staff to the Convention Center and another portion to the Emergency Operations Center on the 9th floor of City Hall.

Meanwhile, Chief Nicholas and I would keep a contingency of officers with us. Our likely operational spot would be the overhang at Harrah's Casino, one of the few places in the city still functional due to a powerful generator.

I instructed Captain Weathersby to get in touch with Joe Herbert, a former NOPD Lieutenant now heading security for the New Orleans Convention Center (NOCC), and check for a suitable operations area. "Tell Herbert that HQ is submerged!" I exclaimed. The New Orleans Convention Center was located at the foot of the Mississippi River and was 8 feet above sea level and would remain high and dry, one of the few areas in the city that would not flood. We would need a place to relocate the person we rescued.

Captain Weathersby was not only one of my closest friends but also a minister. I respected him both as a friend and a man of faith. In the weeks to come, I would call on him to lead many prayers that would offer hope and comfort to me and numerous officers. The unrelenting force, cruelty, and mercilessness of Hurricane Katrina were starting to wear down my civility and patience in my speech.

The unending challenges and intricacies that Katrina continued to unleash upon us led me to use more profanity publicly than I had throughout my entire career! Why? Did I believe that shouting a bunch of expletives would make things better? No, I didn't.

In fact, it was my principle to refrain from using profanity in a professional environment, and my officers and staff were well aware of this about me. However, Katrina presented us with a unique set of circumstances, and the 'motherfuckers' I uttered were deliberate and tactical, conveying just how grave the situation was.

Katrina was a more than formidable adversary, and it certainly brought out my fiercer side. I wanted action, and I wanted it immediately, so in the days ahead, a fair number of 'motherfuckers', 'assholes', and 'sons of bitches' would escape my lips. On occasion, even Captain/Pastor/Good Friend Weathersby would bear the brunt of my frustration. While I respected Weathersby as a pastor and friend, we were confronting a formidable adversary, and there were times when polite discourse wasn't the order of the day. Fortunately, Weathersby was like family, and I knew he understood.

As we continued to outline our operations, an officer from the 8th District entered the room. Captain Kevin Anderson led the 8th District, which was currently stationed in the French Quarter, encompassing Canal Street and the Central Business District (CBD).

"Chief, Captain Anderson asked me to inform you that looters have breached Saks Fifth Avenue on Canal Street and several nearby buildings," the officer reported. "Damn," I muttered, my frustration evident as the officer proceeded. He went on to explain that the 8th District officers were vastly outnumbered and had to retreat due to looters overrunning them.

According to the 8th District officer, the metal sheets placed over the store's large front windows to prevent entry had been ripped off, allowing looters easy access. He recounted how a group of around 25 looters emerged from Saks carrying various items. Instead of being deterred, they charged through the opening, knocking down four officers. One looter even assaulted a female officer, while others kicked some officers as they fled. The officers had no choice but to pull back.

My immediate reaction was that the people at these stores were, indeed, looters. The items they were taking weren't necessities like food or water. None of these items were critical for their survival. And reports suggested that this type of looting was spreading across Canal Street. "Weathersby, can you confirm if the 8th District is without backup out there?" I asked, my anger evident.

"I mean, where the hell are the 200 National Guard troops that were requested and assigned to the 8th District?" I exclaimed. "Sure thing, sir," Captain Weathersby replied, leaving the room. "Where the fuck are the 200 National Guardsmen, we were told would help patrol Canal Street and the CBD?" I asked rhetorically. The situation was dire. "Sir, there's one more thing," the unidentified officer added. "Saks Fifth Avenue is on fire."

WHAT THE FUCK, I screamed internally. There were reports of citizens with bags of clothes and jewelry in garbage cans, carrying them up and down Canal Street. Reports continued to pour in – some looted pharmacies for food and medicine, claiming it was for survival, while others seemed to be looting just for the sake of it. There were even reports of looters stealing big-screen TVs and stereo systems. The looting was rampant.

Captain Weathersby returned to the conference room, his face showing annoyance. "I'm still waiting for a solid location report on the National Guard assigned to Canal Street," he said with an exasperated sigh. "What did Captain Anderson say?" I inquired, referring to the 8th District Commander. "They're trying to keep control, but it's spiraling. There are too many looters to handle," Captain Weathersby replied. "The fucking National Guard is M.I.A.," Reserve Sgt. Andre Menzies muttered disgustedly from across the room. "Total bullshit," I concurred.

Turning to Chief Nicholas, I commanded, "I want every officer leaving this building to be ready to load up on the National Guard truck and assist with the looting on Canal Street." "Every District Commander needs to deploy officers to every pharmacy in their area," I continued. "Officers must go to every drugstore and gun shop to prevent looting at those sites." "Emphasize that pharmacies and gun stores are top priority. We must maintain control over those spots," I concluded. Sergeant Menzies sarcastically quipped,

"Chief, the radio system is down. How do we get them the message?" "I'm well aware of that," I retorted. "Put it out over the air the mutual aid radio system is working. It's hard to get the message out with all the traffic on that system, just put it out over the air." "If need be, you might have to drive your ass to each commander, so watch your mouth." Gather the recruits and meet me at the second-floor elevator in fifteen minutes." As Captain Weathersby exited to relay the information to the 8th District Commander and Sergeant Menzies left to gather the recruits, Orleans Parish Sheriff Marlin Gusman entered the conference room.

Sheriff Gusman was usually immaculately dressed, but today he appeared disheveled, wearing red and white vertically striped runner's shorts, sneakers, a simple t-shirt, and sporting a five o'clock shadow. He looked like a man who'd weathered a storm – much like the rest of us grappling with surviving Katrina. "Sheriff Gusman," I acknowledged, meeting him halfway across the room for privacy. "Chief, I need your assistance," he stated. "We must get the prisoners out of jail, but they're rioting and it's becoming uncontrollable." "We received a call from one of your deputies' wives, informing us of the prisoners' riot," I responded.

"To be honest, Sheriff, our men are fully engaged. We're overwhelmed rescuing citizens and officers all over the city," I explained. "Our primary duty is to protect and serve the people of New Orleans. Right now, we're stretched beyond recognition. Reports indicate rioting and looting on Canal Street, and our officers are outnumbered." "I understand that, Chief, but I need any help you can offer," Gusman implored. "Here's what I can do," I replied.

"If you can get them to the Broad Street Overpass and position them opposite the citizens, our officers can assist your deputies in overseeing them until you can arrange buses to transport them to other facilities."

"Place a call to Sheriff Cane from Angola State Prison," I instructed. "We need prison buses and correctional officers here as soon as possible. Get the prisoners to the bridge, and we'll help you guard them for as long as we can." I reiterated my suggestion for him to contact other sheriff's offices across the state for deputies to assist with buses and manpower, as our resources within NOPD were severely limited. I desperately wanted to provide more help to Gusman. However, the fact remained that our resources were stretched thin, and the city was currently underwater and ablaze.

Reluctantly, Gusman agreed and set in motion the necessary steps to bring his inmates to the Broad Street Overpass. Armed officers would be present to support his deputies in watching over the prisoners until buses arrived to transfer them to their new holding location. I then headed to the second floor to meet with the police recruits that I had asked Sergeant Menzies to gather.

There, about 35 recruits were waiting, having taken refuge in headquarters. As I approached, I heard a commanding female voice call out "attention," and every recruit swiftly snapped to attention. "Who's the lead recruit?" I inquired. "Recruit Nicola Cotton, sir!" a female recruit stepped forward. She was a petite woman, standing at 5'2" and weighing around 115 pounds, radiating enthusiasm, professionalism, and confidence.

"At ease, recruit!" I announced before proceeding to walk and shake each recruit's hand. I wanted them to feel at ease, given the challenging circumstances. They needed to sense they were part of the team. While shaking their hands, I noticed some standing confidently, while others appeared apprehensive. Both reactions were understandable. After all, none of us knew exactly what lay ahead. "Recruit Cotton, you and your team have a crucial assignment," I explained.

"Follow Sgt. Menzies. He will guide you to the Command Desk, which is just down the hall." "The dispatch supervisors have removed vital radio and communication equipment for us to establish communication once we locate a suitable site," I continued. "Dispatch Supervisor Mary Knight will provide you with materials to securely wrap the communication equipment in plastic to keep it dry." "This is of utmost importance. Do you understand?" I asked.

Recruit Cotton and the entire class hung on my words. It was evident they were eager to contribute. "Sir, yes, sir!" they chorused in unison. "Recruit Cotton, your team will take the equipment and store it under the overhang at the Aquarium of the Americas at the foot of Canal Street. We'll have transportation for you in about two hours," I informed her. "Sir, yes, sir!" she affirmed promptly. As I concluded my instructions to the recruits, Captain Weathersby entered the area. He was present as I finished briefing the recruits, carefully listening to my words and observing their responsiveness. "We'll need this equipment once we establish a remote operational base. Is that clear?" I asked, locking eyes with Recruit Cotton.

"Sir, yes, sir!" she responded confidently, once again. I immediately gained a profound respect for this young woman. Her determination was evident. Turning to Captain Weathersby, I inquired, "Captain Weathersby, before we evacuate headquarters, could you please share your spiritual wisdom with us?" "Yes, sir, Chief," Captain Weathersby responded. He then led us in a powerful prayer, as we all bowed our heads in reverence.

"Heavenly Father, we implore your grace today to empower us supernaturally to accomplish what we cannot do on our own," Captain Weathersby began, his prayer resonating with a conviction that connected with each person in the room. "In times when our natural strength is exhausted, we call upon you for encouragement, strength, and your guiding wisdom," he continued.

"Grant us the courage to tackle the seemingly impossible tasks ahead and bolster us where we are vulnerable," he went on. "We seek your protection during these trying times."

"And Lord, we beseech you to extend your mercy to our city and the countless families who are still relying on us to reach them," Weathersby fervently prayed, the cadence of his voice building to a crescendo.

"Even amid all of this, we express our gratitude for sparing our lives and granting us the privilege to serve our fellow human beings," he concluded, wrapping up his prayer. "Now guide us throughout the remainder of these challenging times. In Jesus' name, we pray. Amen." "Amen," we echoed collectively, signifying our alignment with his prayer as we dispersed from the area. As we walked away, I said to Captain Weathersby, if my Pastor Fred

Luter wasn't as great a pastor as he is, I might have joined your church after that prayer I said as Captain Weathersby smiled. Pastor Weathersby's prayer was a great spiritual boost of energy and confidence for all of us.

It took a total of 4 ½ hours to evacuate everyone from Headquarters and transport them to the Broad Street Overpass. My team and I were the last to board the final boats that would ferry us to the overpass. Stepping onto the boat, I caught sight of Officer Chris Abbott on another vessel about 15 yards away, aiding in the last evacuations. A smile crept onto my face. A surge of joy and hope overwhelmed me at the sight of Chris. Officer Chris Abbott had certainly proven his resilience.

One day, we were here at Headquarters, fearing he had taken his last breath in his attic. Today, he was ensuring our safe passage. He met my gaze with an enormous smile, tapping his heart and clasping his hands together, a gesture of love, praise, and thanks to us and to God. I reciprocated his gestures and pointed heavenward.

As our boat pulled away from NOPD Headquarters, the blazing sun and stifling humidity enveloped us. Though we had navigated the city's water-logged streets in boats for hours the previous day, the experience remained surreal. Katrina had unquestionably left an indelible mark on New Orleans, a mark that would endure for eternity.

"Chief, look over there," Sgt. Menzies called out, pointing to our right as we made our way up Broad Street. Following his gesture, I saw two bodies floating in the water along the side of the Broad Street Overpass. The chilling reality was that we had no way of identifying them, their origins, or how many more bodies lay nearby. "Damn," I uttered in frustration.

We had labored tirelessly to prevent loss of life, and while we recognized some casualties were inevitable, in my perspective, any loss was unacceptable. Upon reaching the Broad Street Overpass, four M35 trucks were being loaded with dispatchers and staff, destined for the Convention Center.

Scattered around were suitcases, likely containing the three days' worth of supplies and clothing that staff had been advised to bring. With no room on the trucks for baggage, those suitcases would remain there for quite some time.

I promptly coordinated with Mary Knight and her team, including Levette Joseph, to clarify the forthcoming plan concerning our communication strategy. Just when we didn't need any more complications, we discovered that our primary radio systems were offline, temporarily severing communication.

We had relied on our backup radio system for nearly 18 hours, only to find that the backup cell towers were now down as well. Our sole remaining means of radio communication was the mutual aid frequency, shared by every law enforcement agency and sheriff's office in the Greater New Orleans area.

A sequence of unforeseeable calamities triggered by the storm had forced us to lean entirely on our mutual aid radio frequency. Within 18 hours of Katrina's landfall, our main radio system had collapsed, and several towers were destroyed. Even our backup tower, situated on the 44th floor of the Entergy Center Building at 639 Loyola Avenue, succumbed within 30 hours of the storm's onslaught.

It would take nearly 80 hours before that system could be restored. At this juncture, our only means of interoperable radio communication was the mutual aid frequency, a lifeline shared by every law enforcement agency and sheriff's office in the Greater New Orleans region.

The radio chaos was at its peak. With over 5,000 officers and deputies from various agencies in New Orleans, Gretna, Jefferson Parish, Plaquemines Parish, and Westwego all attempting to utilize the same frequency, conversations often overlapped, making transmissions unclear.

It felt as if we had regressed several decades, and I eagerly anticipated the moment when communication would be fully restored. Assuring these exceptional women that everything would be alright, I bid them farewell as the truck transported them to the Convention Center. Our dispatchers and 911 Operators were undoubtedly among the hardest working individuals in New Orleans, true unsung heroes.

Observing that Sheriff Marlin Gusman and his deputies were assembling the inmates on the opposite side of the overpass brought a sense of relief. As our team lined up to board the M35 trucks, the Sheriff's Office arrived with several boats carrying inmates, loading them on the western side of the bridge. Our staff occupied the eastern side.

While on the Broad Street Overpass, I inquired with one of the sheriffs about Deputy Oscar Boutin. A deputy pointed him out, standing around 20 feet away. "Deputy Boutin played a significant role in regaining control over the inmates," the sheriff informed me. "He and a group of other deputies, including some volunteers from across the state, worked tirelessly to subdue and evacuate the inmates within a few hours." Approaching Deputy Boutin, I greeted him warmly.

"Chief, how are you holding up?" he inquired, and despite never having met before, our initial exchange felt familiar. "The better question is how are you?" I responded. "I heard you all were facing a tough situation in the prison." "How did you know?" he asked, surprised. "Your wife reached out to me and expressed that you were in a dangerous situation," I explained.

A thoughtful expression crossed his face as he likely recollected those moments. "She mentioned you called her," I continued. "Yes, I did," he confirmed. "We managed to regain control over a section of the prison." "It was chaotic," he added in a hushed tone. "Once we secured the safety of all the remaining deputies, we contained the more aggressive inmates in specific sections of the prison." "These inmates here are non-violent and from Templeman II," he mentioned.

"I'm relieved you're alright, Deputy," I remarked. "Have you been able to reach your wife?" I inquired. "No," he replied, frustration evident. I offered my phone, but, like his, it couldn't find a signal. Others attempted with similar results. The situation was clear – most phone communications were down. "Damn," Is this really happening, or am I in a dream? The thought crossed my mind. Standing there, pondering my next steps, Sheriff Deputies arrived with some positive news: Sheriff Cane from Angola State Penitentiary was en route with buses and guards.

"Thank God," I exclaimed, relieved by the prospect of additional resources for the Sheriff's Office. "Amen," echoed Deputy Boutin in agreement. Those needing medical attention, including Deputy Lena Williams, were being assessed by medical staff. I relayed Deputy Boutin's wife's role as our initial source of information and commended her resilience. "You've got a courageous wife, Deputy," I praised him before leaving him and the deputies.

Gazing across the overpass, I surveyed the scene, preparing to outline our next steps, which would involve addressing the ongoing looting on Canal Street and assisting the 8th District. Three M35 trucks were loaded with officers, but we lacked communication, recent intelligence on the current looting situation, and I admittedly didn't have a clear plan for what lay ahead.

I approached the M35 trucks and began to address the officers on the spot. "Listen up, everyone," I declared. "Our destination is Canal Street," I stated, making eye contact with each of my officers. "We don't know exactly what we'll encounter, but remember, these are our fellow citizens facing an incredibly tough situation."

"Our goal is to put an end to the looting, but your actions must be reasonable and necessary," I emphasized. "Make them drop the items and let them go. Move them away. We won't be making arrests unless a violent act occurs. Our city doesn't have the facilities to hold them." I paused, letting the gravity of my words sink in for each officer. "Stay sharp, be wise. Let's move out!" I concluded my impromptu speech and headed towards one of the M35 trucks. As I approached, I heard Captain Weathersby exclaim, "Chief, do you see that?"

About 30 feet away, Captain Weathersby pointed skyward. A sizable plane was flying above the city, noticeably descending in a circular pattern. "I think that's Air Force One," Sgt. Menzies suggested.

I joined Captain Weathersby, Chief Nicholas, and Sgt. Menzies, gazing up at the descending plane. It was indeed Air Force One, as confirmed by Sgt. Menzies. The plane's flight path indicated it was surveying various areas to assess the damage. A shared sense of relief and pride was evident on our faces. It felt like the cavalry had arrived – the President of the United States was present, showing concern for our city. As Air Force One passed overhead, the presidential seal emblems were visible from our vantage point, no more than 5,000 feet above us. Fist bumps and high-fives circulated among us and the other officers on the bridge and in the M35 trucks. The arrival of help was cause for modest celebration. The President's presence offered a glimmer of hope, with the expectation of significant change for the better on the horizon.

A feeling of optimism welled up within me, bolstered by the President's arrival. We believed that the Federal Government and the President now had firsthand awareness of the devastation within our city and the assistance we urgently required. In the midst of all the chaos, there was a small yet powerful pleasure in anticipating a positive shift. We thought that things were about to improve significantly. How wrong we were!

To my astonishment, federal boots on the ground wouldn't materialize for another excruciating five days.

Chapter 15:
Chaos on Canal Street

August 30, 2005

The sight of Air Force One soaring above instilled a renewed sense of determination within Chief Riley, Captain Weathersby, and the other officers. The impromptu response team was now loaded into the three M35 trucks, poised to quell the rampant looting plaguing the 8th District. While the situation still seemed chaotic, the presence of federal assistance hinted at a turning point. Chief Riley held on to optimism, believing that they could coordinate effectively with the incoming support and regain control.

Our group, including Chief Riley, Captain Lawrence Weathersby, Sergeant Menzies, and roughly twenty officers, boarded one of the M35 trucks. Deputy Chief Steven Nicholas led another twenty officers onto a second M35, and approximately twenty more officers filled the third M35. Though overall radio communications were down, they managed to communicate through the Mutual Aid System—a shared communication resource among first responders, including police, fire, and EMS, and neighboring agencies. It was a challenge to navigate amidst simultaneous urgent messages, but it was their sole means of communication.

Just as our first truck, with Chief Riley and his team, was about to depart for the 8th District, scattered communication reached us that a group of troublemakers was attempting to seize control of the 1st District.

"Damn it!" Chief Riley's immediate concern shifted to managing the immediate crises. He understood the urgency of assisting the overwhelmed officers in the 8th District, but he also realized the potential danger in the 1st District. A decision needed to be made quickly.

"Lieutenant Allison," Chief Riley called out, making his way towards the M35 containing Lieutenant Gervais Allison and fifteen other officers. "I need your team to head to the 1st District, check on Captain Jimmy Scott, and make sure they're holding up," he instructed. "While the looting might not be as severe as the 8th District, it could escalate quickly. We need to prevent that from happening."

"Understood, Chief," Lieutenant Allison confirmed. "We'll assess the situation on arrival and report back."

"Excellent," Chief Riley acknowledged, and then headed back to his own truck to finalize preparations.

Approximately ten minutes later, all three trucks departed from the Broad Street Overpass. Chief Riley's anxiety had subsided somewhat, though it was hard to gauge whether it was due to desensitization from the constant stress or a newfound resilience. Despite the uncertainty, he felt compelled to rise to the occasion once again, driven by the magnitude of the challenge they faced. Evacuating NOPD Headquarters, rescuing citizens from submerged homes, and dealing with the prison evacuation—all in the wake of the catastrophic hurricane—had made them realize that they were part of something far bigger than themselves.

The journey to Canal Street was brief, offering a stark view of the city's post-apocalyptic landscape. Floodwaters persisted throughout, while the relentless heat and stifling humidity weighed heavily on them. The forceful winds and tornado activity had left their mark, damaging buildings and leaving behind a scene reminiscent of a bomb blast.

As we reached the 400-800 block of Canal Street, a few stragglers lingered about. Sergeant Menzies pointed to a group of around twenty men attempting to breach the metal gate of the Rubenstein Brothers building, presumably to loot. Chief Riley's eyes narrowed; his determination unwavering. There was no way they would let these looters destroy a longstanding institution like Rubenstein Brothers.

"Pull over!" Chief Riley ordered, and the truck came to a halt. Rubenstein Brothers held historical significance, having been part of Canal Street for generations. It was a part of the community that deserved protection. In response, twelve officers swiftly disembarked from the truck, their weapons aimed at the looters. One officer commanded, "Step away from the building!" Faced with the officers' stern presence, the would-be looters scattered in every direction. A few officers moved to pursue them, but Captain Weathersby intervened, advising them to stand down.

Chief Riley and Captain Weathersby conferred briefly. It was agreed that stationing eight to ten officers along each block of Canal Street would be strategically wise. Even though this specific block showed signs of heightened activity, a stronger police presence across the area could help deter further chaos. The plan was set in motion, as they worked to regain control over the disarray that had befallen the city.

After assigning a group of officers to guard the vicinity of Rubenstein Brothers, Captain Weathersby gathered the remaining officers and addressed them sternly. "Listen up, everyone. As Chief Riley has emphasized, we're in a situation with no holding cells. Our objective is to control the looting without resorting to arrests," he asserted. "Use your judgment and stay reasonable. Remember, these are desperate times." He continued with instructions: "If they're grabbing essentials like medication or necessary clothing, let them go but make sure they leave the area. If they're taking nonessential items like electronics or TVs, make them drop it and disperse."

With their guidance relayed, the two M35 trucks departed the scene. Chief Riley and Captain Weathersby concentrated on strategically positioning officers along different points of Canal Street. While much of the area remained relatively calm, the closer they ventured toward the Mississippi River, the more densely populated the street became, accompanied by a surge in looting incidents. Among these challenges, Chief Riley's frustration over the National Guard's absence resurfaced. Where were they? The promise of 200 National Guardsmen to aid in maintaining order seemed empty, leaving him both baffled and irritated.

Furthermore, it had been two days since Chief Compass's last communication. A sense of unease gripped Chief Riley, urging him to prioritize finding his colleague once the looting situation was resolved and a new command post established.

As they proceeded up Canal Street, they noticed a young man exiting a drugstore, carrying a large garbage bag over his shoulder. The absence of substantial water on Canal Street facilitated his progress. While he appeared nonthreatening, the officers needed to verify the contents of the bag. Captain Weathersby's team halted him for questioning. The man, expressing no intention of causing trouble, carefully lowered the bag to the ground and raised his hands, revealing a nursing home ID badge.

"I work at a nursing home nearby," he explained, pointing at his badge. "These are medical supplies and medications we need for the residents— matter of life and death. Otherwise, I wouldn't risk being out here."

An officer inquired about his medical background, to which he admitted he was a nursing assistant and caretaker. "Most of this is sedatives and antibiotics. I have a lot of scared seniors in my care," he shared.

Reassured by his explanation, the officers showed empathy and support. "You're doing important work. Stay safe," they reassured him. Although he declined their assistance, a few officers accompanied him to ensure his safe passage back to the nursing home, protecting him from potential threats along the way.

As the trucks ventured further toward the Mississippi River, the atmosphere shifted noticeably. With less water on the streets, people moved more freely, and unfortunately, so did looters and criminals. Chief Riley observed broken into and even burned stores and buildings. He couldn't fathom the rationale behind destroying the city even further during such a crisis. The concept of stealing, vandalizing, and setting fires in response to disaster baffled him.

In the distance, faint traces of smoke emerged, likely from the reportedly looted Saks Fifth Avenue. Though firefighters had subdued the active fires, the scene bore witness to the havoc that had unfolded. A sense of determination surged within Chief Riley—a fervent resolve to quell the chaos and regain control. Saks Fifth Avenue had become a focal point, its windows unprotected after looters had torn away the metal grating meant to withstand hurricane force winds. Streaks of soot marked sections of the building where flames had once raged.

The scene outside Saks Fifth Avenue was one of utter chaos and lawlessness. The shattered windows, particularly the grand display window at the storefront, had been smashed in, granting looters easy access to the high-end retail store. A wide array of individuals, spanning across different ages, genders, and races, emerged from surrounding shops, their arms laden with stolen clothing, electronics, and various goods. Inside Saks, looters boldly entered through the shattered entrance, completely disregarding any semblance of authority. The store became a frenzied hub of activity, with looters streaming in and out without restraint. In an effort to restore order, four officers from the 8th District hurried to the scene, determined to curb the rampant looting. However, their valiant efforts were quickly overshadowed by the overwhelming number of looters, rendering their intervention largely ineffective.

Officer Tracye Wilkes, accompanied by Officers Verina Baptiste, Dennis Feldman, and Karl Palmer, confronted a group of thieves exiting Saks Fifth Avenue. Officer Wilkes, weary from a day spent dealing with looting, struggled to maintain her composure as she confronted the criminals. Frustration and anger simmered beneath her facade of restraint. The officers' families were far away, and instead of assisting those in dire need, they were grappling with lawbreakers.

Despite the officers' presence, the looters exhibited a brazen disregard for authority. A few of the thieves hesitated, momentarily considering relinquishing their stolen goods. However, the majority remained undeterred, continuing their pilfering as if the police were nonexistent. The sheer volume of criminals overwhelmed the officers, making it impossible to address every instance of theft. Among the looters emerging from Saks, a particularly audacious group boldly made their way through the shattered display window.

Officer Wilkes issued a stern command, demanding the looters drop their stolen merchandise and leave. Yet, her words were met with contemptuous defiance. The situation escalated rapidly as one of the looters, a muscular figure, hurled profanities and charged towards the officers. Chaos ensued as the officers found themselves outnumbered, with two of their own knocked to the ground and brutally assaulted. Amid the chaos, one officer drew his weapon and issued a desperate warning, seeking to quell the violence.

The commotion attracted the attention of nearby officers, prompting a swift response. The approaching reinforcements caused some of the looters to flee into the nearby French Quarter, scattering in various directions. However, the scene remained unsettling as some looters brazenly continued to flaunt their stolen goods.

Officer Palmer, standing tall and formidable, asserted his authority while closely surveying his surroundings. He demanded that the looters abandon their loot and step away. Yet, defiance persisted, and one of the looters challenged the officers' authority. The situation teetered on the brink of confrontation, heightening tensions and evoking a sense of urgency among the officers.

Officer Wilkes' efforts to intervene were abruptly cut short as she was struck from behind with a jarring blow to the head. The pain radiated through her, leaving her disoriented and vulnerable. In the chaos, her attempts to rise were met with a trampling force, inflicting further injury. The ambush left Officer Wilkes incapacitated, prompting her fellow officers to form a protective circle around her.

Officers Palmer, Baptiste, and their comrade positioned themselves defensively, guns aimed at the crowd. The onslaught of looters continued, exiting the store and scattering in all directions. The officers' valiant stance and readiness to use force served as a stark reminder of the dire circumstances they faced—overwhelmed by a wave of lawlessness and outnumbered by those they were sworn to protect.

Officer Wilkes's attempts to regain her bearings were hindered by the chaotic scene unfolding around her. Meanwhile, two looters seized the opportunity to challenge Officer Palmer. Palmer's authoritative command fell on deaf ears as the looters defiantly approached. Palmer's heart raced as he surveyed the situation, realizing that he was on his own in this critical moment.

A sense of urgency gripped Palmer as he glanced around, seeking aid from his fellow officers who were similarly entangled in confrontations with the marauding looters. The two officers who had been with him instinctively shielded Officer Wilkes, recognizing the gravity of her likely injuries. Focused on the immediate threat, Palmer shifted his attention back to the approaching looters who were now just a few feet away.

As one of the looters brazenly closed the gap, Palmer grappled with his options. The weight of his shotgun in his hands was a stark reminder of the responsibility that rested on his shoulders. He desperately wanted to avoid aggressive force, especially given that the looter was unarmed. Making a split-second decision, Palmer lowered his shotgun, releasing his left hand from its grip. In one fluid motion, he stepped forward with conviction and delivered a powerful punch to the aggressor's face.

The forceful blow sent shockwaves through the looter's body, causing him to crumple to the ground. The immediate threat neutralized, the second looter recoiled and fled in the opposite direction, deterred by the fate of his companion.

Palmer's frustration and anger simmered beneath the surface, ignited by the audacity of the looters and the limitations of their response options. He recognized the precarious balance they needed to maintain—a delicate dance between order and catastrophe. Resorting to deadly force was a last resort, an outcome that would have profound repercussions.

Amid the chaos, Officer Palmer's upbringing and empathy emerged as guiding forces. He understood the challenges faced by marginalized communities and the deep-rooted issues that drove desperate actions. The thought of taking a life, even that of an aggressive looter, weighed heavily on him.

Suddenly, a shift in the looters' behavior caught Palmer's attention. The crowd that had posed an imminent threat abruptly scattered, their flight directed away from Palmer and his fellow officers. Confusion settled over the scene, and Palmer's gaze fell upon the sight that had prompted this sudden change.

Three trucks filled with officers rolled down Canal Street's neutral ground, a formidable show of force that deterred the looters and turned the tide. The arrival of fellow officers galvanized by the call for help infused new energy into the chaotic situation.

As more than three dozen officers spilled out of the trucks, Palmer's relief was palpable. Their synchronized actions communicated a resounding message: law and order would be upheld, and chaos would be quelled. The sight before him offered a glimmer of hope, a testament to the strength of their unity.

The newly arrived officers swiftly took control, enforcing compliance among the looters. The looting that had run rampant was brought to a halt as officers compelled the thieves to return stolen items and cease their destructive spree. The delicate balance between maintaining order and addressing necessity guided their actions.

Amid this controlled chaos, Chief Riley, Captain Weathersby, and Deputy Chief Nicholson approached the officers who had teetered on the brink of confrontation. Concern etched their expressions as they checked on the officers' well-being and the situation they had faced. Officer Palmer recounted the events, expressing gratitude for the timely intervention that had averted a dire outcome.

Chief Riley's authoritative presence offered a sense of stability amidst the turmoil. He turned his attention to Officer Wilkes, ensuring her condition and instructing Captain Weathersby to summon EMTs. As Officer Wilkes received medical attention, Officer Palmer's thoughts turned to the challenges that lay ahead.

Chief Riley's leadership was a beacon of guidance in this tumultuous moment. He reaffirmed the mission, directing Officer Wilkes to remain vigilant. The call to assist Captain Anderson of the 8th District echoed through the chaos as officers mobilized to extend their aid beyond Canal Street.

A few moments later, Captain Weathersby returned with crucial information from Captain Anderson regarding the state of the French Quarter. According to Captain Anderson, the French Quarter was relatively secure, experiencing minimal instances of looting. However, Canal Street bore the brunt of the looting activity. Chief Riley swiftly assessed the situation and, upon his command, allocated additional resources to survey the Quarter and ascertain whether further officer deployment was necessary.

Chief Riley, flanked by Chief Nicholas and Captain Weathersby, stood with furrowed brows as they deliberated the evolving crisis. In the midst of this tense moment, Chief Riley's phone unexpectedly vibrated on his hip. Given the communication challenges they faced, the incoming call was a rare and welcome occurrence. Answering the call, Chief Riley's expression shifted from surprise to disappointment, ultimately settling into an expression of disdain. His voice remained steady; his frustration palpable as he conversed with the caller.

Both Chief Nicholas and Captain Weathersby exchanged concerned glances, recognizing the gravity of the situation unfolding on the other end of the line. Chief Riley's stern words revealed a troubling incident involving two NOPD officers who had been stopped by a Texas State Trooper just outside of Houston. Chief Riley realized that these officers were deserters, no officers had authority to leave the city in a marked vehicle for Houston. Riley's facial expression clearly indicated that he was pissed. Riley instructed the trooper to confiscate their credentials, vehicle and equipment. The officers' official business had been dismissed.

The implications of this event were not lost on Chief Riley and his team. The news struck a nerve, representing a stark betrayal of their duty and a blow to the morale of the officers who remained steadfastly committed to the city. Chief Riley's frustration was substantial as he vented his anger, his voice carrying a mix of disappointment and disgust.

As the conversation ended, Chief Riley turned his attention back to his immediate surroundings, his gaze settling on Officer Clarence Cornelius as he confronted a group of looters further up Canal Street. Officer Cornelius's composed demeanor and firm, yet measured, approach exemplified the delicate balance officers needed to strike in this tumultuous environment.

Chief Riley observed the scene, a mixture of relief and admiration welling within him. Officer Cornelius's authoritative yet empathetic handling of the situation diffused the tension. With his guidance, the would-be looters relinquished their stolen televisions and, heeding his advice, sought essential supplies instead. The encounter demonstrated the potential for effective communication and resolution amidst the chaos.

Lieutenant Allison and his team, having returned from assessing the First District station, approached Chief Riley. Their report confirmed the district's intact state, with Captain Scott overseeing efforts to curb looting and maintain order on the periphery of the French Quarter.

Acknowledging the reliability of accurate information amidst the rampant rumors, Chief Riley directed Lt. Allison to secure the 200 – 400 blocks of Canal Street, bolstering their efforts to deter further looting.

A short while later, Captain Kevin Anderson of the 8th District joined Chief Riley's side, flanked by six officers from his district. Grateful for the support rendered to his area, Captain Anderson provided a succinct update on their actions. He detailed their efforts to manage the security of Canal Street and the French Quarter, highlighting their decision to allocate officers to the Quarter to safeguard against looting, especially in the absence of the expected National Guard presence.

"We made a few arrests when it was absolutely necessary and have them handcuffed and detained in the 8th District station," Anderson added. Chief Riley leaned in, curious for details. "How many is a 'few' arrests?" he asked, his voice tinged with urgency. "About 30 to 35 people," Anderson replied. A sense of admiration crossed Chief Riley's face. "Damn! Good job!" he commended Anderson. Captain Anderson took a moment to emphasize that these arrests were exclusively for cases of severe looting or instances of violence against officers. Chief Riley, however, quickly pointed out the predicament of the flooded jail, leading him to instruct Anderson to document the arrested individuals' information and release them unless there were serious acts of violence involved. Detaining people wasn't a luxury they could afford now; the officers overseeing detainees were needed out on the streets.

"Yes, sir," Captain Anderson agreed, fully comprehending the situation's complexities. "Chief, we also secured one of the pharmacies in the area in case anyone needs medicine," Anderson reported, adding a note of practicality to the conversation. Chief Riley's eyes reflected approval. "Excellent idea, Captain! We could be in this dire situation for God only knows how long," he responded. "Great job, Anderson!"

With the necessary protocols established, Captain Anderson and his team departed for the 8th District station. The increased police presence, now totaling around one hundred officers on Canal Street, had substantially curtailed looting activities. Deputy Chief Nicholas, perched on the back of an M35 truck, made his way up the Canal Street median, overseeing the hard-won order that had been established over the past couple of hours.

"Chief, we have Canal Street and most of the French Quarter on lockdown," Nicholas reported to Chief Riley, his tone reflecting a sense of accomplishment. He continued, "I've patrolled Chartres Street, St. Peters Street, and Esplanade Avenue." The gravity of the events hung heavy in the air. "That's not surprising," Chief Riley acknowledged, understanding the chaos they were grappling with. Deputy Chief Nicholas then shared a light-hearted detail amid the chaos. "A few bars are still open on Bourbon Street, Chartres, and St. Peters," he revealed with a hint of amusement. "They never closed down. Some of those folks are so drunk I don't think they know Katrina has come and gone."

A chuckle resonated from Officer Andre Menzies, offering a brief respite from the tension. Chief Riley, looking at Menzies with a smile, appreciated the officer's ability to inject a bit of humor into the situation. The chief's focus shifted to the issue of communication as he asked Deputy Chief Nicholas for an update. "We still only have the mutual aid system at this time," Nicholas confirmed, his tone tinged with frustration. "We're still unsure what the problem is. My staff is headed to the Entergy Center to repair the backup system and see what failed."

The Entergy Corporation Headquarters on Girod Street and Loyola Ave housed the backup radio system, antennas, and generators on its 44th floor. Restoring communication was crucial, and Chief Riley's attention turned to his phone once again. Despite the prevailing lack of service, his phone rang, connecting him with an unfamiliar male voice. "Is this Chief Riley?" the voice queried. Chief Riley confirmed his identity. "Who is this?" he responded; his curiosity piqued.

"This is Officer Kasher from the Memphis Police Department," the voice identified itself. "I have stopped two of your New Orleans Police Department vehicles with four officers inside." Riley's brow furrowed, his expression a mix of disbelief and frustration. "Two male officers and two female officers," Officer Kasher continued, providing specific details. Chief Riley's exasperation was palpable as he listened to the unfolding account. It was another instance of officers attempting to leave the city.

Firmly, Chief Riley instructed Officer Kasher to seize their credentials and impound their vehicles. The matter would be addressed later. "Thank you for contacting me, Officer Kasher," Chief Riley said, his voice a mixture of appreciation and concern. As the conversation concluded, Chief Riley couldn't help but ask the question that had surfaced in his mind. "How did you get my number?" he inquired, his tone tinged with curiosity and intrigue.

"I contacted the National Organization of Black Law Enforcement Executives located in Washington, D.C.," Kasher answered, providing the source of his information. Chief Riley nodded in understanding. "Copy that. Thank you, Officer Kasher," he replied, appreciative of Kasher's diligence. Turning his attention to the next steps, Chief Riley instructed, "I will put you on the phone with Captain Weathersby. Please provide him with all the necessary information." With that, the conversation shifted as Chief Riley handed over the responsibility to Captain Weathersby.

Once the call with Officer Kasher ended, Chief Riley let out a heavy exhale, the weight of the situation evident in his demeanor. Surrounded by his staff of officers, he addressed them with a mix of frustration and resolve. "That's about the ninth or tenth call that we have received about our officers from Texas, Atlanta, Arkansas and now Memphis, Tennessee," he remarked, a touch of weariness in his voice. The numerous reports of officers leaving the city weighed heavily on him.

In the midst of the chaos, Chief Riley allowed himself a moment of introspection, his thoughts drifting into a contemplative realm. The city was plunged into darkness, devoid of power and communication, while the aftermath of the disaster continued to unfold. Yet, amidst all these challenges, it was the defections of officers that gnawed at his conscience the most.

"What the hell is next?" he wondered, the question echoing his thoughts. In a moment of quiet reflection, Chief Riley turned to a higher power, offering up a heartfelt prayer. "Dear Father God, please give me the strength, wisdom, and courage to do what must be done," he prayed, his voice a mixture of earnestness and determination. "Please carry me through these difficult times and allow me to elevate my wisdom and determination during these perilous and ever-changing times. In the name of Jesus, I pray. Amen."

As the echoes of his prayer faded, Chief Riley's gaze refocused on the task at hand. The challenges were immense, but he was resolved to navigate them with unwavering dedication, seeking strength from within and guidance from above.

Chapter 16:
Critical Decisions

August 30, 2005

Chief Riley's emotional state had been a seesaw between determination and anger over the past hours. He had diligently supervised his officers, orchestrating their efforts to restore order within the 8th Police District and a substantial portion of the Central Business District (CBD) in New Orleans. The rest of the city remained an enigma, a landscape of unknown challenges and adversities.

Riley's measured strides traced the sidewalk before Saks Fifth Avenue, his brows furrowed in deep thought. He paced purposefully, covering a span of 10 to 12 feet in each direction, his demeanor a reflection of both intensity and resolve. To some, his countenance might signify anger; to others, it might exude unwavering determination. Yet, all could concur on one thing—he was wholly engrossed in the gravity of his contemplations.

"Hmm..." Riley exhaled, a quiet murmur to himself as his footsteps echoed his introspection. He empathized with his officers, understanding the weight of their burdens. However, he recognized that their stresses were shared by every officer in these dire circumstances. The shadow of concern for their families loomed over all, prayers uttered for another day's survival, and the dread of what might befall their loved ones if something went awry. The indelible images of lives they couldn't rescue would forever haunt them. Yet, despite these collective fears, officer after officer chose to remain and confront the tempest. They stood united, steadfast in their mission to safeguard the city's soul and its populace. For them, abandoning their posts was inconceivable; the solemn oath they had taken bound them, rendering desertion unthinkable and tantamount to sacrilege. Those who abandoned their duty would be held accountable for their lapse in courage.

When the looting tide finally receded, Chief Riley swiftly issued the command for comprehensive updates from all districts, seeking a comprehensive view of the city's condition.

"Chief, the Special Operations Division has established a makeshift post at Harrah's and has been operating from there for over 24 hours," reported Captain Weathersby. Riley promptly decided to head to Harrah's Casino, and before doing so, he rallied all officers nearby.

In an assertive yet composed tone, Chief Riley disseminated orders and instructions. A quick call to action drew officers to him, their focused attention riveted on his words. With calm authority, he assigned tasks—Sergeant Menzies and Officer Barnes were dispatched to the 3rd and 6th Districts. Their mission: to liaise with commanders and compile a comprehensive headcount of officers, accounting for the present, the missing, and any injuries. The scope of their responsibilities spanned the Lakeview area and Mid-city, regions that Menzies and Barnes would cover with haste. Unbeknownst to Chief Riley, the NOPD Third District was entrenched at the LSU Dental School, engulfed by eleven feet of water. Fortunately, the Dental School was housed in a towering seven-story structure.

Chief Riley's directives didn't cease. He turned to Lieutenant Allison, tasking him to visit City Hall with an officer to locate key figures—Chief Compass, Mayor Nagin, and Terry Ebbert. Riley emphasized the importance of notifying them of his whereabouts once confirmed. Officer Osborne was next, entrusted with visiting the Fourth District. Captain Kirsh was to assist in conducting a headcount, a vital assessment of officer presence, and any absences. Each district commander was charged with providing a comprehensive status report, shedding light on strengths, weaknesses, and challenges that needed immediate attention.

As Chief Riley's instructions unfolded, Sgt. Cynthia Landry and Officer Derek Brumfield approached, their update offering a significant shift in the narrative. Sgt. Landry conveyed news from the National Hurricane Center—Hurricane Katrina had waned, its once-menacing winds now dwindling to a maximum of 35 miles per hour over Tennessee. The storm's diminished force signaled a turning point, an opportunity for the city to shift from immediate survival to ongoing recovery.

Chief Riley, his resolve unyielding, pressed forward with measured steps, a steadfast leader navigating the city's tumultuous waters.

Chief Riley nodded affirmatively, expressing his gratitude upon receiving the positive update. Sgt. Landry added, "Sir, news reports indicate that Governor Blanco has issued an evacuation order for the Superdome. It's estimated that over 20,000 residents are sheltered there." Chief Riley's response carried a mix of disbelief and concern, "Damn, 20,000 people? And it's surrounded by at least five feet of water?"

Another piece of information came from Sgt. Landry, "Chief, Sheriff Gusman has approximately 200 inmates on the Broad Street Overpass, guarded by only about six deputies. Several inmates have jumped into the water to escape." Chief Riley's reply was pragmatic, "Sheriff Gusman will have to manage that for now. We have too many other pressing matters. Once we gain control, we'll allocate resources to assist him." Officer Brumfield promptly affirmed, "Copy that, Chief."

Refocusing, Chief Riley instructed Sgt. Landry and Officer Brumfield to proceed to the Second District. Their task was clear: assess officers' headcount and status. Concurrently, he mandated a mandatory staff meeting at seven the following morning under Harrah's valet. Each district commander was to provide comprehensive reports on strengths, weaknesses, challenges, injuries, accounted officers, the missing, and potential attic-trapped personnel.

Though Chief Riley disliked dispatching officers as messengers akin to the 1800s, given the defunct communication systems, resourcefulness was paramount. The only modern divergence was the use of cars and boats instead of horses. Strategizing further, Chief Riley surveyed the vicinity. Amid the officers were unfamiliar faces, including Officers Tracye Wilkes and Verina Baptiste, who had confronted looters near Saks Fifth Avenue. Chief Riley inquired about their well-being and received resolute assurances. He tasked both Officers Wilkes and Baptiste to visit the First and Eighth Districts for status updates, to which they promptly affirmed, "Yes, sir."

Both districts were within a mile, making foot travel more expedient. The officers swiftly departed for the French Quarter without a word. Captain Weathersby sought information on the Seventh and Fifth Districts, to which

Chief Riley responded, "Currently, they are submerged. We'll address them later. The Fifth District is in St. Claude Hospital, and the Seventh District is at Methodist. However, the water levels prohibit immediate action. Once Wildlife and Fisheries teams arrive, deploy them to these locations. We must relocate those officers to ensure city control."

Chief Nicholas interjected, "Chief, I'm attempting to contact commanders through mutual aid channels. However, transmission is intermittent due to multiple agencies communicating simultaneously. I can't establish a clear message." Chief Riley resolved, "We'll persist, Chief Nicholas." With that, Chief Riley directed everyone to Harrah's Casino. Returning to the M35, they departed Saks Fifth Avenue, heading southbound on Canal Street toward Harrah's Casino. Chief Riley observed officers deterring looters, aided by the influx of over forty officers. This intervention curbed looting and restored order. Satisfied with the progress, Chief Riley then directed his driver to Harrah's Casino.

Harrah's Casino sat at the foot of Canal Street, a mere block away from the Mississippi River and just off Poydras Street. A swift ride would take Chief Riley, Chief Nicholas, Captain Weathersby, and five other officers to Harrah's Casino. Their truck smoothly navigated the short distance, drawing closer to the casino. As they approached, they immediately spotted Special Operations officers stationed along the driveway overhang. The once opulent scene of luxury vehicles awaiting elite gamblers was replaced by SWAT officers utilizing the pillars for temporary shelter and strategy discussions post-Katrina.

Within the overhang, the hanging lights illuminated the area. Chief Riley speculated that perhaps this was the sole location in the city with functioning electricity. A notion formed - Harrah's might serve as a suitable command post, considering the available amenities. Welcomed by the camaraderie born of shared adversity, Chief Riley's team connected with the Special Ops officers. Within the past 48 hours, their experiences had encapsulated a spectrum of events that some never encountered in a lifetime. They had witnessed both the city's noblest acts and darkest moments, rescued lives, and faced the wrenching losses of those they couldn't save. These shared moments indelibly marked their souls, forging an unbreakable bond.

Chief Riley inquired about Lieutenant Winn's whereabouts, to which SWAT Officer David Shipp responded that Lieutenant Winn was engaged in a search and rescue mission in the Lower Ninth Ward. The Special Operations Division had used the area as an operational hub while unofficially safeguarding Harrah's General Manager, John Payne. Payne was tending to casino administrative matters and shared concerns about potential looting. The operational benefits were twofold - it provided a launch point for search and rescue missions, and one of Harrah's operational generators supplied electricity. The illusion of downtown New Orleans having power was fleeting; this tiny oasis was a rarity. A few moments later, John Payne emerged from the casino with four hefty duffle bags on a cart. The grey SUV parked nearby was ready for loading. Several officers hastened to assist him with the bags, Chief Riley recognizing Payne from their prior interactions.

Engaging Payne in conversation, Chief Riley learned of the urgency. Payne needed to transport cash and valuable items to Baton Rouge before potential looters struck. The casino's assets demanded safeguarding against a potential multi-million-dollar loss. Chief Riley empathized with the dilemma and offered a solution, "What can we do for you?" Payne explained his need for an escort to Baton Rouge, ideally four police officers and two cars for protection. Chief Riley promptly agreed, ensuring a safe passage for Payne. Grateful, Mr. Payne added that he would leave the generators running, illuminating the valet area for the next week. Confirming the escort and power supply with a tactical sergeant, Chief Riley greenlit the operation. The tactical lieutenant, already apprised by Payne, offered four tactical officers for the escort, their unmarked cars ensuring a discreet journey.

With the arrangements made, it became clear that the Harrah's Casino overhang/valet area, roughly fifty yards long and twenty yards wide, was the designated Field Command Post for the immediate future. Chief Riley acknowledged that this oasis of electricity was rare in the city, likely to remain so for the next week.

As Payne and the four SWAT officers prepared to depart, Chief Riley noticed Lieutenant Allison arriving at the overhang. "Chief, Mayor Nagin and Terry Ebbert are in City Hall," he reported. "I didn't see Chief Compass, and no one knew his whereabouts at the moment." Discussing Chief Compass, Lieutenant Allison added, "Several people in City Hall mentioned that

Mayor Nagin and Chief Compass had a major argument the night before Katrina hit." Curious, Chief Riley inquired, "Any idea what it was about?" "I'm not sure, sir," Lt. Allison responded. "Well, at least they're all okay," Riley commented. "Captain Weathersby, join me at City Hall," Chief Riley directed. "Chief Nicholas, let everyone know this is our Field Command post for now. Collect status reports from the officers who went to the districts. If I'm not back in two hours, meet me in City Hall." "Understood," Chief Nicholas replied affirmatively.

"Hey chief!" a voice called from Chief Riley's left. He turned to see Captain Jimmy Scott of the First District approaching. Captain Scott quickly reported, "No takeover or widespread looting near our station, but we had a tough time here on Canal Street." Concerned, Chief Riley asked, "What happened to the National Guard?" "Wish I knew," Captain Scott replied. "Good to hear your station wasn't taken over," Riley noted. "Early this morning, someone fired shots at the station. We determined the shots came from a building on Rampart Street, about a block away. Thankfully, no one was hurt," Captain Scott explained. "It happened twice last night," he added. "Some of my officers investigated and found two .223 casings. About ten shots were fired the first time, and fifteen to twenty the second time, two hours later. Bullets hit the station's walls and cars. It felt like Fort Apache. Fortunately, no injuries." Reflecting on the analogy, Chief Riley mused about Captain Scott's reference to the historical military post.

"No injuries is a relief," Riley acknowledged. "Stay cautious and safe. I'm off to City Hall to catch up with the Mayor and Director Ebbert. Hopefully, I'll reach Chief Compass too. I'll return in a few hours. Thanks for the update." "Copy that," Captain Scott responded. Moments later, Chief Riley watched John Payne and the four SWAT officers drive away from the Harrah's valet area, headed for Baton Rouge. Reserve Sergeant Menzies approached him a few minutes later. Chief Riley inquired, "Did you reach the districts I assigned you?" "We attempted to reach the Third District, Chief, but the LSU Dental School is surrounded by high water. We couldn't get close," Menzies explained. "I believe the levees broke." Chief Riley signaled for Captain Weathersby to join the conversation. "Contact Captain Paisant or anyone from the Third District," he instructed. "Use cellphones, radio, whatever it takes. We need a status report." Captain Weathersby immediately acted on the directive, trying to establish communication with the Third District. Moments later, he returned to Chief Riley with an update. He had managed to reach Captain Paisaint by phone, who confirmed that the first two floors of the LSU Dental School were submerged, and their vehicles were drifting away.

"In some areas, he mentioned that the water is at least ten feet high," Weathersby reported. "Goddamn! This fucking shit keeps getting worse by the minute!" Chief Riley exclaimed in frustration. Back on the M35 truck, en route to City Hall, he noticed another M35 pull up near the Aquarium of The Americas, just 40 yards from the Casino at the foot of Canal Street. Recruit Commander Nicola Cotton emerged from the back of the M35 and swiftly directed recruits to unload communication equipment they had brought from headquarters. The recruits efficiently organized the equipment under the overhang. Amid the recruits, NOPD dispatchers were also present, including Senior Police Dispatch Supervisor Mary Knight. Chief Riley instructed his driver to approach the dispatchers for a conversation.

"Chief, the stormwater has overtopped the levees in New Orleans East, flooding the area," Ms. Knight informed him. "Additionally, the Lakeview levees have breached, leading to flooding in Lakeview as well." Curious, Chief Riley inquired, "How did you receive this information, Ms. Knight?" She responded, "My pager is operational, and I received a text from the Emergency Operation Center in City Hall." "Thank you, Ms. Knight," Chief Riley acknowledged, his brow furrowing in disbelief at the distressing news.

Preparing to head to City Hall, Chief Riley instructed Officer Brumfield to meet them there with his Expedition SUV. As their M35 departed for City Hall, Chief Riley contemplated the constant stream of distressing news flooding his mind. Citizens trapped in homes, over 20,000 residents needing evacuation from the Superdome, New Orleans East submerged in floodwaters, and reports of officers abandoning their posts. "What the fuck else could happen?" he pondered internally, bracing himself for a debrief with Mayor Nagin, Director Ebbert, and Chief Compass at City Hall. Unbeknownst to him, another catastrophe was unfolding on the Westbank of New Orleans, destined to shake them all to their core.

Chapter 17:
Officer Down

Fourth District NOPD Officer Kevin Thomas and his partner, Officer John Mitchell, eased their police vehicle to a gentle stop beside a Chevron gas station nestled within the 2600 block of General DeGaulle Drive. The Fourth District, situated on the Westbank of New Orleans across the Mississippi River bridge in Algiers, was their jurisdiction. Arriving at the gas station, their eyes were drawn to the shattered large front window, with movement discernible in the grocery section of the station. Earlier, citizens had alerted NOPD about ongoing looting at this location. Given the shattered window, the overall state of disarray, and the apparent activity within, their conviction grew that the reports of looting held truth. The parking lot, strewn with debris and shards of glass, further solidified their suspicion that illicit activities were afoot. While an air of lawlessness had not entirely blanketed the vicinity, a sense of vulnerability hung in the air – a clear signal that venturing without protective company was inadvisable.

Officer Thomas, a seasoned 20-year police veteran, had weathered his fair share of crises during his tenure. His commitment to upholding the law and serving the community was unwavering. This was complemented by Officer Mitchell's straightforward approach, providing a counterbalance that enhanced their partnership. In the wake of Hurricane Katrina, although the Fourth District had escaped the worst of the structural damage and flooding, their challenge lay in quelling the looting and criminal activities rampant in the area.

"Goddamn, these looters wasted no time hitting this place," Officer Mitchell murmured as he surveyed their surroundings. The two officers exited their vehicle, their scrutiny meticulous and thorough. Officer Thomas, a man of principled beliefs, expressed his dismay at the act of looting during such dire circumstances. He firmly believed that an individual's potential was limitless regardless of their circumstances, asserting that choices, not fate, dictated the heights one could achieve. Officer Mitchell, pragmatic in his outlook, replied, "Desperate times lead to desperate measures, Kevin." Officer Kevin Thomas nodded, acknowledging the grim reality of the situation. "Yeah, you're right."

The officers observed several subjects about 20 yards from the gas station and one, a female flagged them down and advised them that the four men near the station were robbing the looters.

"Stay alert, Thomas," Officer Mitchell cautioned, subtly gesturing towards four individuals emerging from the gas station and approaching the parking lot. The officers intercepted the subjects, four African American men three spanning early to late twenties and much older. Following protocol, they instructed the men to place their hands against the adjacent wall and conducted a standard pat-down for weapons. Their belongings were in line with their claim – bags containing chips, bottled water, and soda. Satisfied that no further action was warranted, the officers allowed the men to leave. Officer Mitchell ventured into the store while Officer Thomas scrutinized the surrounding area for any signs of irregularity. A few moments later, his attention was drawn to three African American males advancing toward him – later identified as Vincent Walker, Sye Carter, and Jamil Joyner. The trio ambled nonchalantly toward the lot. The angle of approach left little doubt that they had already spotted Officer Thomas and his marked police vehicle. Each clutched a plastic bag, unfurling them with intent. Their actions, combined with the officer's presence, confirmed their intentions.

"NOPD!" Officer Thomas bellowed with authority, as if his uniform bore invisibility.

"Ah, damn it!" one of the men exclaimed in frustration as the trio abruptly halted their steps. "What brings you out here?" Officer Thomas queried. Instantly, tension crackled in the air. "Man, seriously? We can't just be out here?" spat Jamil Joyner, the youngest of the trio, his fury evident. Standing at about 5'9" and weighing around 150 lbs., he had a lean build, his anger palpable from the moment he laid eyes on Officer Thomas. "Easy there," interjected Sye Carter, an older man among them, his voice carrying a mature calmness. Aged around 50, he stood at 6'4" and weighed about 250 pounds. "Just listen to your friend and cooperate," Officer Thomas urged, his tone even. "We're looking into reports of looting and crime in the area, so we're checking out any suspicious behavior or anything that appears unusual," he explained. "So, just because we're walking through the parking lot, we're automatically suspects?" Jamil Joyner retorted, his frustration boiling over. The others remained quiet, while Joyner vehemently protested, his rage evident. "What's bothering you?" Officer Thomas inquired. "If you're clean, you'll be free to go."

"Forget that noise, this is ridiculous," Joyner persisted. "I'll need to perform a routine pat-down on all three of you. If nothing comes up, you can leave," Officer Thomas stated. "This is nonsense!" Joyner exclaimed in defiance. "Relax! You need to calm down. We haven't done anything wrong," Vincent Walker, who had yet to speak, advised Joyner. Following the procedure, they had used with the previous group, Officer Thomas instructed the three men to place their hands on the gas station wall. Forming a line, he proceeded to conduct a methodical pat-down on each one, step by step. Meanwhile, Officer Mitchell remained inside the station, scanning for potential looters. Walker, Carter, and Joyner were unaware of Officer Mitchell's presence. "You guys are on some bullshit!" Joyner angrily ranted as the pat-downs commenced. Amid Carter and Walker's searches, Joyner's torrent of invectives and curses continued unabated. "Screw all of you, damn police officers! You Uncle Tom motherfucker!" Positioned third in line, Joyner would be the last to undergo the frisking. Fully anticipating his profanity-laced tirade, Officer Thomas strained to maintain his composure.

"Shut your mouth and look straight ahead," Officer Thomas ordered, his patience worn thin by the young man's blatant disrespect. As he bent down to conduct Vincent Walker's pat-down, a sudden shift in the situation unfolded. "Screw you, nigga!" Joyner explosively shouted. The deafening 'bang' characteristic of a .45 caliber handgun eclipsed all other sounds in the vicinity. In the span of a heartbeat, Officer Thomas was robbed of any chance to react as the projectile from the .45 caliber firearm pierced his NOPD baseball cap and struck the crown of his head.

Struck at almost point-blank range, Officer Thomas crumpled to the ground, his body limp and lifeless. Unconsciousness swept over him in an instant, leaving him devoid of movement or awareness. The trio of men wasted no time, bolting away toward the west, their destination set for Jefferson Parish. Inside the service station, Officer Mitchell was making his way to the exit door when the sickening 'pop' of the gunshot pierced the air, a sound that seemed to grip his heart and send it racing at an impossible speed. Rushing to the doorway, his eyes locked onto the figures of the three fleeing men, their forms diminishing into the distance as they headed westbound towards West Jefferson Parish. Among them, Jamil Joyner and Vincent Walker clutched firearms in their hands. Officer Mitchell exploded through the exit, the urgency of the situation propelling him onto the lot. A dreadful sight met his eyes—his partner, Officer Thomas, lay motionless on the ground, a pool of thick crimson blood oozing from his head. "NOOOOO!!!" his anguished cry reverberated; each syllable laden with raw desperation.

Drawing his service weapon in a fluid motion, Officer Mitchell responded with a barrage of rounds aimed at the escaping figures. The gunfire found its mark, striking Sye Carter in the shoulder. Carter tumbled to the ground, his resolve unwavering as he swiftly regained his footing and pressed on, sprinting alongside his companions towards the distant horizon. "One-oh-eight, one-oh-eight!" Officer Mitchell's voice crackled through the radio waves, signaling the dire situation. "We have an officer down," he continued, his voice quivering with urgency. "I need an ambulance on a code three. Officer shot in the head! I need an ambulance at the Chevron gas station located at 2600 General DeGaulle. Officer down! Officer down!" Despite his racing heart and the uncertainty surrounding his partner's condition, Officer Mitchell's training kicked in. He knew that accurately describing the assailants and their escape route was paramount if they were to have any hope of capturing these cold-blooded criminals.

Summoning an unexpected reservoir of composure, Officer Mitchell relayed detailed physical descriptions and clothing particulars of the suspects via his police radio, even as the traumatic scene played out before him. His voice wavered at times, the terror and exhaustion a persistent undertone in his transmission. "Suspects are armed and dangerous," he repeated urgently, his words a desperate plea for assistance. The NOPD radio system was plagued by static, rendering transmission unreliable. However, the lifeline came from the functioning radio system of the Jefferson Parish (JP) Police. Within mere blocks of the scene, Deputy Gregory Joerger and Deputy Darin Groas, both Jefferson Parish law enforcement officers, heard the distress call and swiftly responded. The call for backup resonated through their radios, propelling them to rush to Algiers.

The Jefferson Parish Sheriff's Office initiated an urgent call for assistance at 2600 General DeGaulle, reaching officers from Jefferson Parish, Gretna, and the Louisiana State Police assigned to the Westbank. Deputies Joerger and Groas arrived within minutes, armed with detailed descriptions provided by Officer Mitchell. The ambulance arrived in tandem with the two deputies, ready to tend to Officer Thomas. Amid the chaos, Officer Mitchell made his intentions clear—he would accompany his wounded partner to West Jefferson Hospital, determined to ensure his friend received the care he desperately needed.

With astonishing composure amidst the tumultuous scene, Officer Mitchell continued to provide vital details to Deputies Joerger and Groas, even as the EMT workers swiftly and carefully loaded his injured partner into the ambulance. He relayed the belief that he had managed to shoot one of the assailants—the tall figure standing at about 6'4"—and he further described the suspects' escape. "They can't be too far from here," Deputy Groas declared, determination etched on his face. "We'll find them." In a matter of moments, the ambulance sped away, carrying Officers Thomas and Mitchell towards West Jefferson Hospital. Simultaneously, the two Jefferson Parish Deputies embarked on a relentless pursuit of the fleeing suspects.

Unbeknownst to most NOPD officers, one of their own was in grave danger. Amid the flurry of static-filled radio transmissions and disjointed information, they grasped the gravity of the situation unfolding but remained uncertain about the specifics— "who, what, or where."

In the corridors of City Hall, Chief Riley and Captain Weathersby had just entered, seeking out Mayor Nagin, Homeland Security Director Terry Ebbert, and NOPD Superintendent Eddie Compass. An officer present at City Hall delivered grim news— a Fourth District officer had been shot at a Chevron station on General DeGaulle Drive. Shock and concern exchanged glances between Chief Riley and Captain Weathersby, their determination unwavering. "Let's go," Chief Riley's directive was succinct. Without hesitation, they pivoted, retracing their steps to the waiting SUV. Flashing lights and blaring sirens on a Code Three, granting them the right of way through red lights and intersections, propelled them towards the Greater New Orleans Bridge.

As their SUV raced across the Mississippi River Bridge, they overtook a convoy of Regional Transit Authority (RTA) buses ferrying evacuees westward. Sergeant Menzies, at the wheel, pointed out that NOPD RTA Officers were leading the caravan, escorting people out of the chaotic city. The sight momentarily diverted Chief Riley's attention before his focus snapped back to the dire situation at hand—the potential severity of the Fourth District incident loomed heavily. This was mentally and emotionally draining, a stark reminder of the exhaustion that had settled over him.

Meanwhile, in another part of the city, JP Deputies Joerger and Groas had tracked the three shooting suspects to a residential subdivision on Wabash Street. Deputy Groas pointed out a handgun discarded in the street, likely one of the suspects' weapons. The evidence suggested that it might have been the very weapon used in the assault on Officer Thomas. Leaving their vehicle behind, the two deputies advanced on foot, their vigilant eyes scanning the surroundings with guns at the ready. As they neared a cul-de-sac, Deputy Joerger spotted movement in the nearby bushes, approximately 50 feet away. He conveyed the discovery to Deputy Groas with a subtle nod of his head, cautious not to alert the potential suspects.

In the dim illumination cast by the streetlights, Deputy Groas affirmed the visual confirmation with a subtle nod. He discerned the outlines of the three men, crouched behind the bushes. Proceeding cautiously, the two deputies strategically positioned themselves around the bushes, using nearby cars and trees as cover, prepared for any potential violence that the suspects might initiate. Once they were strategically situated, Deputy Joerger issued a firm command, "Place your hands in the air and make no sudden moves!" Despite the darkness, the deputies observed the three sets of hands slowly ascending into the air. "Step out where we can see your hands!" Deputy Groas ordered. "Keep your hands raised!" added Joerger. Gradually, one by one, the three suspects rose to their feet, hands raised, and cautiously emerged from behind the bushes.

Shortly thereafter, three additional Jefferson Parish officers arrived at the scene, their guns aimed at the suspects. As the suspects emerged from the bushes, the deputies instructed them to turn around for a thorough visual inspection of their bodies and clothing, searching for any concealed weapons or objects. With their hands on the backs of their heads, the suspects were directed to kneel and space themselves apart. Deputy Joerger holstered his firearm and retrieved his taser, approaching the first suspect for handcuffing. Deputy Groas, along with another deputy, maintained a vigilant watch over the subdued suspects.

Working efficiently, Deputy Joerger handcuffed the first suspect, followed by another deputy who handcuffed Jamil Joyner in the same manner. With all three subjects now securely handcuffed and kneeling, another deputy carefully searched the bushes adjacent to a house at the center of the cul-de-sac, in search of discarded weapons. It was a tense moment as the officers remained vigilant and prepared for any potential threat.

However, Jamil Joyner, facing the inevitability of his arrest, grew agitated. In a fit of anger, he brazenly declared, "I killed one motherfucking officer, and I'll kill another!" His actions behind his back heightened concerns, prompting Deputies Joerger and Groas to cautiously approach. As they moved closer, they observed Joyner's attempt to retrieve an automatic weapon from the rear of his pants.

"Gun! Gun!" Deputy Joerger's urgent cry echoed through the scene. In unison, both deputies discharged their tasers. The shock of 20,000 volts surged through Joyner's body, causing him to convulse and struggle. Despite the excruciating voltage, Joyner clung onto the weapon, his determination to harm another officer unyielding. "Release the weapon now!" both deputies commanded, yet Joyner persisted in his defiance.

In a decisive action, both deputies activated their tasers once more, unleashing an additional 20,000 volts into Joyner's body. The cumulative effect of 40,000 volts incapacitated him, rendering any further aggression futile. Groaning from the ordeal, Joyner lay on the ground, his intent to harm thwarted. His accomplices, Sye Carter and Vincent Walker, looked on, each with their own reactions—Carter, despite his own injuries, appeared empathetic toward Joyner, while Walker seethed with anger.

Rushing to secure the situation, Deputy Joerger disarmed Joyner and ensured his immobilization. The confrontation left Joyner temporarily incapacitated, his threats now silenced. As he regained his awareness, the barrage of profanities resumed, with Joyner unleashing vitriol towards the officers.

"This night just keeps on giving," Deputy Joerger commented with a rueful tone, encapsulating the ongoing challenges they faced.

Upon reaching the Chevron shooting scene, Chief Riley and his team swiftly arrived, a mere twelve minutes after departing City Hall. The sight of Officer Thomas's blood-soaked surroundings was overwhelming, almost inconceivable that he could have survived such a brutal attack. A small contingent of State Police officers, along with Jefferson Parish Deputies and Gretna officers, were present. Chief Riley's immediate concern was Officer Mitchell's location, and he was informed that Mitchell had accompanied Officer Thomas in the ambulance, an understandable decision.

Soon, Jefferson Parish Deputies Joerger and Groas returned to the scene, having successfully tracked down and apprehended the three assailants just two blocks away. Deputy Joerger conveyed the details of their swift capture, explaining that the suspects had been hiding in nearby bushes. Two of them were en route to the Jefferson Parish Correctional Facility, while the wounded third suspect was being transported to the hospital. Chief Riley inquired about the circumstances of the suspect's shoulder wound, and Joerger explained that Officer Mitchell had fired at the suspect in response to the shooting of Officer Thomas. While the suspect was injured, his condition was not deemed life-threatening.

Reinforcements from the Fourth District NOPD soon arrived at the scene, greeted by the grim sight of Officer Thomas's blood staining the ground. The scene was disheartening, leading many to fear for Officer Thomas's survival. As Chief Riley observed the blood-stained crime scene, he offered a silent prayer, hoping that Officer Thomas's injuries were less severe than they appeared. NOPD spokesperson and Public Information Officer, Paul Accardo, arrived shortly afterward, ready to gather the necessary information to relay to the media.

Chief Riley directed Officer Accardo to confer with JP Deputies Joerger and Groas for a comprehensive account of the events leading up to the apprehension of the suspects. While Officer Accardo delved into the details, Chief Riley and some of his officers made their way to West Jefferson Hospital. There, they were met by an emergency room nurse who delivered the grim news that Officer Thomas was in critical condition and undergoing surgery. The wait for updates was agonizing, and despite their efforts, they couldn't locate Officer Mitchell at the hospital.

Recognizing the need for further action and acknowledging their powerlessness while waiting, Chief Riley decided to return to City Hall to contact Chief Compass, Mayor Nagin, and Director Ebbert. During the drive, Chief Riley's fatigued mind reflected on the latest catastrophe, replaying the details of Officer Thomas's shooting. He imagined the excruciating pain of the bullet's impact, visualizing Officer Thomas's final conscious moments as a rapid series of fragmented images.

In an instant, Chief Riley's mind raced through a series of vivid flashes, attempting to piece together Officer Thomas's last moments. He envisioned Thomas's ears catching the desperate cry of his partner's voice, shouting his name in alarm. Another image flashed, depicting Thomas's body hitting the ground with a sickening thud. Amid the chaos, he likely heard the frantic chorus of "Officer down! Officer down!" piercing the air. And then, a final mental snapshot emerged – Thomas witnessing a blinding burst of light before being engulfed by an overwhelming darkness, succumbing to the grip of unconsciousness. Chief Riley's imagination delved deep into the harrowing experience, grappling with the magnitude of the situation.

Chapter 18:
Resilience Amidst the Nightmare

Chief Riley, Captain Weathersby, and Sgt. Menzies continued their journey towards City Hall, the weight of recent events pressing heavily on Chief Riley's mind. It felt surreal, as if the world had been thrust into a nightmare that refused to relent. Officer Kevin Thomas, a fellow officer, who was popular and a highly respected officer now fought for his life in a hospital bed. The notion that this could all be a nightmarish fabrication flitted through Riley's mind, but the harsh truth remained unyielding. This was the grim reality they faced – a city ravaged by Katrina and its aftermath, and now a comrade fighting for survival.

City Hall loomed ahead, a mere few blocks away. Chief Riley's head throbbed relentlessly, each pulse a reminder of the mounting stress. The pain seemed to radiate from behind his eye, coursing through his skull. He battled through it, taking deep breaths to keep his discomfort hidden from his companions. Was it anxiety? The scorching heat, combined with the relentless humidity, only added to the physical strain. Riley's thoughts turned to his own well-being, a quiet prayer escaping his lips for protection and strength.

As they approached City Hall, a barrage of distressing images flooded Riley's mind. The haunting cries of citizens trapped in their attics echoed, followed by the grim sight of lifeless bodies adrift in floodwaters. The mental reel shifted abruptly, and Officer Thomas's wounded form took center stage. The memory of the blood-soaked crime scene intensified Riley's headache, driving home the harsh reality they all faced. This wasn't just a crisis – it was an ongoing nightmare, each chapter darker than the last.

The agonizing journey to City Hall felt like an eternity, a tumultuous mental odyssey that forced Chief Riley to confront the depths of his own resilience. Amid the chaos and despair, a spark of determination ignited within him. Greatness, he reminded himself, often emerged from the crucible of pressure. With his leadership training at the forefront of his mind, Riley tapped into the wisdom gained from recent courses at Boston University. The Senior Management Institute for Police had been a crucible of its own, a melting pot of law enforcement leaders from around the world, united by a shared commitment to effective leadership.

Riley's thoughts retraced the lessons learned, focusing on principles that transcended adversity. Leadership was about more than just navigating calm waters – it was about weathering storms and steering through uncharted territories. He remembered discussions on crisis management, policy development, and the profound impact of public perception. These insights converged as a beacon of guidance, reminding Chief Riley that even in the darkest moments, his leadership could be a source of strength.

The SUV came to a stop outside City Hall, and Chief Riley stepped out, his resolve renewed. He knew that while the challenges ahead were daunting, the capacity for leadership within him was unwavering. The nightmare they faced was all too real, but so was his determination to navigate it, draw upon his training, and lead his team through the turmoil that Hurricane Katrina had unleashed upon their city.

During his time at the forum, Chief Riley had absorbed valuable lessons from esteemed professors, some hailing from Harvard University's Kennedy School of Government. These courses had been a crucible of knowledge, demanding and enlightening in equal measure. Strangely enough, the wealth of insights he had gained during those sessions seemed tailor-made for the present crisis. Among these lessons, a particular course taught by Dr. Herman "Dutch" Leonard resonated deeply. This course delved into the leadership wisdom derived from the exploits of the Great Antarctic Explorer, Sir Ernest Shackleton – a beacon of exceptional leadership and crisis management.

Shackleton's story had become a template for effective leadership during unexpected crises. He had led a perilous expedition to the South Pole in 1914, steering a team of 28 through treacherous terrain. The mission took a dramatic turn when their ship became ensnared in ice off the Caird Coast. Enduring a grueling ten-month drift at sea, they faced unfathomable cold, scarcity of provisions, and severe weather. Shackleton's leadership came to the fore as he fostered camaraderie, loyalty, and unyielding determination among his crew. Chief Riley recalled a poignant quote from Shackleton that lingered in his mind: "When things get bad, who do you want to be?" Remarkably, Shackleton's leadership ensured the survival of his entire crew, all of whom eventually returned home safely after more than two years.

Suddenly, Sgt. Menzies' voice jolted Riley from his reverie. They had arrived at City Hall, the same location they had departed from merely hours ago. Lost in thought, Riley felt as though he had traversed the distance alone. Shaking off his mental haze, he looked up to see the familiar entrance of City Hall. His attention was drawn to the surroundings – the water levels had surged significantly since their earlier visit. What had been a two-foot depth now appeared to reach up to five feet. The Superdome and Hyatt Hotel, once on solid ground, now stood surrounded by the rising waters. Riley's concern shifted to the 20,000 citizens sheltered in the Superdome – how would they be evacuated from this watery quagmire?

Recalling Shackleton's tenacity and his own unshakable attachment to New Orleans, Riley's demeanor transformed. From the depths of despair, he summoned inspiration and resolve. This was an unrelenting nightmare, but Riley was determined to fight tooth and nail. He remembered his father's advice – a hardworking man who had instilled in him the grit to confront adversity head-on. As the words echoed in his mind, Riley made his stand: he would find a way to triumph.

Stepping out of the vehicle, Riley rallied his resolve. His bearing exuded confidence, strength, and unwavering determination. His mission was clear – he needed to convene with the city's key figures, Mayor Nagin, Chief Compass, and Director Ebbert. He would marshal his inner strength to lead his officers strategically through this crisis, an essential factor in prevailing over the onslaught of nature's fury. Emerging from the SUV, Riley and his team waded through the contaminated waters that engulfed the building. The grim reality of the city's ordeal was palpable, each step a reminder of the havoc Katrina had wreaked. The murky waters seemed to whisper tales of tragedy and loss; a haunting reminder of the lives claimed by the relentless hurricane.

In response to the devastating impact of Hurricane Katrina, City Hall's ninth floor had been transformed into a specialized Emergency Operations Center. Here, representatives from various vital agencies like the Coast Guard, National Guard, Criminal Sheriff's Office, Civil Sheriff's Office, Fire

Department, NOPD and Fire Department Dispatchers, City Attorney's Office, Mayor's Staff, and the Chief Administrative Officer's Staff collaborated to address the urgent needs of the city. As Chief Riley and his team entered, they noticed the presence of power and lighting, a clear result of a generator's operation. Yet, they were immediately struck by the oppressive heat inside – the sweltering atmosphere was reminiscent of the outside temperatures, making it hard to distinguish between sweat and moisture.

Stepping through the main floor, having navigated the waterlogged environment, the men were relieved to find a functional elevator. While Sgt. Andre Menzies and two other NOPD officers remained on the main floor, Chief Riley and Captain Weathersby rode the elevator to the ninth floor. The doors opened, revealing the hub of Emergency Operations – the CAO's conference room. Inside, Mayor Ray Nagin and Sally Forman, a member of the mayor's Public Information Office, were seated at a long conference table, laptops open before them. The visible signs of exhaustion etched on their faces spoke volumes, emblematic of the shared weariness they all bore.

Greeting them, Sally Forman's radiant smile stood in contrast to the fatigue that underscored their shared experience. Mayor Nagin welcomed Chief Riley and Captain Weathersby with his characteristic easy charm and collected demeanor, even in the face of adversity.

Chief Riley succinctly recounted the chain of events from the past 48 hours. He relayed the dire news of Officer Thomas, critically injured and fighting for his life at West Jefferson Hospital. He detailed the challenges faced in evacuating and rescuing stranded officers from various locations, such as the LSU Dental School, New Orleans East Methodist Hospital, and St. Claude General Hospital. Informing the mayor of rampant looting on Canal Street, he noted that Saks Fifth Avenue had been set ablaze, though New Orleans Fire Department had managed to contain the fire. Capt. Weathersby chimed in, sharing the ongoing predicament of at least 12 officers, along with their families, trapped on rooftops and in attics throughout the city.

Concluding his report, Chief Riley touched on a disheartening aspect – reports of some officers abandoning their posts. The mayor's astounded reaction mirrored the collective shock and sorrow over the unfolding tragedies within the city, juxtaposed against the disheartening revelation of officers failing in their duty to stand by the city during its darkest hour.

Amid the collective processing of the shared information, Colonel Terry Ebbert, the Director of Homeland Security, made his entrance, juggling a laptop and phone in his hands. After exchanging greetings with Chief Riley and Captain Weathersby, Ebbert conveyed the results of his recent meeting with the National Guard. The news of 10,000 National Guardsmen in position to assist, with requests for reinforcements from FEMA, brought a sense of relief. The focus shifted to the urgent need to evacuate the approximately 20,000 citizens seeking refuge in the Superdome, which had transformed into a chaotic environment due to rising temperatures and instability.

The prospect of federal assistance finally arriving was met with a mix of acknowledgment and hopefulness, with Mayor Nagin confirming President Bush's response and the appointment of General Russel L. Honoré to manage the Department of Defense's involvement. Amid the discussions, the absence of Superintendent Compass was noted, with Col. Ebbert revealing that Compass and his team were assessing the city for damage. However, the strained expression on Mayor Nagin's face in response to this news hinted at underlying tension, evident to Chief Riley.

Sgt. Menzies' entrance brought another unexpected development – reports of the Gretna Police Department blocking entry to black New Orleanians. The room's collective shock and disbelief was palpable, shared by all present. As Chief Riley vehemently expressed his disbelief and frustration, the unsettling news highlighted the breakdown of order and compassion within the crisis. It was later learned that St. Bernard Parish had blocked Claiborne Ave with crushed cars to limit access to New Orleanians and Jefferson Parish had done the same on Airline Highway.

Meanwhile, several miles north of City Hall, the New Orleans Regional Transit Authority (RTA) building on Canal Street was engulfed in chaos. The RTA staff, numbering close to 100, including family members, RTA Dispatchers, and New Orleans RTA Transit Officers, had taken shelter in the building before Katrina's impact. However, the situation had rapidly deteriorated. The water level had surged to five or six feet outside the building, flooding the main floor, while nonfunctional generators had robbed them of power and water for the past 24 hours. Inside, the stifling heat, exacerbated by the lack of cooling systems, added to the discomfort.

RTA Transit Officer Sherese Harper, along with her colleagues, had convened to strategize the preservation of lives in the building. With their critical role in evacuating citizens and maintaining transportation services, the RTA staff had hunkered down at their headquarters. As the storm ravaged the city, the employees stood as a determined and essential force, continuing their efforts even in the midst of their own dire circumstances.

Inside the dimly lit conference room, illuminated by scattered battery-powered flashlights and streaks of outside light filtering through open windows, a gathering of nine officers, predominantly RTA Transit Officers with dual NOPD assignments, formed an impromptu tactical unit. Their immediate mission: the safe evacuation of both RTA staff members and their families, now trapped within their Canal Street headquarters as encroaching floodwaters threatened their refuge.

Officer Sherese Harper provided a succinct yet dire overview of the situation. Power had been lost for over 24 hours, rendering restrooms inoperable, and rising floodwaters permeated the building's lower floors. RTA Officer William Huckabee echoed what was likely on everyone's mind, questioning what more could be done to persuade those inside to abandon their current shelter.

The facts were clear: there was no sustenance, no functional restrooms, and water levels surged ominously. Yet, as Officer Harper acknowledged, the sheer terror of drowning persisted, hampering the decision to evacuate. RTA Officer Merrell Merrick attempted to offer a glimmer of hope, pointing out the presence of ten large air mattresses that could accommodate several individuals at once. However, Officer Harper empathetically understood the psychological hurdle these individuals faced – the prospect of floating on these mattresses through waterlogged streets was terrifying, given the surrounding chaos and devastation.

Officer Harper candidly shared her understanding, validating the overwhelming fear gripping those considering this mode of escape. She illuminated the paradox – while the air mattresses provided potential salvation, they also symbolized a harrowing journey through submerged streets. RTA

Officer William Huckabee intervened, reinforcing their duty to ensure safety and providing a pragmatic perspective. The consensus crystallized around prioritizing women and children for evacuation, with non-swimmers relying on the air mattresses, each capable of accommodating multiple people, to navigate the watery expanse of Canal Street.

The plan was outlined: women and children first, non-swimmers would take to the air mattresses, and together they would forge a path to the Cleveland Street and Claiborne onramp, a gateway to the Westbank. The anticipated outcome was a convergence in a more hospitable environment, where nourishment and dry clothing awaited. As the strategy coalesced, Officer Harper couldn't help but marvel at the resilience displayed by her colleagues, each confronting the most challenging circumstances they had ever faced.

In a city battered by the unrelenting fury of Hurricane Katrina, their resolve stood as a testament to the unyielding spirit of the people of New Orleans. As they prepared to embark on this perilous journey, Officer Harper couldn't help but recall the events of the past few days, the heart-wrenching phone calls from colleagues and their family members – conversations that would forever echo in their hearts as testaments to the relentless turmoil Katrina had wrought.

They had already saved countless lives through their dedication to duty, their willingness to face danger head-on. As they ventured into the murky waters of Canal Street, they did so with the unwavering determination to overcome adversity, to save not only themselves but also the lives of those entrusted to their care. In the face of unfathomable challenges, they were a beacon of hope, a testament to the strength that resides within the human spirit when confronted with the darkest of times.

"Now all we have to do is convince the holdouts that evacuating is better than staying and drowning," Officer Merrick said. "I think the ever-deteriorating conditions here might be a great motivator," Sheresc Harper replied. Strategically dividing the staffers and their families into smaller groups, the RTA Officers began convincing them that it was imperative for them to evacuate the building for everyone's safety, and that they were likely to find food and dry clothes on the Westbank.

"The restroom facilities are inoperable at this point and because the power has been out for more than 24 hours, we've lost most of the food in the building," Officer Sherese Harper summarized for the other officers. "With no food, no restrooms, and water pouring into the building every hour, what more do we need to convince these people to leave?" RTA Officer William Huckabee asked. The other officers nodded in agreement with what he was saying.

"It's a slam dunk case to me too, but they're scared and many of them can't swim," Sherese responded. The officers had approached the staff about possible evacuation of the building but received a lot of resistance from those who were debilitatingly afraid of water and drowning.

"Listen, we have ten air mattresses here that can fit at least two or three people on it at once," RTA Officer Evan Merrick said slightly frustrated. "The people who can't swim have nothing to worry about."

"Lisa, I know you're afraid, but we can't leave you here," Sherese said compassionately. Even in the dim lights coming through the window of the small room where they had stepped aside to speak to Lisa, Sherese could see tears cascading down her face. "We need everybody to head to garage exit on the third level. We will exit from there," an officer could be heard announcing loudly.

"I just can't do it, Officer Harper," Lisa said with sad resignation. "Everything in my heart tells me that I'm going to drown out there. I can't do it." Sherese's heart broke as she watched this woman who'd been such a consistent and loyal coworker break down in tears. She was afraid and her spirit was broken.

"Lisa, listen," Sherese said softly. "We can't leave you here." "I've accepted it Sherese," she replied. "Just leave me behind." Sherese couldn't believe the resourceful and vibrant Regional Transit Authority dispatcher that she had come to know and care about over the years had been resigned to wait for the flood waters or dehydration to overtake her.

"Lisa we aren't leaving anyone behind," Sherese responded. "You have children to live for and an entire life ahead of you. It will not end like this." Lisa was quiet as tears continued to stream down her face. It wasn't just the fear that immobilized her and caused her to surrender her strength to survive. It was everything working in concert with her fear.

"The second floor has been compromised. We gotta get everybody out of here now," Sherese heard one of her RTA Officers say as he passed by the room looking at her pointedly. She could see through the doorway of the room that she and Lisa were in that the RTA officers had begun escorting staff members and their families toward the garage exit on level three.

"Because the building was surrounded by at least ten feet of water the idea was to float individuals from the garage level onto Canal Street and allow them to swim or float up the street where hopefully the water wasn't as high. Once they reached the on-ramp for the Westbank at Cleveland Avenue and Claiborne they would wait until everybody from RTA was there and as a collective unit they would make their way to the Westbank for drier territories, food, and clothing. It was a smart and strategic plan that might actually work," Sherese thought.

"Lisa in all the years that we've worked together, have I ever lied to you?" Sherese asked.

"Never," Lisa answered tearfully. "Today is no different. I can't promise that it will be easy, but I promise you that I will get you out of this building safely," Sherese said to her emphatically. Lisa said nothing but began to sob heavily as she shook her head yes, in affirmation.

Relieved, both women embraced each other as Lisa continued to sob. "Good, because my next move was to drag you out of here kicking and screaming. No way was I leaving you here," Sherese said with a laugh of relief. "I know," Lisa laughed nervously.

The evacuation from the RTA building had been anything but easy. The water around the building was at least ten feet which meant anyone that couldn't swim had to use the air mattresses to float past the 2800 block of Canal Street en route to the Westbank on-ramp. Even those who could swim had the challenging task of swimming two blocks up Canal Street, where the water level dropped to chest-level for the most of them – enabling them to slowly walk through the water.

Though Officer Harper's height was only 5 foot 4 inches, she had swum professionally throughout high school and college and therefore was proficient to assist others for the task ahead. As promised, her first order of business was to get RTA Dispatcher, Lisa Evanston out of the building to a safe space. She placed Lisa on one of the mattresses outside of the garage with four other staff members who couldn't swim and swam alongside the mattress as it made its way slowly up Canal Street. When she was convinced that Lisa's group was sufficiently making their way up Canal Street in the direction of the Westbank on-ramp, she turned around to continue helping with the building evacuation.

As she swam through the warm waters on Canal Street, Sherese could feel what felt like a slow burn on her back. Though she had sustained some minor cuts and bruises while aiding in the expedition of the RTA evacuation, she was also aware that there were likely many toxins in the waters from chemical and oil spills and even raw sewage. Oh, what she would have given from a fresh bath in clean water at this moment! Sherese continued to deftly slice through the water with the nimble agility and efficiency of a professional swimmer as she reentered the 2800 block of Canal Street.

She felt an object brush up against her arm distracting her attention from the RTA building, which was now less than one block ahead.

The RTA Officers had their work cut out for them during the two-hour evacuation from the RTA building. Those who were proficient swimmers played a vital role in pushing and guiding those on the air mattresses further up Canal Street. It took them another half hour of progress before the water level subsided enough for everyone to begin walking. The collective RTA group, officers, staff, and family members, finally reached the Westbank on-ramp, marking the beginning of their journey across the Crescent City Connection Bridge and into Gretna, Louisiana.

The less-than-five-mile journey was physically and mentally taxing due to the challenging conditions and uncertainties. The relentless heat and stifling humidity made it difficult to distinguish between physical fatigue and mental exhaustion as they trudged across the bridge. After over an hour of walking, they began their descent down the ramp into the Westbank, where the flooding was significantly less severe. This side of the riverbank provided a suitable location to organize a fleet of buses that could transport everyone to Baton Rouge after providing necessary supplies.

As they descended the off-ramp near the Westbank Expressway, close to a bus stop designated for Jefferson Parish buses, they noticed a fleet of six Gretna Police Department cars rapidly approaching. Richard Step, Officers William Eddington, and Sherese Harper moved to the front of the group, hoping for assistance from their fellow police colleagues. However, relief turned into shock and confusion when the Gretna Police officers emerged from their vehicles with guns drawn, aiming at Officer Harper and her companions. Officer Harper found herself staring down the barrel of a shotgun, held by one of the six Gretna Police officers who had their weapons trained on the group of evacuees.

Officer Harper was taken aback, her damp NOPD polo shirt and service weapon clearly identifying her as a police officer. Lt. Step and Officer Eddington were also in full police uniform, making their law enforcement affiliation evident. The tension was palpable, and Officer Harper sensed Lt. Step's' controlled fury. This wasn't the time for his usual confrontational demeanor; something more complicated was at play.

In the midst of surviving floodwaters, navigating the bridge, and undertaking a strenuous hike, the group had found themselves facing an unexpected threat from those who were supposed to protect and serve. Officer Harper pondered the motives behind Gretna PD's actions. Political agendas or racism could be underlying factors, or perhaps a combination of both. The situation was far from clear, and the uncertainty of the moment only added to the growing sense of unease.

Lt. Step stepped forward, engaging in a calm conversation with the Gretna PD's corresponding supervisor. Despite his apparent anger, he remained composed. The other Gretna officers holstered their weapons but maintained their blockade. The NOPD officers worked diligently to keep the RTA group calm and assured them that the situation would be resolved peacefully. "Unbelievable, isn't it?" Officer Eddington remarked to Officer Harper. "We have to be the voice of reason here, but if things were different, we know how this would play out," Officer Harper responded. "Their lack of empathy and common sense is astonishing," she added. The discussion between Lt. Step and the Gretna PD supervisor went on for about ten minutes before the standoff ended, and the RTA group was allowed to continue into the city.

Meanwhile, back at City Hall, Sgt. Menzies provided a status update to Chief Riley, Mayor Nagin, Captain Weathersby, and Colonel Ebbert. The tense situation involving Gretna PD and the group of black New Orleanians, which included RTA officers, staff, and their families, had been successfully resolved. Lt. Richard Step reported that the RTA building evacuation had been completed, and plans were in motion to transport many of them to Baton Rouge using RTA buses. A short while later, Sergeant Menzies requested a private conversation with Chief Riley. In another office, he informed the chief of a call he received from Mrs. Rockson, the executive assistant for billionaire oil tycoon Carson Jimmy Rockson.

Mrs. Rockson had urged Menzies to travel to Houston within the next 24 hours. Chief Riley found this request intriguing, given that he knew Mr. Rockson was currently at Baptist Medical Hospital in the flooded 2nd District, in need of a serious surgery. Chief Riley couldn't help but wonder if it made more sense for Menzies to stay in New Orleans in case Mr. Rockson required his assistance. "Does that sound logical to you, Menzies?" Chief Riley inquired. He knew that the 2nd District was heavily flooded, and the roads were likely impassable. Furthermore, Baptist Medical Hospital was surrounded by almost five feet of water.

"Chief, I'll be honest with you. Mrs. Rockson expressed deep concern for his well-being, and she's aware of the dire situation at the hospital," Menzies replied. "Given Mr. Rockson's connections and influence, it seems they have plans to get him to Houston," Menzies added frankly. Chief Riley silently acknowledged the accuracy of Menzies' assessment. Carson Rockson held significant political power and had ties to influential figures, including the White House. If anyone in New Orleans had the means to mobilize resources and navigate through various levels of government, it was Carson Jimmy Rockson and his family. No more words were exchanged between the two men. The unspoken understanding between them was clear, and Chief Riley gave a slight nod of acknowledgment. Some things didn't need to be spoken aloud; they were mutually understood.

Menzies exited the room, and Chief Riley remained lost in thought. The intricate web woven by Hurricane Katrina was becoming increasingly convoluted and hazardous with every ticking hour.

Chapter 19:
Alligators?

September 1, 2005

The oppressive heat and stifling humidity clung to Officer Glenn Madison as his fiberglass boat glided silently through the warm, murky waters of the Ninth Ward. The aftermath of Katrina had left streets in chaos, houses demolished, and trees ripped from their roots, leaving the city resembling a war zone. It felt like ages had passed since he joined Chief Riley in the daunting task of evacuating NOPD Headquarters, transporting staff and their families to safety at the Broad Street Overpass. Following his role in the evacuation, Chief Riley had directed Madison to assist a family in Carrollton, ferrying them to the New Orleans Convention Center for shelter.

Amidst the daily routine of deploying his boat to search for survivors and aid citizens, the staggering scale of the disaster was a constant reminder of their dire circumstances. Even in the days following the hurricane's onslaught, the true extent of its devastation was still unfolding. The Ninth Ward bore witness to heart-wrenching devastation and loss. Madison had recently come across a heartbreaking scene – a home where the lone survivor was a young boy, around six or seven years old. His mother and two other adults had managed to keep him safe atop a tall dresser on the second floor, above the floodwaters that inundated their home. The child's cries echoed through the silence, providing only fragments of the tragedy that had unfolded. Despite scouring the vicinity, Madison found no trace of the mother and the other adults, who had likely been swept away by the merciless flood.

In a surprising turn of events, the previous night, Madison had encountered fellow citizens engaged in rescue efforts. These ordinary individuals had mobilized their own motorized boats for rescue missions and had received fuel from Wildlife and Fisheries, who generously supported their compassionate efforts. These kind-hearted residents highlighted areas where Madison could refuel if needed, a gesture that reinforced his faith in the goodness of his fellow New Orleanians. Madison navigated his boat onto Arts Street, guided by information that families were stranded and awaiting help. As he approached, he spotted figures atop a rooftop, frantically waving a white sheet. The time had come for another rescue.

Vanessa Rowland and her ten-year-old son, Bobby, had been trapped in their powerless home on Painters Street since the hurricane hit. Relief finally arrived in the form of a Good Samaritan, who arrived with a boat to transport them to the safety of the Convention Center. "Thank you so much," Vanessa expressed, her gratitude evident as she stood on her porch, water up to her waist, her street transformed into a watery expanse. The Good Samaritan, a middle-aged white man named Blake, paddled towards them. He had been tirelessly navigating the inundated street, calling out for those in need. For Vanessa, Blake was an answered prayer, a savior who had come to their aid after days of isolation, lacking power and sustenance. Vanessa observed as Blake drew closer, his boat navigating the murky waters. His age was hard to pinpoint amidst the collective disarray – everyone appeared disheveled, bearing the signs of days without proper grooming or care.

"Bobby, stay inside until I come get you," Vanessa called out to her son, who remained on the dry second floor. "Okay," Bobby responded from upstairs. After days of flooding, the sight of a man paddling a boat towards her house on the submerged street still felt surreal. Most of the block had evacuated, but a few residents, like Vanessa and Bobby, had stayed behind due to financial constraints or an attempt to weather the storm. His absent father and distant extended family left Vanessa and Bobby alone, relying on a bathtub filled with water to sustain them for the past 48 hours. However, the stifling heat and humidity inside the house, coupled with the lack of power, made their situation increasingly dire. Nights were pitch black, punctuated by distant gunfire and unrest. Despite the absence of valuable possessions, Vanessa knew that her vulnerability as a single mother made them potential targets for looters and troublemakers.

As Blake's boat approached Vanessa's home, he stowed the oars and waded through the chest-high water, unable to navigate the narrow space directly to the porch. "Ma'am, I'll help you and your son onto the boat from your porch," he offered as he sloshed through the water. "Thank you so much, sir," Vanessa expressed her gratitude. "We'll need to lift or carry my son into the boat. He can't swim, and the water is too high for him to walk in." "That's fine," Blake reassured her. "I'll assist you first, and then I'll carry him to the boat."

"Bobby! Come on down, baby!" Vanessa called up to her son. Blake reached Vanessa just as Bobby appeared at the doorway. "Hi," Blake greeted Bobby in a soothing tone. "I'm here to help you and your mom get to a safe, dry place with power." Bobby exchanged nervous glances between his mother and Blake. Although he was afraid of the water, he trusted his mother's judgment and found comfort in her assurance. Vanessa addressed Bobby, explaining the plan: "So, Bobby, Mr. Blake will help me onto the boat first and then come back for you, so you won't be alone in the boat. I'll be watching you the whole time. You'll be okay."

"Yes, ma'am," Bobby replied, his voice tinged with nervousness but also obedience. "Stay right here," Vanessa instructed Bobby as she and Blake waded into the murky water. "Mr. Blake will be right back for you." The journey from the porch to the boat, though short, felt interminable to Vanessa. The warm, murky water made her uneasy, the thought of countless pathogens lurking in the water unsettling her mind. As much as she understood the practicality of leaving Bobby on the porch, the idea of being separated from him gnawed at her. She watched as Blake returned to her house, his progress slow and deliberate, Bobby's nervous eyes shifting between them.

"Alright, baby. You don't have to be afraid," Vanessa reassured Bobby. However, her words were cut short as she noticed a murky brown silhouette moving towards Blake from beneath the water.

Her mind raced to comprehend the swift-moving silhouette, even though a part of her refused to believe it. Fear gripped her soul, leaving her momentarily voiceless, a paralysis that proved fatal. In her helpless gaze, a monstrous twenty-foot alligator leaped from the water, jaws wide open, revealing rows of menacing teeth. Blake, caught off guard, never stood a chance. The alligator's jaws clamped around his right arm and upper torso, and he let out a piercing scream of shock, disbelief, and agony as the beast thrashed violently. Vanessa's voice returned to her, a heart-wrenching scream escaping her lips, "NOOOOO!!!!!!" Her desperate plea was directed both at Blake and her son Bobby.

"BOBBY, get back inside and close the door!" she shrieked, her maternal instinct overriding her own terror. Bobby hesitated for a moment, eyes fixed on the nightmarish scene before him, until his mother's urgency snapped him into action. He darted inside the house, slamming the door shut behind him.

"Blake!!!" Vanessa's voice trembled with fear and desperation as she called out to him. Blake's agonized screams filled the air, mingling with the water and the monstrous struggle unfolding before her. Vanessa could only watch in helpless horror as the alligator, driven by primal instinct, dragged Blake beneath the surface, his screams silenced by the murky water. The water's surface calmed, leaving Vanessa in a nightmarish silence, the remnants of the horrifying scene playing out before her eyes.

For what felt like an eternity, Vanessa stood paralyzed, her gaze fixated on the water, Blake's blood intermingling with the surrounding liquid, a haunting testament to the tragedy that had just unfolded. The silence finally snapped her out of her shock, a chilling reminder of her vulnerability. Panic surged through her veins as she realized that she was now stranded in a small boat, far from her porch, and potentially within the sights of the same alligator that had claimed Blake's life. With no way to bring the boat closer to safety, she faced a harrowing choice: remain in the boat or wade through the treacherous waters towards her home.

Almost half an hour later, the sound of Brandon Gaynor's boat echoed through the air as he and his brother Robert navigated Painters Street. Despite the devastation of Katrina, the brothers had stayed behind to protect their homes and assist in rescues. As they approached the scene, the distant sound of a woman's voice pleading for help caught Brandon's attention. Guiding his boat closer, he and his brother realized that a woman was stranded in a small boat, her voice conveying a mix of relief and urgency. "I think there's someone in trouble up ahead," Brandon alerted Robert, directing his attention towards the small vessel. Without hesitation, the brothers steered their boats towards the distressed woman, their sense of duty propelling them forward. As they drew closer, the woman's grateful expression told them that their arrival offered a glimmer of hope amidst the chaos.

"Ma'am, is everything okay?" Brandon's voice held a mix of concern and compassion as he brought his boat to a stop alongside Vanessa's. She introduced herself as Vanessa Rowland, her tearful account describing the tragic encounter with the alligator that had taken the life of their rescuer. Her son, Bobby, remained inside their home, terrified and alone. Robert scanned the area for any signs of the man who had been attacked but found nothing – as if he had simply vanished. Despite the absence of physical evidence, Vanessa's words painted a chilling picture of the ordeal. Brandon assured her, "We'll bring you and your son to safety in our boat, but we'll need your help to reassure him." Brandon picked up his shotgun, as he gazed into the water rotating 360 degrees, his head was on a swivel as he looked for the alligator or signs of any other alligators possibly lurking nearby.

"Did he witness what happened?" Robert inquired; his voice empathetic.

"Yes," Vanessa replied, her tears continuing to flow. "I don't think either of us will ever forget what we saw." The weight of the traumatic experience hung heavily in the air.

"We're deeply sorry for what happened, ma'am. But we need you to help him trust us. Can you do that?" Brandon asked, seeking her commitment to ease Bobby's fear.

"Yes," Vanessa responded, her voice determined. With her help, they hoped to convince Bobby to join them.

Calling out to her son, Vanessa's pleas went unanswered – Bobby was hesitant to open the door. The situation required them to bring him out. "I'll go get him and bring him to the boat," Brandon declared, addressing both Vanessa and his brother. "Just keep an eye out, Robert. If anything seems off, shoot first and ask questions later." Robert nodded in agreement, a reassuring gesture accompanied by the double barrel shotgun and his eyes fixated on the water. Assisting Vanessa into his boat, Robert positioned her to receive her son once they brought him out. Meanwhile, Brandon prepared himself mentally for the task at hand – retrieving a frightened child from their home in the aftermath of a horrific incident.

Stepping down into the chest-deep water, Brandon could feel the adrenaline coursing through his veins. He only had about a 20-foot walk to the porch but the fear of a twenty-foot alligator began to creep into his mind with each step. He knew that his brother had his back, but the danger posed by a potentially submerged aggressive alligator kept him on high alert. The slow and deliberate steps he took were driven by the urgency of reuniting a scared child with his mother. Robert's voice offered reassurance from the boat, affirming his support and vigilance.

Finally reaching Vanessa's porch, Brandon knocked gently on the door. After some coaxing from his mother, Bobby cautiously opened the door. "I'm going to bring you to your mom, alright? You'll be safe, and my brother and I will make sure the alligator won't harm you," Brandon spoke with conviction, hoping to convey a sense of security.

With Bobby securely on his back, Brandon looked into the boy's mother's eyes and saw a combination of love and terror as she trembles watching Brandon entering the water. Bobby felt an ounce of security as he watched his brother's eye's heavily focused with an obsessed look into the water in search of any strange movement as he navigated the water back towards the boats. The added responsibility of carrying the young boy heightened his awareness of potential threats. Gazing into the worried eyes of Bobby's mother, he felt a deep sense of duty – a determination to protect the child at all costs. The return journey felt quicker, driven by the urgency of the situation. Reaching the boats without incident, Brandon handed Bobby over to his mother's waiting arms, her tears of relief and gratitude pouring out.

As they embraced, Brandon let out a sigh of relief. The immediate crisis was averted, but the lingering concern remained – if one aggressive alligator was lurking nearby, it was possible that others were as well. The havoc wrought by Katrina still loomed over New Orleans, a reminder of the ongoing challenges they faced.

Across town, NOPD Superintendent Eddie Compass gazed down at the grim tableau of devastation that stretched before him, visible through the window of the neighboring Jefferson Parish Sheriff's Office helicopter in which he was flying. The helicopter carried a small team, including Lieutenant Marlon Defillo, and two other sheriff deputies as they conducted observational operations over parts of the Ninth Ward. Below them, a haunting landscape of submerged homes and buildings sprawled out. The once-famil-iar streets had disappeared beneath the rising waters. Amidst the destruction, there were pockets where the flooding was less severe, yet the overwhelming majority of the area was engulfed, the rooftops of surviving structures barely peeking above the waterline. In certain blocks, the ferocious hurricane winds had torn roofs from buildings or reduced them to ruins.

A grim reality had materialized, a true nightmare unfurling before their eyes. The Coast Guard's helicopters were a beacon of hope in this dystopian scene, as they observed police and civilians in their boats below tirelessly rescuing stranded citizens from rooftops in neighborhoods like the Ninth Ward, a community that had been ravaged by the relentless forces of Hurri-cane Katrina.

As the helicopter hovered over a neighborhood, I can only imagine Chief Compass's thoughts were a maelstrom of anguish. The sight of every roof on a whole block ripped off by Katrina's furious winds weighed heavily on his heart. How many lives were disrupted? How many families had chosen to brave the storm, hoping against hope for survival within those now-wa-terlogged homes? The homes that once symbolized safety and comfort were now transformed into potential watery graves. The weight of these uncer-tainties pressed on Chief Compass's mind, adding to the already immense burden of managing this disaster.

Compounding his stress was the concern for his pregnant wife, Arlene, and their three-year-old daughter, who had evacuated to Denham Springs at the first whisper of danger. Arlene's safety was paramount, especially con-sidering her advanced pregnancy, but the thought of being separated from his family during such a crucial time was deeply unsettling for Compass. He could practically feel the tension tighten around his thoughts as he consid-ered the distance between them and the impending birth of their child. The dichotomy of his duty to the city and his yearning for the safety of his family tugged at him relentlessly.

"Chief, any word from Mayor Nagin today?" a helicopter crew member asked: the question interrupted Compass's introspection. The chief's face momentarily registered a blank expression, revealing an underlying tension. Unbeknownst to the public, the relationship between Eddie Compass and Mayor Nagin was far from harmonious. Even before Hurricane Katrina, their differing tactics and personal dynamics had strained their interactions. The unprecedented challenges posed by the disaster only intensified their existing discord. Chief Compass couldn't help but feel that Nagin was pushing for his departure from the position.

With a heavy sigh, Chief Compass responded to crew member's inquiry, his voice carrying the weight of both professional and personal burdens. "No, not today. But we have a lot more pressing matters to attend to right now." The urgency of their mission refocused his thoughts, momentarily setting aside the complex web of relationships and emotions that entangled him amidst the chaos of Katrina's aftermath.

"No, I haven't heard from him today," Chief Compass responded, his voice carrying a sense of urgency. "We should reach out and inform him about the situation in the Ninth Ward." "I've been receiving reports of alligator attacks in the Ninth Ward," a crew member added, his tone grave. "There are multiple accounts of these attacks, and it's believed that one man may have been fatally wounded." An overwhelming sense of dread gripped Chief Compass, churning his stomach. "What in the world?" he exclaimed; the shock evident in his voice. "SOD has already rescued a woman who witnessed a man being attacked and consumed by an alligator," Charbonnet informed him. Before Compass could react, the pilot interjected. They watched several Coast Guardsmen's helicopter team's extraction process which involved lowering a ladder and baskets from the helicopter to reach stranded residents on rooftops. They would guide the individuals onto the helicopter, which would then transport them to a designated drop-off point, facilitating their journey to the Convention Center for further evacuation.

As the helicopter continued its five-thousand-foot observation, Chief Compass peered out of the window, surveying the Ninth Ward below. The devastation was overwhelming—homes reduced to ruins, neighborhoods reshaped by the unforgiving forces of nature. His attention was drawn to a haunting sight: more than a dozen lifeless bodies floating face down in the floodwaters of a neighborhood they passed over. Their genders were indistinguishable at this distance, but the tragic reality was undeniable—all the individuals, still clothed, adrift in the water that had consumed their community. These were lives lost, families torn apart. The image weighed heavily on Compass's heart, a poignant reminder of the unrelenting toll of the disaster. The Chief's grip tightened on the edge of his seat as he struggled to suppress the anguish welling up inside him. For each person they observed, it seemed that the floodwaters claimed even more lives. The cycle of loss and destruction was relentless. In the midst of this chaos, his thoughts turned once again to his wife, Arlene, and their impending child. Their well-being remained his driving force, urging him to persevere through the ongoing turmoil.

Under the scorching ninety-degree heat, sixty-six-year-old Millie Reed sought refuge on the rooftop of her Ninth Ward home. Below her, floodwaters reached the second floor, forcing her to the highest point they could reach. The relentless sun beat down on her, exacerbating her exhaustion and hunger. Yet, it was the terror of recent events that weighed most heavily on their minds. Her tears soaking into Millie's embrace. The memory of what she had witnessed just moments ago was etched in her mind, a source of unshakeable fear. Not daring to look down, she was haunted by the vision of the floodwaters tainted with blood. Millie could still see the remnants of the man who had met a gruesome fate, torn apart by the jaws of two monstrous alligators. The man had been a stranger to her, a familiar face in the neighborhood, but now reduced to pieces in the water. The waters below prevented any attempt to reach safety or to assist him. Desperate and frightened, the man had sought refuge on top of submerged vehicles, only to meet his tragic end.

For over twenty minutes, Millie had been observing the man's progress up their flooded street. Millie's attention sharpened when she spotted two alligators advancing toward the man just as he slipped back into the water, attempting to swim further up the block. Her mind struggled to reconcile the reality before her with the surreal image one might expect from a nature documentary. Acting swiftly, she urgently called out to the man, warning him of the approaching danger. The heart-wrenching part was witnessing the raw terror that overtook the man's face as he comprehended the peril closing in on him. His desperate cries filled the air as he fought to reach safety, grappling with a stranded van in a futile attempt to escape the relentless predators. Tragically, the alligators proved swifter, latching onto his legs, and dragging him beneath the water's surface. Millie's scream pierced the air, as she witnessed the horrifying scene below. The sight induced hysterical sobs, as the anguish gripped Millie.

Millie's arms enveloped herself as she shook with terror from the nightmarish reality unfolding below. Powerless, she bore witness as the alligators mercilessly tore apart the man's body, a grotesque spectacle of violence and brutality. His anguished cries echoed briefly before being silenced by the grisly fate that awaited him. The ghastly tableau etched itself into Millie's mind, triggering waves of nausea that manifested in dry heaves, her body recoiling from the unimaginable horror. In her grief and terror, Millie, finding no solace remained terrified for the next two hours.

Over two hours later, Millie's weary eyes spotted two small boats navigating the waters of her street. Relief surged within her, albeit tinged with cautious apprehension. The recent deluge of disasters had left her wary of harboring hope. Still, she grabbed the white sheet she had brought to the rooftop, frantically waving it to catch the attention of the approaching boats. Randolph and Phillip, dress in hunting attire and wearing coon skin hats, utilizing their personal boats and with a hunting dog were conducting rescue operations, they were first to arrive from the Cajun Navy and a hunting dog, immediately spotted Millie's signal. They adjusted their course to reach her location, their unwavering commitment to aiding their fellow citizens evident.

During a refueling stop with Wildlife and Fisheries, Randolph and Phillip had been informed about alligators being spotted in the Ninth Ward and reports of partially eaten bodies being recovered.. This knowledge heightened their vigilance but did not deter their mission. Upon arriving at Millie's home, she recounted the harrowing encounter with the alligators, leaving them to contemplate whether the same predator might be responsible for the recent reported attacks. With determination, Randolph and Phillip worked together to assist Millie off the rooftop and onto Phillip's boat. Millie breathed a sigh of relief as the immediate threat of alligators seemed to have receded, her gratitude for their rescuers overwhelming her.

On the other side of the town in uptown New Orleans, SWAT Officers LeJon Roberts, Darrel Shuerman, Savadore Castelon, and Valintine Emery navigated through the waters of the Calliope Housing Development, off of South Galvez Street in uptown New Orleans, accompanied by Wildlife and

Fisheries officers. Their mission was clear: scour the area around I-610 and St. Bernard Avenue and then head further uptown to the Broadmoor area for survivors and those in need. An almost imperceptible bumping sound and faint voices drew their attention to a submerged two-story home. Cutting their engines, they followed the sounds until they reached the rooftop of the house.

The family inside cried out for help, revealing their dire circumstances. The officers quickly went into action, utilizing hammers, crowbars, and saws to breach the roof. The intense heat and dehydration had taken a toll on the trapped family of seven, including an elderly woman and two children. After twenty minutes of teamwork, a hole was opened in the roof, and the officers carefully lifted the children out of the attic. The focus then turned to the elderly woman, who remained unresponsive and slumped over on a stack of boxes. Concerned, Sergeant Roberts and his team inquired about her condition, determined to provide the necessary medical assistance.

"She's okay," the woman replied. "She's just been resting." Sergeant Roberts felt a sinking sensation in his gut upon hearing her words. "We'll prioritize getting all of you out first, and then we'll need to assess your mother," he informed them. Initially met with resistance, the woman and two other adults eventually agreed. Within five minutes, everyone except two adults remained on the boat, opting to wait on the rooftop while Officer Roberts and a Wildlife and Fisheries officer went to assess the mother in the attic. As Sergeant Roberts touched her, he immediately recognized the truth – her skin was cold, and rigor mortis had set in. He knew the family likely had an inkling, but denial held them. "I'm deeply sorry," he uttered. "Your mother didn't survive." Devastated, the woman collapsed to her knees on the rooftop, her cries echoing in the air. The man's pacing and disbelief underscored the tragedy. He called out to his mother in the attic, attempting to reach her, only to be stopped by the officers. Once they had regained composure, Sergeant Roberts broke the news that they would have to leave her there. Again, protests erupted from the grieving family members. It was a painful decision, but their focus was on ensuring the safety and well-being of the living. Retrieval for those who didn't make it was a task for another time. It took another twenty minutes of patient reassurance for the family to accept the reality and reluctantly leave their matriarch behind, deceased in the attic. As the woman and her brother finally boarded the boat, she continued to utter broken sobs, repeating, "That's my mother. That's my mother." With everyone secured and ready to depart for safe shelter, Sergeant Roberts used a spray paint can to mark "1/D" on the rooftop, a grim indicator of the body left behind. He cast one last glance at the roof before descending into his boat. In his mind, Katrina epitomized heartlessness.

As they guided their boat another sixty feet, a mother and two children were on a balcony waving and pleading for help. They navigated the ship to the edge of the second-floor balcony, which was difficult because the water was at least four feet below the balcony. The lady, her 3-year-old daughter, and a baby in an infant car seat appeared disheveled, with a look of desperation and exasperation coloring her face. Sergeant Roberts and his team assisted the 3-year-old boy into the boat first. The mother desperately clung to the baby in the car seat and refused to let go. The officers assisted the female into the boat not knowing the baby was not strapped into the car seat. As she stepped onto the boat, the boat leaned one way, and the mother struggled to maintain her balance and hold on to the baby at the same time. The boat rocked again, and the mother unintentionally leaned, trying to balance herself, and the baby slid out of the car seat and into Katrina's murky, dirty waters.

The mother yelled with fear and anguish and attempted to go overboard. One officer grabbed her and stopped her as the entire boat almost flipped over. They watch in horror as the three months old baby began to sink into the water. Officer Sheurman immediately removed his gun belt and dove into the water, following the baby as she sank deeper into the nasty water. The officer located the baby within twenty seconds and returned to the surface with the baby. The officer handed the baby to the officers on the boat, and another officer immediately performed CPR, reviving the baby. The mother, who was hysterical, quickly exhaled with relief and repeatedly thanked the officers. When that almost catastrophe was over, the officers with a can of spray paint painted onto the balcony door the letters 3/R/ 0/B, indicating three recovered and zero bodies.

Chapter 20:
Nagin's Cry for Help

In the midst of citizens falling prey to alligators, perishing in attics, looting rampant across the city, officers abandoning their posts, and the federal government conspicuous by its absence, the deluge of Katrina raged on relentlessly.

As the NOPD grappled with an onslaught of tragedies, ranging from racism and classism to sheer misery, pain, and both acts of cowardice and heroism, they remained unaware of the desperate plea Mayor Ray Nagin was making for his drowning and devastated city. The damage wrought by Hurricane Katrina was beyond human imagination, exceeding the capacity of any preparedness measures.

Mayor Nagin, who had become increasingly desperate and exhausted, found himself on the Garland Robinette Radio Talk/News Show hosted by the long-time, revered news anchor turned radio talk show host. His frustration, coupled with the perceived lack of support from the Federal government, boiled over during the broadcast.

Nagin, in a voice thick with exasperation, articulated his urgent needs, saying, "I need troops, I need 500 buses." When informed about the prospect of school bus drivers being sent, he incredulously replied, "Are you kidding me? This is a national disaster." His frustration grew with each word, as he implored, "Get every Greyhound Bus line in the country down here, get them to New Orleans."

He highlighted the fact that rampant looting had taken hold because the majority of available resources had been directed towards the monumental task of rescuing thousands of people stranded in attics and, in some cases, elderly individuals found clinging to life in dire conditions.

Nagin expressed his deep dissatisfaction with the government's response, noting that they had made a single visit to the area two days after the catastrophic event, accompanied by a multitude of media personnel. The absence of government officials, resources, and troops in the aftermath of America's greatest disaster left him profoundly dismayed.

Even Garland Robinette, a seasoned television anchor, could not contain his emotions, breaking down in tears as he reflected on Mayor Ray Nagin's impassioned tirade. The collective frustration and disbelief among the people of New Orleans, including parish presidents and the Governor, were palpable due to the slow response of the Federal government.

While Chief Riley remained oblivious to the radio broadcast and Nagin's frustration, rumors of the mayor's outburst began to circulate within the police department. As the story spread, many officers perceived it as if the mayor had forcefully voiced his frustrations, perhaps even cursing out the President of the United States, for the failure to dispatch the anticipated and much-needed federal support.

Chapter 21:
Algiers Point Community

Racist Whites murder Black Citizens

On September 1, a crucial roll call was conducted, marking the first gathering of officers since the devastating landfall of Hurricane Katrina. This roll call carried immense significance, functioning as a lifeline of communication in the midst of chaos. With communication networks obliterated and officers scattered throughout the city, it was imperative to gauge the situation and account for personnel. The calls received on August 29, the day Katrina unleashed its fury on New Orleans, had already painted a grim picture of citizens trapped and lives lost.

Chief Riley recognized the urgency of assessing the status of each police district and unit. In the absence of functioning cell phones or radio communication, this roll call emerged as the most effective means of coordination. The gathering drew a mix of high-ranking officers representing various districts and units across the city, but it was notable that many other officers disregarded formal protocols and attended. The situation was too dire to wait for official summons; they craved information, desperately needed to comprehend the unfolding crisis.

Convening under the shelter of the Harrah's Casino overhang, officers waited with a blend of hope and apprehension for Superintendent Compass to arrive. The Superintendent's presence was pivotal, despite the absence of communication since the eve of Katrina's arrival. His leadership was essential in this critical hour, a beacon of guidance amidst the tumultuous sea of uncertainty.

In the midst of the gathering anticipation, patience emerged as an essential virtue, given the extraordinary challenges of traveling downtown. The journey to this rendezvous was anything but ordinary. Commanders embarked on a multi-step odyssey involving boats, cars, and more boats. Some persevered through blocks of chest-high water, braving an arduous path. As officers steadily congregated, forming a growing assembly, Chief Riley moved among them, personally connecting with each one. He extended handshakes, inquiring about their well-being and the safety of their families. This genuine concern mirrored the worry he held for his own loved ones.

Even before the formal meeting commenced, the murmurs of officers circulated through the air, filled with a mixture of frustration and determination. Conversations unveiled a stark contrast in perspectives. Some voices carried tones of exasperation, threatening the possibility of departure. Simultaneously, others expressed an urgent need for resources, eagerly questioning the whereabouts of FEMA and the military, yearning for the tools to execute their duties effectively.

The undercurrent of restlessness was palpable even before the meeting's initiation. Several officers approached Chief Riley, seeking permission to exit the situation. In response, Chief Riley delivered a resolute message: unity was paramount. In these dire times, they were all that the citizens of New Orleans had, a shared responsibility that couldn't be forsaken. He spoke with fervor, empathy, and comprehension, understanding their desire while offering a dose of reality. He made it clear that leaving was not an option, at least for the foreseeable future, which he knew would likely span several weeks. The expressions of disappointment were evident, with one female officer audibly expressing her intention to depart in frustrated resignation. Captain Weathersby moved to intervene, but Chief Riley calmly advised against it, understanding the depth of emotions in this high-stress moment. Sometimes, allowing an outlet for such sentiments was the best course of action.

While conversing with Captain Weatherby by my side, two young officers from the Fourth District, one white and the other black, approached me with a request to speak. Chief Riley gave them a reassuring nod, encouraging them to share their concerns. Despite their evident nerves, their words were forthright. These clean-cut, unfamiliar faces had something urgent to communicate. It was a moment that Chief Riley had not anticipated.

With a blend of candor and trepidation, the officers recounted an unsettling discovery they had made in the Algiers Point community. Chief Riley's interest was piqued as he probed deeper, seeking clarity. What unfolded was an alarming picture: barricades erected by residents, vehicles strategically positioned to seal off the streets entering their neighborhoods, and armed individuals brandishing shotguns, assault rifles, and pistols. The young officers relayed their observations matter-of-factly, a stark contrast to the disturbing scene they had encountered.

Chief Riley's inquiry led to a critical revelation. The day prior, these two officers had encountered an incident where two black men sought refuge and sustenance at the Algiers Ferry Landing. Their intention was simple – to access food and water. However, their encounter took a distressing turn when confronted by armed white men. In chilling detail, the officers recounted the ominous warnings issued to the black men, laced with threats of violence. It was a harrowing encounter, with the white men menacingly discharging a shotgun into the air. The message was unmistakably clear: black people were not welcome, and dire consequences awaited if they ventured any closer.

Driven by a sense of duty, the officers ventured into Algiers Point to validate the claims. Their investigation painted a stark reality. The entrances to Algiers Point were fortified with vehicular blockades, cars and trucks positioned deliberately to obstruct access. Trees felled purposefully added an extra layer of obstruction. Algiers Point had become a fortress, a segregated enclave where the message was unmistakable: outsiders, particularly those of a different race, were not only unwanted but were met with hostility.

The officers' account painted a chilling portrait of a heavily armed and menacing group of at least fifteen white men. Upon Chief Riley's inquiry into their numbers, interjected with a fervent expletive, expressing his outrage. The officers shared that the group was not only armed but also brazenly displayed a rebel flag from a car window. Chief Riley pressed for further details, specifically whether they had reported the incident to their commander. Their response indicated that they had informed their sergeant the previous night, citing a stark reality: they were outmatched, outgunned and outnumbered.

Navigating the precarious circumstances, the officers chose caution over confrontation due to the absence of communication and backup. Chief Riley interjected, commending their judicious decision-making. He affirmed that their actions were astute given the circumstances, a validation that visibly lifted their spirits. Bolstered by Chief Riley's support, the officers continued, revealing another disconcerting piece of information: Gretna Police Department was obstructing New Orleanians from entering Gretna, particularly targeting black individuals. Chief Riley acknowledged this concern, assuring them that the matter would be addressed.

A subsequent officer stepped forward, offering his account. He disclosed that he had driven through Algiers Point in a marked car, investigating reports of armed white individuals. His discovery was nothing short of horrifying – two black men lay lifeless on the ground. One had suffered a gruesome head wound, while the other appeared to have been shot in the back. Attempting to call for backup proved futile due to the radio system's overwhelming congestion. He shared the locations of the bodies with Chief Riley's staff.

Gretna, a suburb of Jefferson Parish adjacent to Algiers in New Orleans, was becoming a hotbed of disturbing incidents. Captain Weathersby's solemn expression mirrored Chief Riley's growing concern. The situation had spiraled into chaos. Chief Riley expressed gratitude for the officers' revelations and requested that they inform their commander to contact him urgently. Promising that decisive action would be taken to address the disturbing reports of racism and violence, Chief Riley resolved to quell the rising tide of unrest.

However, the unsettling revelations were far from over. Another officer stepped forward, sharing a shocking account involving three white officers, including a certain Henninger, who were seen entering a black Cadillac truck. One of them was armed with a high-powered assault rifle. The chilling overheard comment, "it was time to hunt some black people," reverberated in the air, eliciting a mix of shock and anger. Chief Riley demanded clarification – was it a fact or a mere rumor? The officer affirmed that he had witnessed this himself near the First District Station on South Rampart Street. The gravity of the situation was undeniable, leaving Chief Riley both outwardly composed and inwardly infuriated.

Riley's urgency was palpable as he fired off a rapid succession of questions: "Where did you see them? What type of truck? What color was the car? Were they in NOPD uniforms?" The officer, hailing from the 4th District in Algiers, provided details, recounting that the officers had uniform shirts and blue jeans, riding in a black Cadillac pickup truck. Their location had been Rampart Street, near the Saenger Theater. The officer overheard one of them being referred to as Finniger or Henniger, a name that struck a chord with Riley, who recollected Officer Finger from his earlier years. Fueled by a mix of concern and suspicion, Riley promptly contacted Public Integrity to initiate an immediate investigation into these concerning allegations.

Public Integrity swung into action, mobilizing to locate and apprehend the implicated officers. Riley's directive was clear: take them off the streets, seize their weapons, and launch a thorough internal investigation. However, despite intensive efforts over the ensuing days, the trio remained elusive. The officer's testimony stood as a testament to the credibility of their account, even if the culprits themselves were not yet captured.

In the midst of the tense wait for Superintendent Compass, Chief Riley's attention shifted to a presence at the rear of the gathering. A high-level U.S. attorney from the Eastern District of Louisiana and a lead FBI's New Orleans Office Special Agent in Charge were both present, standing among the multitude of NOPD ranking officers. Riley seized the opportunity to share the alarming reports of possible hate crimes in Algiers Point – the alleged presence of armed skinheads threatening black individuals and reports of a shooting involving two black men. The lead FBI agent's swift proclamation characterized it as a potential hate crime. Riley appealed to the high-level US attorney and the FBI agent for assistance, acknowledging the strained resources and crippled communications that hindered the NOPD's response. Their immediate pledge to address the situation was a welcome relief for Riley, providing a glimmer of respite amid the chaos.

With the US attorney and the FBI agent taking charge of the potential hate crimes investigation, Riley turned his attention back to his officers. He stepped forward, taking the lead amidst the assembly of ranking officers, his intention clear: to gather and assess the current conditions. Before him stood the commanders from various districts, all under the shadow of escalating challenges. Riley called for each district commander to present a briefing on their respective areas, elucidating the conditions, challenges, and resources at their disposal.

Amid this dynamic exchange, two commanders were notably absent: Captain Bob Bardy of the Seventh District and Captain Rose Durea of the Third District. Riley recognized the need for clarity and instructed the crowd, "Explain what they were doing." With attention firmly focused, Chief

Weathersby's commanding voice rang out, rallying everyone's attention. Assistant Chief Riley, positioned at the back of an NOPD pickup truck, addressed the assembled officers, acutely aware that they were on their own in a time of unparalleled crisis. The ominous silence was broken as Riley began to brief them, proceeding with the knowledge that communication with Superintendent Compass remained severed. The uncertainty hung heavy, but Riley's determination to provide guidance and leadership persisted. He forged ahead with the briefing, offering a sense of direction in an otherwise chaotic and uncertain landscape.

Ladies and gentlemen, your presence here amidst the chaos and devastation speaks volumes about your commitment and resilience. I know the journey here was no easy feat—traversing through treacherous waters and unforgiving circumstances. In this moment, we are united as survivors of an unprecedented storm, the mother of all storms. Each of you is now a chief in your own right, entrusted with the responsibility of leading your divisions and districts through the challenges that lie ahead. Why, you might wonder? Because our communication lines have been severed, leaving us without the crucial lifeline of police radio comms and cell phones. We stand in uncertainty, uncertain of when we will regain these vital connections. In this interim period, your leadership and sound judgment will be our guiding light. You must exhibit unparalleled leadership, making decisions that are both astute and principled.

Our fellow citizens are in dire straits, stranded on rooftops and ensnared in attics. Among them are members of our very own NOPD Family, including civilians who find themselves in perilous situations. The medical facilities that our city once relied upon are now incapacitated. In the face of this dire reality, you must tread carefully yet display unwavering courage. We are confronting an adversary that shows no mercy—a situation that demands our utmost resilience and resourcefulness. Amidst the chaos, our survivors, who have lost loved ones and homes, are turning to us for guidance and strength. We are, in many ways, their only hope.

Yet, we must also acknowledge the presence of malevolent forces. There are brutal and violent individuals who seek to exploit the vulnerability of our city. Reports of racism and skinhead activity are surfacing, alongside opportunistic looters who are driven by both desperation and ill intent. It falls upon us to restore order, beginning with Canal Street and our pharmacies. But let's be clear: we lack a functioning jail and a proper facility to detain these hardened criminals. Deputy Chief Burkhart is working tirelessly to convert the greyhound bus terminal into a Central Lockup, an effort that will soon come to fruition. In the meantime, our Special Operations teams, alongside makeshift units, are engaged in the critical task of rescuing citizens via boats from perilous rooftops.

Our approach must be strategic and collaborative. We're coordinating with neighboring parishes to decide where and when we can apprehend violent or dangerous individuals. Remember, each arrest involves someone's son, daughter, grandparent, sibling, or child. While ensuring law and order, I implore you to treat these individuals with respect and dignity. For violent offenders, if necessary, handcuff them until we can arrange transportation. For others, gather their names and information for processing later. Our fellow citizens, thousands displaced from Lakeview, Gentilly, the ninth ward, and beyond, are seeking refuge. Direct them to the convention center until further notice. Be mindful that the Superdome's roof is compromised, surrounded by water.

In these trying times, let compassion guide us. If you possess extra water, extend it to our elderly citizens in need. Help is on the way from the Federal government and other law enforcement agencies; their arrival is imminent. This is the moment you've trained for—the moment to be the embodiment of the police force. As I surveyed the room, I saw a range of emotions etched on the faces of officers and ranking officials. Some displayed unwavering courage, while others grappled with confusion. Everyone make sure your actions are reasonable and necessary. The citizens of New Orleans need us now more than they ever have! In that moment, I signaled to Captain Weathersby, who donned his reverend hat. With heads bowed, we sought solace in prayer, grounding ourselves in the shared belief that resilience, unity, and courage would light our path forward.

After the solemn prayer, a group of officers, both male and female, approached Chief Riley with a heartfelt request. They expressed their fear for their families and their desire to leave the city, as their kids were away with relatives. As much as Riley empathized with their concerns, he knew that their duty to the city came first. He addressed them, explaining the gravity of the situation and the critical role they had to play. While he understood their anxieties, he urged them to remain focused on the task at hand. Promising that as soon as the situation improved, they would be able to reunite with their families. Riley could sense a mix of disappointment and frustration among the officers, their eyes reflecting a blend of sadness and, in a couple of cases, subtle anger at his denial.

As their SUV pulled away from Harrah's Casino overhang, Riley's team embarked on their mission toward Algiers Point. Just then, Mayor Nagin's SUV arrived at the scene, accompanied by his security detail. Riley's vehicle came to a halt, and both men stepped out to exchange greetings. Taking a moment to connect, Riley proceeded to apprise Mayor Nagin of the ongoing, harrowing events that continued to unfold throughout the city. The mayor appeared visibly worn down, his disheveled appearance reflecting the toll of the crisis. In a polo shirt and jeans, with an unshaven face, he exuded a palpable weariness, much like his security team.

Riley wasted no time in briefing Mayor Nagin on the disturbing reports that had surfaced. He shared concerning rumors about racial tensions surfacing in various parts of New Orleans. Specifically, he highlighted the alarming situation in the Algiers Point community on the Westbank, where white individuals were reported to have shot at black residents, claiming to be safeguarding their property from looters. Riley acknowledged the complexities of the situation, recognizing the need for people to protect their belongings in such dire circumstances. However, he also relayed accounts from young black men who had encountered armed white men, some possibly resembling skinheads, firing shots in their direction. These incidents occurred as they tried to navigate through the Algiers Point community, where streets had been blocked with cars. The alleged perpetrators were said to reside on Opelousas Street, spanning from old Algiers into the Algiers Point Community.

Riley assured Mayor Nagin that he had alerted U.S. Attorney and FBI agent about the potential hate crimes in Algiers Point. He conveyed their commitment to addressing the matter. Riley also informed the mayor about reports from cities like Memphis, TN, Waco, TX, and Arkansas, where NOPD officers had been stopped with marked NOPD vehicles and had left the city. He elaborated on the dire situation in specific police districts, such as the Seventh, Fifth, and Third, which were currently submerged underwater due to the catastrophic flooding.

Amid the unfolding chaos, Chief Riley detailed the dire state of affairs to Mayor Nagin. He began by describing the widespread destruction, including the ruin of the Special Operation Division complex. Riley emphasized that even the Police Headquarters' basement and first floor had been inundated, rendering the power and backup generator useless. Evacuations had been necessary for submerged police district stations. Mayor Nagin's concern and determination were palpable as he inquired about potential injuries among officers. Riley conveyed that, thankfully, there were no serious injuries reported, though some had narrowly escaped harm.

Mayor Nagin inquired about Superintendent Compass's whereabouts, his voice reflecting a mix of worry and urgency. Riley admitted that he hadn't seen Compass for days, and he had no knowledge of his current status. Mayor Nagin shared a forthcoming development: General Honore of the 82nd Airborne would be arriving to provide assistance with thousands of troops. He instructed Riley to prepare to brief General Honore on operational priorities. Riley affirmed his readiness to do so.

Mayor Nagin then urged Riley to locate Superintendent Compass and find out where he was. Riley assured him that he would take immediate action. Rallying his commanders, Riley called for an executive staff meeting, seeking input on the top ten operational priorities from each district. Captain Weathersby was tasked with contacting FBI Agent in Charge to receive an update on the reported hate crimes in Algiers.

Unbeknownst to them, a disturbing incident was unfolding in Algiers Point. In close proximity to their meeting, a deeply troubling event was taking place. Roland Bourgeois and a group of like-minded white men had taken it upon themselves to enforce a disturbing agenda. With racist intent, they erected barriers and barricades to prevent anyone darker than a paper bag from entering Algiers Point. This historic, picturesque community held a dark secret beneath its nostalgic façade.

Algiers Point was a charming district with its vintage homes and inviting ambiance. It offered a glimpse into the past with its classic pubs, Creole cottages, and quaint coffee shops. Overlooking the Cresent City Connection

Bridge and New Orleans' skyline, it sat adjacent to the Westbank ferry landing, a mere ten-minute ride from downtown. While many residents embodied the warmth of neighborliness, some harbored less benevolent sentiments. These individuals held deep-seated prejudices, longing for an era of white dominance over minorities.

Algiers Point and greater Algiers were divided by Opelousas Street, a symbolic boundary between different classes and races. The stark contrast between the two neighborhoods was a stark reminder of the city's history of racism and classism. The insular community within Algiers Point was where the white individuals who held such beliefs resided, while predominantly black neighborhoods existed beyond its borders.

At the center of this disturbing narrative were three white men, led by Roland Bourgeois. Bourgeois, bearing a striking resemblance to a skinhead with his bald head, was the apparent leader of this group. Joining him were two other white males, each in their late thirties or early forties. Their actions following Katrina's landfall spoke volumes—driven by fear and prejudice, they hastily barricaded their community. Fallen tree branches, cars, and any available obstacle were used to create barriers, signaling their intent to keep non-white individuals out.

These individuals, armed with shotguns, AR15 assault rifles, and handguns, patrolled Algiers Point, explicitly targeting black people and people of color. Reports began to circulate of violent confrontations and intimidation, with several black men allegedly shot or killed at the hands of these racists. Victims recounted horrifying encounters, including the brandishing of weapons and threats of violence.

As these events transpired, the true extent of the horrors remained concealed, shrouded in secrecy and prejudice. It would take years for the full truth to emerge from the shadows.

Henry Glover Shooting

September 2, 2005

Amidst the turmoil consuming the East bank of the Mississippi River, Chief Riley and his command staff remained oblivious to the unfolding dilemmas on the West bank. In Algiers, a community known for its affluence and charm, an entirely new set of tragedies was taking shape. As Chief Riley grappled with the myriad challenges brought on by flooding, rampant looting, and breached levees, a parallel crisis was quietly emerging in Algiers, which had largely managed to evade the initial wave of looting due to its relative safety.

Algiers, encompassing a mere 2.0 square miles, was characterized by its compact geography and diverse communities, ranging from upper-middle-class enclaves to opulent neighborhoods. However, looting was beginning to spread its grip even here. The Fourth District officers were tasked with combating this growing menace that threatened homes, schools, and businesses across Algiers. Two key locations stood out in this story: the Fourth District Sub-station and the Habans Elementary school.

The Fourth District's efforts to curb looting were centered around their substation on General Degaulle Drive, located within an outdoor strip mall in Central Algiers. Officer David Warren, an unconventional rookie cop at the age of 47, was appointed to safeguard this crucial outpost. Warren's unique background set him apart – a highly educated individual with a Master's Degree in Business Administration and specialized training in lethal force tactics. Despite being assigned to the Seventh District in Eastern New Orleans, he reported to the Fourth District due to the impassable floodwaters that prevented access to his designated precinct. The hope was that Warren's presence would serve as a deterrent to potential looters.

Nearby, Habans Elementary school had become a stronghold for the NOPD SWAT teams. The usual SWAT facilities had succumbed to eight feet of floodwater, prompting their relocation to Habans. In these dire circumstances, the SWAT teams demonstrated their exceptional skills, rescuing individuals stranded on rooftops and in attics. Their resourcefulness and commitment were evident as they transformed the school into makeshift quarters, providing citizens with food, water, and cots.

As the desperate search for essentials persisted, two citizens, Henry Glover, also known as Ace, and Bernard Calloway, ventured out from the Garden Oaks community in search of sustenance for their families. They scoured various locations, including gas stations, pharmacies, and supermarkets, only to encounter empty shelves and fellow citizens in similar predicaments. In their quest for supplies, they arrived at a strip mall located at 3701 General Degaulle Drive.

This intricate tapestry of events continued to weave together, revealing the challenges faced by individuals and communities across the city. While Chief Riley and his team grappled with the monumental task of restoring order and providing leadership, the residents of Algiers found themselves confronting a new form of adversity, as looting and desperation seeped into even the most resilient corners of the city.

Glover and Calloway, steering a commandeered red pickup truck to carry their supplies, pulled into the strip mall. Leaving the engine running, they hastily exited the vehicle, darting towards various businesses to scavenge for necessities. From his elevated vantage point, Officer Warren spotted their actions and urgently commanded them to stop. A moment later, a gunshot reverberated through the air, and in the ensuing panic, Glover and Calloway fled the scene. Officer Warren, armed with a .40 caliber handgun and a rifle, had discharged his weapon. The intention behind the shot was unclear; was it aimed at the subjects or meant as a warning? It was unequivocally not a warning shot, as the NOPD strictly forbade and didn't train officers to employ such measures. Regardless, the gunshot prompted the frightened pair to scramble back into their truck, driven by Calloway. In their desperate flight, it soon became evident that Glover was wounded, bleeding from his chest and abdomen. Racing to their destination on Garden Oaks Drive, Calloway parked the truck haphazardly on the street and rushed to assist Glover, who had collapsed outside his girlfriend's apartment. Shouting for help, Calloway's frantic cries reached Rolanda Short, Glover's girlfriend, who emerged from her apartment in alarm.

Rolanda sprinted to the scene and discovered Glover lying face down on the street, blood staining the pavement from his injuries. In the midst of her anguished cries, a police car pulled up, disgorging two officers who hastened to Glover's side. However, Rolanda refused to be moved away from her injured boyfriend, her grief and distress rendering her immovable. The officers, met with her refusal, directed her to step back, a command that she adamantly resisted while continuing to wail in sorrow. Amid the chaotic scene, the officers endeavored to communicate for assistance via their police radio, grappling with the interference that plagued the transmissions. Despite their efforts, the situation remained dire, and Glover's condition continued to deteriorate.

With a growing crowd of onlookers, the officers faced increasing hostility and tension. Unable to ascertain the details of the incident amidst the chaos, and confronted with the harsh accusations from the gathering crowd, the officers retreated to their patrol car, bewildered and uncertain. Unable to establish contact through their police radio due to the communication breakdown, and faced with the mounting tension and accusations, they chose to abandon the scene, driving away with a sense of confusion and trepidation.

Meanwhile, in the midst of the turmoil, Glover's brother Edward King stood in the street, attempting to flag down passing vehicles for assistance. Many vehicles chose to disregard the unfolding tragedy, ignoring Edward's desperate pleas for aid. Some slowed down briefly, only to witness the dire situation and accelerate away, unwilling to become involved.

After agonizing minutes that felt like an eternity, a white Chevy Malibu driven by Tanner came to a halt. Tanner, on a mission to find fuel for his car, was swayed by Edward King's plea for help. The trio swiftly and carefully loaded Glover's wounded form into the back of the Malibu. As they sought a hospital, the closest option, West Jefferson Memorial Hospital in Jefferson Parish, seemed too distant. In a change of plans, Tanner suggested an alternative – Habans Elementary, where the NOPD SWAT team had set up camp. It was a decision made out of compassion and a desire to aid a fellow human in need, standing in stark contrast to the indifference exhibited by so many others. With a wounded man in their care, they embarked on a journey to Habans Elementary seeking assistance and medical attention.

Tanner sped towards Habans Elementary, the sight of several police cars and numerous officers dressed in tactical gear providing a glimmer of hope that Henry Glover might receive the help he so urgently needed. Pulling into the exterior driveway, they stepped out of the car and beseeched the officers for assistance. However, their hopes were quickly dashed as they encountered a few officers who were visibly agitated and hostile. Despite their attempts to explain the dire situation, several officers pointed their assault rifles at the trio, commanding them to raise their hands. Their pleas fell on deaf ears as they tried to communicate that Glover was wounded and in the back of the car. An officer approached Tanner and viciously struck him on the head with the butt of his rifle, sending him sprawling to the ground. Accusations of being looters were hurled at them, further escalating the tense situation. Callaway was kicked in the ribs and thrown to the ground by another officer, while King, Tanner, and Callaway were all subjected to brutal beatings before being handcuffed. Despite their pleas and explanations, the officers appeared unmoved, disregarding their urgent appeals for help for Glover. Amidst the chaos, a couple of officers finally intervened, urging a halt to the aggression and demanding an understanding of the circumstances.

However, even as the situation began to be assessed, Tanner's repeated assertions that Glover was in the back of the car and had been shot seemed to go unheeded by some officers. A white male officer seized the car key from the Malibu, which he inexplicably carried in his back pocket, and without regard for the critical situation, drove away in the vehicle with Glover still in the rear seat. Two other officers followed closely behind in a white truck. As Tanner and Callaway endured further questioning for an additional hour, they were eventually released. Fleeing the city immediately, they left behind a trail of unanswered questions and unresolved turmoil.

The officers, meanwhile, departed the scene with Glover's lifeless body in the back of the Malibu, unaware of his fate. Captain Jeff Winn, the commander of the SWAT team, and his assistant, Lt. Dwayne Scheuermann, neglected to report the incident's details to the NOPD leadership, allowing a shroud of mystery to envelop the tragic events. This incident would come to symbolize another disgraceful chapter in the history of the NOPD, marked by the callous disregard for human life, rogue actions, and yet another significant scandal for a department already burdened with corruption and shame. More would pass before the executive leadership of the NOPD would become aware of the incident's occurrence.

It was reported that amidst the chaos of the initial encounter with Tanner, Callaway, and the wounded Glover, no officer attended to Glover's injuries or heeded Tanner's desperate pleas for assistance. As Glover lay there, his life hanging in the balance, Lt. Scheuermann arrived on the scene, working to deescalate the tension that had erupted. Questioning a visibly shaken

Tanner and Callaway, Scheuermann aimed to unravel the confusing and distressing series of events. In the midst of his efforts, a third individual identified as Edward King entered the picture. The reaction was violent, as he allegedly began assaulting King through punches and kicks. It was only when Captain Jeffery Winn intervened, ordering Scheuermann to cease the aggression and remove the vehicle and body from the premises, that the situation began to stabilize. The details surrounding Glover's condition and vital signs, however, remained unclear, leaving lingering questions about the events that transpired that day.

It was rumored that McRae swiftly settled into the driver's seat of the white Malibu, with Scheuermann positioned behind the wheel of a white pickup truck. The engines roared to life, and McRae accelerated away, with Lt. Scheuermann tailing closely behind. The trio sped away from the scene, leaving Tanner alone in the back of the Malibu.

The full extent of the truth would remain concealed for years to come. Unbeknownst to the public, Lt. Scheuermann and Officer McRae transported Glover's body to a location along the Algiers levee. As McRae parked the vehicle on the levee's edge, Lt. Scheuermann silently observed. In a shocking and heartless act, McRae doused the car with gasoline and ignited it, setting both the vehicle and Glover's lifeless body ablaze. The question of Glover's condition at that moment, whether he was still alive or not, hung heavy in the air, casting a dark shadow over the depths of this horrifying incident.

The unfathomable actions of McRae and the passivity of Lt. Scheuermann in allowing such a heinous act to unfold would come to light only after an extended period of cover-up. The revelation of these disturbing events, the discovery of Glover's remains within the charred vehicle, and the grim realization that his head was missing would shock the conscience of all who learned of them. This incident would emerge as a massive cover-up, shrouding the truth for an extended duration before the disturbing details would finally come to light.

The implications of this horrific act were far-reaching, resulting in immeasurable pain and suffering. It forever altered the course of Henry Glover's life, inflicted profound wounds upon his loved ones, and stained the reputation of the NOPD with another indelible mark of shame. The extent of this scandal's impact was profound, leaving an enduring legacy of disgrace that would persist throughout modern times.

Officer Celestine

September 3, 2005

Officer Celestine, the same dedicated officer who had been tirelessly rescuing individuals amidst the chaos of the hospital, swimming through the turbulent waters and encountering lifeless bodies, found himself seeking solace and sustenance.

Learning of a refuge at Algiers, a retirement home offering food and shelter, Celestine and his partner, who had shared the harrowing experience at the hospital, ventured towards this haven of hope. They arrived at the facility, their respite from the relentless challenges they had faced.

Unfortunately, the trials of communication persisted. In their quest for a phone signal, they were informed that they needed to step out onto the balcony to establish a connection. As Celestine settled into a chair on the balcony, his partner made his way to join him.

In a shocking and heartbreaking moment, Celestine's partner heard a deafening gunshot. He turned in disbelief to find that Celestine had taken his own life, a single, tragic shot to the head robbing them all of his presence and courage.

Paul Accardo

September 3, 2005

Paul Accardo, the Public Information Officer, was a constant presence alongside Chief Compass. However, Chief Compass had been notably absent.

It was the morning of September 3rd, around 5:30 AM. I was asleep on a makeshift cot on the 9th floor of City Hall, surrounded by Paul Accardo and approximately 20 other officers. I was roused from my slumber by a fellow officer, who urgently informed me that Chief Compass was trying to reach me on the radio. The early hour was 4:35 AM.

I swiftly got up and began to dress as I listened to the message from Chief Compass. He reported a shooting incident at the convention center.

As I rushed to put on my uniform, I noticed Paul Accardo sitting nearby. Paul, a 38-year-old white male, was a clean-cut, amiable individual who had recently gone through a divorce. At that moment, he was sitting on the edge of his cot, clad only in shorts and a t-shirt, wearing a vacant expression. It was as if life had drained from his gaze. Concerned, I asked him if he was alright, but there was no response from him.

We hurriedly prepared to leave, and that was the last time I saw Paul Accardo.

Upon reaching the convention center with the team, we meticulously searched through the crowd of hundreds of citizens, looking for any sign of a firearm, but none was found.

Approximately four hours later, Chief Compass contacted me again. This time, it was to deliver grim news. I received a notification from another officer stating that Paul Accardo had taken his own life near the Lakeview area, close to his home. They had discovered him in a car.

The vacant, lifeless stare I had observed earlier had been an ominous sign that something was deeply troubling him. The reasons behind his tragic decision to end his life remained a mystery. It was a devastating event that unfolded on September 3rd.

September 4, 2005

Danzinger Bridge

It was September 4, 2005, and I stood there alongside Captain Weathersby, surrounded by members of the New Orleans Police Department Water Rescue teams, National Guard personnel, and FEMA's search and rescue team leader. The scorching heat and high humidity made us repeatedly wipe sweat from our brows, necks, and arms as we gathered to address another challenging task.

Despite the relentless heat, the sun blazed overhead, illuminating our surroundings. We had affixed a city map to the exterior brick wall of Harrah's Casino, just west of Canal Street. Days earlier, I could gaze eastward across the street and see the now-charred Saks Fifth Avenue store, which had been set ablaze a few days earlier. What had once been a bustling shopping district was now occupied solely by an array of large motor homes, news trucks, vans, and cars from major and local television networks. News vehicles from various unfamiliar regions were also present, turning Canal Street's median into a media epicenter, complete with satellite dishes scattered everywhere. Amid this chaos, I tried to concentrate on the map, despite the dozens of news reporters just beyond the barricades, clamoring for our attention. They were merely doing their jobs, seeking breaking news, but I had to muster the mental fortitude to stay focused on the task at hand.

Our team had divided the map into multiple sections, each representing a part of the submerged city. At least five other groups of officers were also diligently working to identify individuals still trapped in their attics. This makeshift outdoor emergency field operation center buzzed with activity.

Several officers, including Lieutenants Michael Roussel and Lieutenant Buford, along with National Guard members and the leader of FEMA's search and rescue team, commanded various teams. We carefully examined the map, noting that areas like the Ninth Ward, Lower Ninth Ward, and Lakeview were submerged in water ranging from 7 to 10 feet deep. The city had been divided into grids, and each team lead reviewed their designated area on the map, verifying the locations they had already searched. It was decided that even areas previously covered would be searched again. In the initial chaos of the first few days, officers had performed rescues wherever they encountered people on rooftops or heard desperate cries from flooded attics. There had been little structure or organization to the process, given the overwhelming scale of the disaster.

FEMA teams had arrived only a few hours earlier. Each water rescue team leader was assigned a specific grid for searching. Lieutenant Roussel's team was responsible for the Ninth Ward, Lieutenant Buford's for the Lower Ninth Ward, and the FEMA team leader was tasked with the Lakeview area of the city. The FEMA leader provided instructions to each team regarding the symbols that would be spray-painted on houses after they were searched. Additionally, FEMA assigned some teams on foot to areas with less than five feet of water to search the interiors of homes for survivors and victims. The briefing was somber as the FEMA leader explained the meaning behind the symbols that would be marked on the roofs and doors of the homes they searched. These symbols would indicate the house searched, the date and time of the search, the number of people rescued, and the number of deceased individuals found in the house, whether it was occupied or empty. Despite the grim nature of this briefing, it represented a departure from the initial chaos and offered a semblance of organization. The first few days had been marked by utter disorder and despair, so even this slight semblance of structure provided a glimmer of hope.

After the briefing, the team leaders gathered their respective teams and set out for more rescue operations. As I turned to glance at Canal Street, I once again saw numerous reporters stationed in the area. We had to establish a barrier to keep them at least 25 yards away from our operations. Reporters from various news agencies were scattered all around, and Canal Street's median was now swarming with even more news vehicles. It was astonishing to see how many reporters had descended upon the scene, not only from the United States but also from countries such as France, England, Japan, China, Australia, and likely many others. Wherever I went, reporters were there, diligently seeking information. As our grid meeting concluded, Captain Weathersby and I headed toward my vehicle to meet with another group of commanders. However, radio communication remained abysmal. We were still using the mutual aid channel, which was overrun with traffic from various local agencies across the greater New Orleans area, making it difficult for any officer to get their transmission through.

Suddenly, a chilling sound pierced the airwaves: police signal 108. The female officer's voice crackled over the police radio, but her transmission was distorted and challenging to decipher. Panic ensued as officers began shouting, "There's a one-oh-eight! One-oh-eight!" This was the police signal that no officer ever wanted to hear because it meant that fellow officers needed immediate assistance, and lives were in grave danger.

The officers on the other end of the radio urgently relayed those two officers were down under the bridge. The Danzinger Bridge, which spanned the industrial canal and connected Eastern and Western New Orleans, was typically a heavily trafficked drawbridge for vehicles. However, in the wake of Hurricane Katrina, it had become a pedestrian lifeline between the floodwaters of Eastern New Orleans and downtown New Orleans, leading to the Superdome and the Convention Center. Most of those on foot were unaware that the city was inundated by rising floodwaters due to breached levees and overflowing canals in Mid City and uptown New Orleans.

I was at Harrah's Casino, and the transmission came through loud and clear: "One-oh-eight, one-oh-eight." The urgency in those numbers was unmistakable, signifying those two officers were in serious trouble. It was a chilling moment, and an eerie silence fell over everyone present as we listened intently to the radio. The concern in the air was palpable, and we all shared a deep worry for our fellow officers.

Sergeant Kenneth Bowen, from the Seventh District Task Force, responded that they were on their way in a 20-foot white Budget Rental truck. This was a stark reminder of the dire situation – most of our police vehicles had succumbed to the floodwaters, with only a few stored high above the waterline at the Superdome, which was inaccessible. These vehicles would remain stranded for weeks.

The Danzinger Bridge, where the incident had occurred, was roughly 10 miles away from our current location. The streets were submerged, with water covering a staggering 83 percent of the city. To reach the bridge, we would have to navigate through flooded streets by car, transfer to boats, and then switch back to cars. It was a logistical nightmare, and we lacked the crucial resource of helicopters, as NOPD did not have an aviation unit.

Despite our fear for the safety of our officers and the innocent citizens involved, we felt helpless. We knew we couldn't reach the scene in time. As we listened to the radio transmissions, I prayed silently for a positive outcome, but deep down, I feared we might lose another officer, if not more. The memory of Officer Paul Accardo, who had taken his own life just hours earlier, was still fresh in our minds.

The day before, reports had surfaced of armed individuals firing at Wildlife and Fishery Agents in the water beneath the bridge. These assailants were targeting those attempting to rescue fellow citizens. A mere 15 minutes before the 108 signals, there had been reports of individuals near the bridge shooting at a convoy of rescue workers. Even in a city like New Orleans, known for its crime and violence, these acts were senseless and perplexing. It was unclear whether these shooters were criminals or desperate citizens trapped in their attics, attempting to shoot their way to safety.

So, when the initial radio transmission indicated that two officers were down under the bridge, it was only natural for most of us to assume that they had been shot. The transmission was fraught with interruptions, broken segments, and static, making it challenging to decipher. "108," "one ooooo," and garbled sounds were all we could make out. Then, amidst the chaos, a clear "108" came through, followed by an unusual surge of static. The officer's identity and call number were indecipherable, and the transmission was marked by heavy breathing and what sounded like someone running. There were roughly forty officers and police-civilian workers at the Harrah's command post when the call came in, but the chaotic radio waves made it difficult to discern critical details. As multiple agencies attempted to work on the same channel, static and fragmented transmissions rendered it nearly impossible to comprehend every word being communicated. Initially, it was unclear whether the distressed officer was from NOPD or another local agency.

I could hear the unmistakable sound of gunshots - bang, bang, bang - echoing through the radio waves. Amidst the chaos, an officer's voice broke through, shouting something about two individuals heading towards a place we couldn't quite decipher, referred to as "the Friendly." Confusion rippled through the command post as we exchanged puzzled looks, wondering what "the Friendly" could possibly mean. Then, a voice over the radio suggested it might be the Friendly Inn Motel on Chef Mentuer Highway, near the Danzinger Bridge. The distorted communication only compounded our stress, making a bad situation even more challenging to comprehend.

It soon became evident that these were NOPD officers in the Seventh Police District, but the distorted transmissions left us hanging in uncertainty. Moments later, another NOPD officer at Harrah's tentatively identified the voice as that of Sgt. Kenneth Bowen, the leader of the Seventh District task force. He relayed information that one perpetrator had been shot and was down, describing a chaotic scene with gunshots, officers in pursuit, and frantic footsteps, all barely audible due to the warped radio transmissions.

Under the overhang at Harrah's, more than 40 officers were gathered, focused intently on their police radios. Groups huddled together, ranging from ten-person clusters to pairs, each fixated on their handheld radios as if they were television screens. The media present sensed that something was unfolding but remained outside the perimeter, unable to hear clearly.

Through fragmented transmissions, we caught snippets of information: an officer reporting a subject down in a hotel parking lot, the sound of running footsteps and heavy breathing, and officers in hot pursuit. The situation was rapidly evolving, and it resembled a running gun battle, unlike anything I'd encountered in my 24 years on the force. The distorted radio waves made it challenging to piece together the unfolding events.

Then, the airwaves fell silent. Anxiety hung in the air as we awaited any sign of what was happening. The officers at Harrah's stood in rapt attention, their eyes fixed on their radios, desperate for more information. The momentary stillness felt excruciating. Worried expressions were etched on every face, as we collectively hoped and prayed that we hadn't lost another officer. The silence was oppressive, and frustration mounted.

Finally, an unidentified officer broke the silence, his voice trembling but calmer than before, reporting another perpetrator down. Yet again, the airwaves fell silent, leaving us in suspense. Minutes passed, although they felt like an eternity. Then, an unknown officer asked if the situation was code 4, indicating that no additional officers were needed, and again, the airwaves offered only silence.

A few minutes later, though it felt like an eternity, Sgt. Bowen's voice came through, confirming that it was indeed code 4, signaling that the situation was under control.

A dispatcher's voice crackled through the radio, seeking to understand Sgt. Bowen's situation. An unidentified officer quickly chimed in, inquiring about the number of perpetrators down. Another voice responded, confirming that two perpetrators had been taken down, and several individuals had been apprehended. I attempted to inquire about any injured officers via radio, but the static and overlapping voices made it impossible to get a clear response.

Moments later, a voice broke through the chaos, asking if any officers were hurt. Another officer instructed Sgt. Bowen to conduct a roll call and ensure all his officers were accounted for. Yet another unidentified voice added, urging Unit 780 (Sgt. Bowen) to gather a status report on his officers and their locations. Sgt. Bowen's voice trembled amid the static as he instructed all Seventh District task force officers to report their status. It became evident that officers from the surrounding parishes, all connected on the mutual add system, were finally realizing the gravity of the situation, as silence blanketed the airwaves, disrupted only by the persistent radio static.

One by one, the officers responded, confirming they were unharmed and accounted for. Sgt. Bowen then conducted a roll call, summarizing the situation: two perpetrators down (fatally shot), four perpetrators apprehended, all officers accounted for, and no injuries reported.

Under the overhang at Harrah's, an eruption of jubilation ensued. Officers exchanged high-fives, hugs, and cheers. Some exclaimed, "Finally, a damn win!" while others voiced their frustrations about the recent losses the department had suffered. Captain Weathersby and I exchanged a knowing glance, our thoughts unspoken, but we shared a sense of bewilderment about what was happening in our beloved city.

For these officers, the celebration marked a stark contrast to the events of the past few days, during which:

- Officer Kevin Thomas had been shot in the head on 8/30/2005 and remained in critical condition.

- Officer Celestine had taken his own life on 9/2/2005.

- Officer Paul Accardo had committed suicide on 9/3/2005.

- Dozens of officers had been stopped in other states while abandoning the city in the midst of the crisis.

I immediately tried to contact Superintendent Compass but without success. I reached out to Chief Lonnie Swain, who was at the Detective Bureau, regarding the need for homicide detectives at the scene. Unfortunately, the detectives assigned to the Superdome were preoccupied with the daunting task of evacuating 20,000 people from the flooded facility. Radio transmissions remained chaotic, and my attempts to reach Captain Bob Bardy, the Seventh District commander, also proved futile.

In the midst of this confusion, Chief Compass's voice came over the radio, directing that the Seventh District handle the situation on the Danziger Bridge. He cited the Detective Bureau's involvement in the Superdome evacuation as the reason for this decision.

Little did I, or the more than 1,500 officers listening in on the radio transmission, know the full extent of what had transpired on the Danziger Bridge that day. It would be years before the facts and truth surrounding the Danziger Bridge shooting came to light. What initially seemed like a victorious outcome in a running gun battle with seven armed perpetrators would ultimately become one of the darkest days in the history of the NOPD. The name "Danziger" would carry a heavy burden for the department in the years to come, as many families had lost innocent loved ones at the hands of those sworn to protect them. This incident would forever live-in infamy.

Chapter 22:
That John Wayne Dude

It was around 3 pm when Mayor Nagin requested his executive team to meet at City Hall for a scheduled meeting with General Russell Honore. When Captain Weathersby and I arrived, we were greeted by Colonel Ebbert of NOLA Homeland Security, General Landreneau of the Louisiana National Guard, Sally Foreman, the Director of Public Information, and several other staff members from the Louisiana National Guard and city government. Several sidebars were conducted just before the meeting began, and casual yet deep conversations continued. Every sidebar dealt with the tragedy of one of America's greatest cities in some form or fashion. The overwhelming destruction, water covering eighty-three percent of the city, dead bodies everywhere, our people suffering from heat and high humidity, and lack of food and water; each conversation was summed up with disbelief and dismay at the constantly unfolding suffering of our people and the ongoing destruction of New Orleans.

As I participated in my sidebar, I noticed the weary look on everyone's face and then the sudden and slowly growing distinct smell of sweat, mildew, and the slight but funky odor of a group of professionals who were always immaculately dressed and pristine. This gradually increasing smell of mold, sweat, and funk emanated from professionals who had not bathed in days. I, too, was one of those who had not bathed in days. Looking around the room, I could see people rubbing their noses slightly as they first recognized the collective filth and the tragedy we were dealing with. Understand that it had been three days with 95-plus-degree heat and no air. The conference room had windows that could not be opened and no air conditioning for three days. We would have to bear the stench; hell, it was to be expected in this never-ending tragedy.

Mayor Nagin walked into the room moments later with a six-foot-three, mature gentleman who walked with swag, wearing army camouflage green fatigues and a black beret, holding an unlit cigar. Following him were three soldiers, all with the rank of captain or above. Mayor Nagin introduced him as General Russell Honore of the Army's 82nd Airborne. Nagin stated that

General Honore had direct access to President Bush. General Honore's presence and leadership should make all the difference in the world to this slow federal response we have been getting.

General Honore spoke with a gruff southern accent and stated, "Ladies and Gentlemen, I am here to help in any way I can. I am more than happy to be here. Louisiana is my state; I am Louisiana-born and bred, from Lakeland, Louisiana, and a graduate of Southern University in Baton Rouge. I am not just here because I am in the military. This is home; I have family and roots here. We are going to turn this around and turn it around fast. I would like you all to brief me and give me details and your priorities, no matter what it is. Ladies and gentlemen, you'd be amazed at your military's capabilities."

Mayor Nagin said, "Before you all begin the briefing, let me inform you of some essential issues. I fully support the men and women who work for this city, not just the first responders. Everyone is valuable."

Dr. Hatfield (CAO) has been working from Baton Rouge, where she and many administrative teams were assigned to work for the storm. Their work is essential. Dr. Hatfield will ensure that every city employee receives a check via an electronic transfer. Nagin instructed that whatever their last regular check with no overtime would be mirrored. He was concerned about the well-being of all of his employees. He stated, "We do not know how long this will last; our people have evacuated all over this country and must get paid to survive." Nagin instructed us to let all the first responders know that they would get paid as usual so they would have no worries; it would be done through electronic transfers to their banks. He also provided a 311 number for all employees and a website that all City of NOLA employees could visit related to getting paid. Nagin was very concerned and passionate about the well-being of his employees. That was super positive news as Captain Weathersby, Director Ebbert, and I all looked at each other with a nod of approval and relief.

At that point, the staff began briefing General Honore. General Landreneau of the Louisiana National Guard advised that 500 additional National Guard troops would arrive later the same day. He suggested that they assist in any way they were needed. Colonel Ebbert and I then leaned into each other and had a momentary sidebar in which we determined that we wanted the National Guard posted at major intersections, shopping malls, and pharmacies throughout the city to show a public military presence; this would be a huge deterrent to criminals. Chief Charles Parent of the Fire Department then gave a briefing, stating that his firefighters had created several boat rescue teams and had rescued over two hundred citizens from rooftops and flooded houses in New Orleans East. Chief Parent reported that firefighters had observed dozens of dead bodies in attics and floating in the water throughout New Orleans East. Chief Parent then made a request that would stretch our resources even closer to their limits. He stated, "Chief Riley, we need a police escort for our fire trucks; idiots are shooting at our fire trucks." Dr. Saussy, the director of emergency services, added, "Chief, we also need escorts. We are having serious issues with people threatening our staff and trying to steal the ambulances." An Emergency Operations Center (EOC) representative advised that underground gas leaks were underwater, and some were burning atop the water. The Emergency EOC Representative reported that they had requested divers to come in and go underwater to cap the gas leaks and extinguish the fires. The divers were expected to arrive within 24 hours. The EOC reps also advised that a Disaster Mortuary Operational Response Team (DMORT) was en route to collect, identify, and process the hundreds of dead bodies around the city.

Captain Weathersby voiced to General Honore about the evacuation challenges at the convention center with over 20,000 people of all ages. Many of the seniors who had evacuated had special needs, and some elderly died, probably from lack of food and water and the extreme heat and humidity.

Chief Riley briefed the General on the evacuation challenges with the Superdome, surrounded by at least 4 feet of water and many elderly citizens. Chief Riley told the General about the increasing looting city-wide and that we had no functioning prison or jail. Each person who briefed brought out something that had all of us shaking our heads in disbelief.

Mayor Nagin advised that in his private meeting with General Honore, "I informed him that we need food, water, buses, and accommodations for about 50,000 people and medical attention for thousands. The General has assured me that he would advise President Bush and ensure that the response moving forward would be made expeditiously."

General Honore stated, "I have already ordered over 100 buses, and we are distributing MREs (Meals Ready to Eat) today. The buses will begin arriving tomorrow. We will have the Superdome and the convention center cleared within 48 hours. I can't tell you exactly where they're going, but it will be much better than the current conditions." I then requested that General Honore deploy troops to as many neighborhoods for visibility as possible. I began to point, name, and identify the areas where we needed his troops the most on the map on the wall. We needed troops' visibility almost everywhere that was dry and did not have severe flooding. I aimed to have them in every residential community, shopping mall, strip mall, and anywhere that was dry. General Honore replied, "I have more than 6,000 troops. I have one requirement: a team of officers with each of my platoons for radio comms to guide us to and through these communities." Chief Riley replied, "Yes, sir." The General was a savior, and I replied, "Sir," because he deserved that, and his aura and sincerity earned the highest respect. We met for more than 4 hours to organize the plans. At one point, the General advised that he had a meeting with the media near the Le Pavillon Hotel on Poydras Street, just a few blocks away, and he and his staff proceeded out of the building.

Captain Weathersby and I left as well. When we got downstairs, we saw two army trucks with at least 20 troops in each truck as General Honore and his executive assistant entered a high-water Humvee jeep and proceeded ahead of us. We arrived about five minutes later and observed the media near the hotel and dozens of citizens wandering around. We observed General Honore ordering troops and police officers who had their weapons in a ready position to put their guns down as he called out with conviction, shouting, "Put your weapons down. These are American citizens." Guns lowered as troops and officers complied. Citizens began to clap and cheer for General Honore. He made an immediate impact! The John Wayne dude had arrived!

On September 15, the looting subsided tremendously as the following days passed with a solid military presence all over the city. NOPD's Major Raymond Burkhart was coordinating a temporary makeshift jail with the help of the City of New York Department of Corrections and Louisiana's Angola State Penitentiary personnel at the downtown Greyhound Bus Station—finally, a place to bring the thugs and looters. Police departments from all over the state and the country arrived, and peace and calm were now present. We still had no power, no lights, and no air conditioning. However, the never-ending fear of thugs that caused uneasiness was now at bay.

Three weeks later, the water had subsided tremendously. It was around 9:15 pm; while downtown on Canal Street, we saw a light at a hotel come on in the distance, and then another light illuminated a building. Then, streetlights slowly began to come on all around us. The lights on overhead beams on the Mississippi Bridge started to go on row by row. The excitement of New Orleans, which had been drowned and submerged for more than two weeks, the darkness that enveloped each evening, began to dissipate; with each flicker of light, we came out of the darkness and uncertainty. NOLA's glitter, the electricity, the shine of a city that never sleeps, darkened for what seemed like an eternity, was back on as cops, citizens, and first responders began to second-line dance in the streets. Many had tears flowing. The joy of the moment was so heartfelt. The lights were a beacon of hope. It ignited each of us; we had a long way to go, but NOLA was on the way back!

We thought!

On September 18, New Orleans Chief Edwin Compass flew to New York for the Saints' home opener that was moved to New York due to Katrina's destruction of NOLA. Chief Compass stated that officials from New York invited him to the game to flip the coin. When Mayor Nagin learned of this, he blew a gasket that Chief Compass went to New York for a football game amid our embryonic stages of recovery from America's greatest disaster. Mayor Nagin advised that he witnessed Chief Compass have an emotional breakdown in the presence of a world-renowned talk show host while he was doing an interview. Mayor Nagin asked the gracious host not to show the tape she and her cameraman had filmed. The elegant host assured the mayor that she would not. She advised the mayor that Chief Compass needed rest and care. The mayor received reports that Chief Compass had another public emotional breakdown when he learned Officer Paul Accardo died from a suicide. The mayor was upset when he knew that Chief Compass had advised him of several incidents of babies being raped that he later learned to be false. Mayor Nagin was concerned about Chief Compass's well-being and leadership ability and could not contact him for several days immediately after Katrina's arrival. He shared his concerns with Chief Riley six months earlier in a French Quarter coffee shop. He stated that politics influenced his decision to move forward with Chief Compass.

That same weekend, while Chief Compass was in New York for the Saints' football game, Chief Riley conducted a senior-level staff meeting with all deputy chiefs and captains. During the meeting, the main topic was the accountability of officers. It was estimated that over 150 officers were unaccounted for, and we had received information from other law enforcement agencies that NOPD officers had deserted to their states.

During the executive staff meetings, it was determined that some had abandoned, some had left as their rank permitted them to seek their families, and some had deserted. Many officers threatened to leave because there were no decent living accommodations, and the stress was unbearable for some. The third-world lifestyle that we were living was unacceptable to many. We discussed how to accommodate the officers better to prevent them from leaving. Another major unexpected challenge was that other law enforcement agencies were actively recruiting NOPD officers in the immediate aftermath of Katrina and offering $5,000 to $10,000 bonuses and six-month rent-free accommodations to join their departments. Even former NOPD chiefs recruited our officers with enticements such as signing bonuses. They were luring officers away.

During the meeting, we discussed ideas to provide better living arrangements, mental health care, and ways to reunite the officers with their families. After much deliberation, Captain Harry Mendoza of SWAT suggested that we request a cruise ship with reasonable accommodations, food, decent sleeping quarters, the ability to shower, and entertainment. There was a palpable shift from solemn energy in the room to positive energy when those comments were made. The thought of having a cruise ship was a great idea. After the meeting, Chief Riley immediately walked across the street from City Hall to The Hyatt Hotel, met with Mayor Ray Nagin, and suggested the cruise ship.

Mayor Nagin asked how he could get a cruise ship here. I replied, "FEMA?" The mayor contacted the City's Homeland Security Director Colonel Terry Ebbert, and within seven days, the first of three Carnival Cruise Ships arrived. It was only for essential personnel and first responders. Normalcy was still a long way off, but this was a big step, closer than it had been for almost a month, which seemed like a lifetime. That ship turned the tide. When the second ship arrived, other city workers returned; when the third ship arrived, first responders were allowed to bring their families back. The cruise ships cost over 200 million dollars, but it was worth it for what NOLA's people went through. Some families were back together. On board the vessels were the U.S. Department of Health and Human Services and Louisiana State University mental health care professionals who made themselves available to all who sought assistance.

On September 28, Chief Compass resigned. On September 29, Assistant Superintendent Chief Warren Riley was sworn in as the new Superintendent of Police. Nagin advised Riley that he appreciated his determination, collectiveness, and leadership throughout Katrina. Riley was charged with the recovery of law enforcement efforts and rebuilding NOPD, from personnel to the many police stations, equipment, and facilities that were damaged and destroyed.

One of my first orders was to investigate those who deserted their posts during Hurricane Katrina. It resulted in the termination of almost 90 officers.

Years later, two police shooting incidents that occurred during Katrina were discovered after federal investigations.

Five officers would plead guilty to killing two citizens and wounding four others in the Danziger Bridge Shooting. They were sentenced to serve seven to 12 years in federal prison.

Two officers were also sentenced to twenty-five years and five months for the killing and burning of the body of Henry Glover during the first days of Hurricane Katrina. These two incidents devastated two families and would forever taint the NOPD.

Epilogue

Hurricane Katrina caused 1,392 deaths (NOLA.com); more than 700 people are still missing or unaccounted for (DoSomething.org).

The word Katrina means pure in many countries and languages. Katrina cleansed New Orleans. We could only hope! Could the crime, corruption, racism, and bad politics that have been pervasive in New Orleans have been washed away? As unfortunate as it was, this cleansing presented an excellent opportunity for NOLA to rebound in a new and improved way. To recreate and improve NOLA in every way. To provide a modern-day Southern Charm that would be inclusive and embrace all people and cultures.

Almost ninety thousand New Orleanians would not return after Katrina over the next 18 years. The vast majority of minorities who evacuated would not return. Many who did not return love NOLA; no one can criticize NOLA but another New Orleanian, that is how much we love NOLA. NOLA's evacuees created a far better and safer life for themselves and their children in other cities. New Orleans' demographics would shift drastically over the next sixteen years from 454,863 citizens in 2005 (U.S. Census Bureau 2005) to 369,749 (U.S. Census Bureau 2021) citizens in New Orleans.

Little did we know that over the 18 years to follow, chaos and the apparent local government mismanagement of FEMA recovery funds, weak leadership, a mayor who foolishly downsized the police department, jeopardizing the safety of locals and tourists, police misconduct, and cover-ups, political corruption from city leaders, and surrounding parishes' leaders, even a handful of NOLA's top federal authorities would be forced to step down for misconduct. A white male in Algiers would be convicted thirteen years later in federal court for hate crimes, shooting blacks evacuating during Katrina for walking through his Algiers Point neighborhood. Some of those in the shadows would allegedly pay off a NOLA chief attorney to step down for his incompetence. He was allegedly frequently releasing hard-core criminals without cause, or was it some other reason? Two highly prominent political families held national political offices: One family would be disgraced through corruption, and the other would thrive.

Over the next eighteen years, many city leaders would talk about the significant reforms of New Orleans and it would be great to believe that in 2023, New Orleans had recovered by having cranes in the sky, progressive and effective economic development, and an increase in new booming businesses. Not!

One of two high-rise buildings under construction, an 18-story building collapsed, resulting in the tragic loss of three lives and injuring 30 others. NOLA leadership allowed the remains of two bodies to sit dormant in the collapsed building for more than ten months, which is hard to process. And inexcusable! This incident has been attributed to the alleged negligence of city inspectors. Moreover, a substantial portion of the streets and infrastructure damaged by Hurricane Katrina remains unrepaired- years later. In contrast to emotionally intelligent and compassionate leadership, in Surfside Florida June 24, 2021 a twelve-story condo in Southside Florida collapsed killing 98 people. All ninety-eight victims' bodies were recovered in 27 days. That is leadership, and compassion!

One would expect that our elected leaders would also prioritize addressing the city's 27 percent poverty rate and reducing homelessness. It is disheartening to witness an elected official making false claims regarding the reformation of the police department and the safety of New Orleans. The New Orleans Police Department was placed under a consent decree on July 24, 2012, and as of 2023, it continues to operate under this decree while earning the unfortunate title of the murder capital of the United States. When I retired in 2010 NOPD had 1595 officers in 2023 it has less than 900 officers. That's negligence.

Considering the billions of dollars in federal assistance and if it had effective leadership, New Orleans should have a thriving economy, attracting people back to the city. While we still enjoy our cherished traditions such as Mardi Gras, professional sports teams, outstanding restaurants, and numerous grand celebrations, New Orleans remains a hub for exceptional food, music, and people worldwide.

However, to believe the political propaganda that NOLA has a thriving economically, citizens were flocking back to NOLA, crime was down, and NOLA was safer, you'd have to be on phencyclidine, yes, angel dust, yes- PCP you'd have to be hallucinating. If you aren't on angel dust, then you have fell for the influence of another type of PCP (Power, Corruption, and Politics) that has ruled and ruined one of America's greatest treasures. NOLA's PCP - The **Powerful** control many politicians; the **Corrupt,** who constantly ruin NOLA via their criminal enterprises; and the weak, paid for, and selfish **Politics** of the city, which refuses to let NOLA progress in the positive, progressive and beautiful way that it should. Eighteen years later, NOLA's PCP lives on. Because of NOLA's PCP, we are still Inside the Eye of the Storm!

Warren J. Riley Author Biography

Warren J. Riley is an accomplished leader with a distinguished law enforcement and disaster management career. Currently serving as the Director of Policing at Delgado Community College in New Orleans, Louisiana, Mr. Riley brings a wealth of knowledge and experience to his role.

With 28 years of dedicated service in the New Orleans Police Department (NOPD), Mr. Riley's career in law enforcement is nothing short of exemplary. He held leadership positions for over two decades, culminating in his appointment as the Superintendent of Police. Remarkably, he assumed this role just four weeks after the devastating Hurricane Katrina struck New Orleans, underscoring his ability to navigate through crisis situations.

During his tenure as Superintendent, Mr. Riley demonstrated outstanding leadership, managing an annual budget exceeding $116 million and overseeing a team of over 1800 commissioned and non-commissioned personnel. His strategic vision and collaborative efforts with federal, state, and local authorities played a pivotal role in the recovery and revitalization of the NOPD following the aftermath of Hurricanes Katrina and Rita.

One of Mr. Riley's key achievements was partnering with the President and executives of the RAND Corporation on essential projects related to pay raises and crisis management. These initiatives significantly contributed to the welfare and progress of NOPD's rank and file, helping transform it into a fully functional law enforcement agency within three years of a catastrophic disaster.

In addition to his distinguished law enforcement career, Mr. Riley served as a Federal Coordinating Officer (FCO) for the Department of Homeland Security Federal Emergency Management Agency (FEMA). During his seven years with FEMA, he was appointed the FCO on thirteen Presidentially declared major federal disasters. In this role, he represented the FEMA on disaster management and recovery operations, ensuring that states and survivors received critical services for a swift return to normalcy.

Notably, Mr. Riley's expertise extended beyond national borders, as he was invited to share his insights on disaster management at international conferences in various countries, including Australia, the Czech Republic, Canada, and Cuba. Mr. Riley also served on the Flood Plain Management Board for the Czech Republic. His knowledge was instrumental in advising on disaster recovery efforts, including his mission to Haiti following the 2010 earthquake as an advisor to the U.S. State Department. Mr. Riley is also a graduate of the Federal Bureau of Investigation National Executive Institute and the Senior Management Institute for Police.

Mr. Riley is a highly educated professional, holding a Master of Arts and Bachelor of Science degrees in Criminal Justice from the Southern University of New Orleans and an Associate of Arts degree in Criminal Justice from Delgado Community College. He has also contributed to academia as an adjunct professor, teaching a range of subjects related to law enforcement and criminal justice.

Throughout his career, Warren J. Riley has exhibited unwavering dedication to public service, leadership excellence, and a commitment to positively impacting communities and disaster-affected regions. His extensive leadership experience and expertise continue to shape and enrich the field of law enforcement and disaster management.